WITHDRAWN

THE HOT GARDEN

Looking back over the first 50 years of my career, I can find nothing that I have done that is worthwhile. At the age of 73, I have at last arrived at the point where I can perceive the true form and characteristics of birds, animals, plants. Thus my true life as an artist is just beginning.

—Katsushika Hokusai, 1760–1849

Rio Nuevo Publishers®
P.O. Box 5250, Tucson, Arizona 85703-0250
(520) 623-9558, www.rionuevo.com

Text and photos copyright © 2009 by Scott Calhoun, except for: javelina photo on page 158 © Tom Vezo.

All rights reserved. No part of this book may be reproduced, stored, introduced into a retrieval system, or otherwise copied in any form without the prior written permission of the publisher, except for brief quotations in reviews or citations.

Library of Congress Cataloging-in-Publication Data

Calhoun, Scott.
 The hot garden : landscape design for the desert Southwest / Scott Calhoun.
   p. cm.
 Includes index.
 ISBN-13: 978-1-933855-31-8 (hardcover : alk. paper)
 ISBN-10: 1-933855-31-2 (hardcover : alk. paper)
 1. Desert gardening—Southwest, New. 2. Landscape design—Southwest, New. 3. Xeriscaping—Southwest, New. I. Title. II. Title: Landscape design for the desert Southwest.
 SB427.5.C35 2009
 712.0915'40979—dc22
                        2008036734

On page 3: Mexican flame vine; on pages 4-5, left to right: vegetable planter at Tucson Botanical Gardens, Santa Rita prickly pear, retro motel chairs backed by a ganglia of slipper plant, Arizona poppies in late summer speldor.

Design and maps: Karen Schober, Seattle, Washington.
Illustrations: © Kevan Atteberry.

Printed in Korea.

10 9 8 7 6 5 4 3 2 1

THE HOT GARDEN

RIO NUEVO PUBLISHERS®
TUCSON, ARIZONA
WWW.RIONUEVO.COM

Preface 7

Introduction to the Hot-Garden Region 10

CHAPTER 1. HOT-GARDEN DESIGN: Approaches for Desert Places 21

   Learning to See: Get Your Desert Eyes On 22

   Design Tips and Tricks 24

CHAPTER 2. DESIGNING WITH DESERT PLANTS: Toward Southwestern Plant Palettes 37

   Trees 40

   Shrubs 45

   Ground Covers 49

   Vines 49

   Wildflowers 52

   Sculptural Plants 62

   Weird Plants 79

   Grasses and Palms 80

   Exotic Additions 82

   Regional Planting Themes 87

   Soil Preparation and the Design Process 91

   Plant Charts 94

CHAPTER 3. OUTDOOR LIFE: Planning for People in the Hot Garden 115

- Colored Walls + Native Plants = Garden Magic 117
- Colored Wall Garden Gallery 121
- The Garden Floor: Paving and Mulching 131
- Seating 135
- Nightscaping and Lighting 138
- Firestyle 139
- Ramadas 140
- Fountains and Water Features 141
- Living with Veggies 143
- A Little Art 145
- Shrines 146
- The Junk Garden 147
- Attracting Desirable Wildlife 151
- Repelling Less-desirable Wildlife 158

CHAPTER 4. PRECIOUS WATER: Conserving H₂O by Design 161

- Watering the Hot Garden 165
- Well-managed Drip Irrigation 167
- Hybrid Rainwater/Drip Irrigation 168
- Desert Raingarden 169
- Raingarden Plant Selection and Considerations 172
- Rainwater-harvesting Cisterns 175
- Plant Charts 178

- Extreme Tools for the Hot Garden 182
- Acknowledgments 184
- Resources 185
- Suggested Reading 186
- General Index 187
- Index of Plant Names 187

Preface

PERHAPS IT TAKES SOMEONE with a warped imagination to see the hot regions of the Southwest as the most beautiful gardens on the planet, but—blessing or curse—that is how I see them. I suppose that I'm in good company: artists, architects, and writers like Georgia O'Keeffe, Frank Lloyd Wright, and Ed Abbey loved these beautiful wastelands for what writer Mark Sundeen calls their "otherworldly geometry and isolation." Brigham Young relied on the formidable topography and climatic extremes as buffers against intrusions by hostile non-Mormon settlers and the U.S. government. But the climate and topography have not been enough to keep people away—millions have voted for the sunny Southwest with their feet. Nearly all of these new immigrants have yards, and many of them are completely perplexed at how to garden in our bizarre North American deserts.

Whether this great migration to the Southwest has been boon or ill is a question that I won't really weigh in on here, except to say

Parry's penstemon in late March splendor in Tucson (Design: Scott Calhoun).

that I recently heard writer Alison Hawthorne Deming comment that "we live in cities which we despise," and I think that despising where one lives cannot be healthy. For this reason, I propose that, beginning with our gardens, we reimagine our home places, thinking back to how visionaries like Frank Lloyd Wright and Georgia O'Keeffe first saw these American deserts. Although we can't easily alter the public infrastructure of our cities, we can radically transform our yards in favor of desert plants and more natural patterns; in so doing, I fervently believe that we can transform how we feel about living in the hot-garden zone. I like to call this reframing of our gardens "getting your desert eyes on," a topic I will discuss at length further into this book.

Experienced designers and plantsmen and -women in the Southwest deserts practice a sort of renegade gardening done outside the view and commentary of mainstream horticulture. Southwestern horticulture and garden design is so different that newcomers may feel as if they've arrived on another planet—someplace like Tatooine, the fictional hardscrabble desert planet in *Star Wars* with two suns, 1 percent surface water, dunes, canyons, sand people, and a notorious resident named Jabba the Hut. The Tatooinians, including one young Luke Skywalker, eke out an existence as "moisture farmers," condensing a couple of liters of water per day from the atmosphere using a cylindrical device called a "moisture vaporator." It is no coincidence that Tatooine evokes some of the spirit of the Mojave and Sonoran deserts—much of the footage of Tatooine was actually shot in Death Valley, California, and the dunes around Yuma, Arizona (as well as in Tunisia and other arid North African locations). And although we know it as water harvesting, moisture farming is an activity that many more real-life desert dwellers are taking seriously as a way to grow plants. After all, when you consider that Arizona has only .32 percent of its land area in surface water (and New Mexico only .2 percent) we surely need to value our water at least as much as the Tatooinians do!

Now that I have confirmed my geekiness with an elaborate *Star Wars* reference, I should return to the business of hot-garden design. What recommends me as an author of this text, more than any formal qualifications, is my abiding affection for North American deserts. I love lacing up my hiking boots and following trails into arid lands; my boots have proven my best design tool—they have led me to spectacularly tough and beautiful plants in remote and rocky canyons, in sandy arroyos, and on the faces of jagged mountains. This book, in essence, is a response to a question that I asked myself as a younger man, on a drive back into suburban

Phoenix in the mid-1980s after a hike in the Superstition Mountains: why didn't I see more of the vivid wildflowers, twisted multi-trunked desert trees, and sculptural cacti—like what I saw peppering the rocky slopes of the Superstition Mountains—growing in home gardens? My quest to address this question has become a large portion of my life's work.

So here is my ecological garden manifesto: I believe in gardens. I believe in wilderness. I believe in saving the few flowing rivers we have left. I believe in preserving our local plant treasures. I hope that in making smart, thrifty gardens we lessen the weight of our footprints in Abbey country. I suspect that the most generic stucco-box tract home can be transformed into a garden teaming with lizards, palo verdes, and penstemons because I have seen it happen. I have a deep and abiding faith in the ability of desert plants to root a poorly executed faux pueblo-style structure to the land, and I know that a well-designed desert garden can bring back some of the diversity we lose to the bulldozers.

Compared with other regions of the country, there is a great dearth of garden-design literature for our desert regions. Although we have a strong tradition of nature writing here, when it comes to garden writing, there are few bold souls willing to venture into the thornscrub—the American Southwest is still largely terra incognita. Except for an occasionally novel suggestion about where to place our barbecue grills and spas, the barrage of cable TV garden-makeover shows and nationally syndicated garden radio programs have little to offer those of us marooned on this barely charted Tatooinesque horticultural planet. Especially when it comes to gardening, things *are* different here.

Because hot gardens are so specialized, even isolated from the conventional American gardening wisdom, I saw a need for a book that further articulates the various wonderful and aesthetically pleasing ways there are to live in deserts, with desert plants. So in writing this, I hope to be your guide on a tour of plants, rocks, colors, and watering methods that bring the grandeur and intricacy of wild Southwestern landscapes into home gardens. I aim to provide a more detailed, expanded, and fortified look at three topics I began to explore in my first book, *Yard Full of Sun*.

Those topics—native plants, water conservation, and outdoor life—are treated here from a garden-design perspective, with a zeal that borders on religious. By the time you finish, I aim to have converted all of you, dear readers, into first-rate Desert Rats, Bedouins, Tuaregs, and Tatooinian moisture farmers.

ON THESE TWO PAGES, LEFT TO RIGHT: Sacred datura flower, artichoke agave, palo brea tree bark, and Mexican blue penstemon (*Penstemon amphorellae*).

Introduction to the Hot-Garden Region

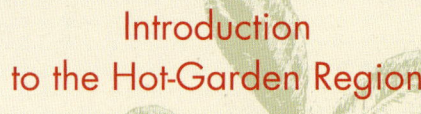

WHEN CONSIDERING THE TERRITORY to cover in a book titled *The Hot Garden*, I deliberated obsessively about how to draw lines around this expansive, occasionally highly urbanized but usually sparsely populated region we call the Southwest, with its many climate zones. Could I cover climates as varied as Denver, San Diego, and Tucson in one book? It seemed unlikely and probably unwise. Denver—which is steppe rather than desert and quite cold in winter—is more similar to western Nebraska or Kansas than Tucson, and San Diego, while semi-arid, has a climate that is considerably milder than most of the Southwest due to its proximity to the Pacific.

The answer came to me early one summer as I was driving south out of Denver toward Albuquerque and finally home to Tucson, along the way stopping to visit friends and photograph gardens. In Denver, with a few exceptions, the gardens I saw were mulched with shredded bark or some other organic material, but

Ocotillo and sideoats grama near Sonoita, Arizona, one of the higher and wetter edges of the hot-garden zone.

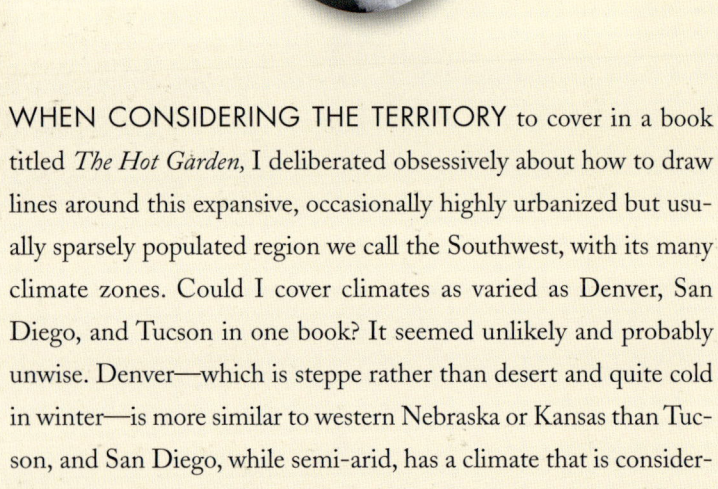

as I drove south, most strikingly in Albuquerque, the predominant ground cover between plants changed to gravel mulch. Right then, I knew that the focus of this book would be the areas of the Southwest where the primary mulch used between plants is composed of rock. The area of the country that extensively employs gravel as a mulch also happens to lie mostly within the boundaries of the three hottest American deserts: the Chihuahuan, the Mojave, and the Sonoran. These deserts are also places where the big sagebrush of the Great Basin gives way to the creosote bush as the predominant shrub. To put it another way, the area I'm covering is arid (the annual precipitation is less than half of the annual evaporation) with high summer temperatures. The majority of the population centers I'm covering in this book average less than 16 inches of annual precipitation, have annual mean temperatures above 55 degrees F, have above-freezing mean temperatures during the coldest month of the year (usually January), and are not adjacent to the Pacific Ocean. In a nutshell: this book primarily covers the part of the Southwest where creosote bush is the most common shrub, gravel is the most ubiquitous mulch material, rain is scant, and summers are hot.

Few would argue that this region—which encompasses cities like El Paso, Las Cruces, Tucson, Phoenix, Las Vegas, St. George, Palm Springs, and Yuma—is the most difficult and extreme area of the United States in which to garden (at least in the traditional sense). It's no surprise that part of this is due to the heat. In fact, Death Valley in the Mojave Desert holds the record for the second-highest temperature ever recorded on earth—134 degrees F—second only to Al'Aziziyah, Libya, where it is purported to have reached 136 degrees F (although the accuracy of the Libyan reading is questioned). Some of the cities in the hot-garden zone, such as Phoenix and Palm Springs, experience a couple of months of what my colleagues David Cristiani and Jim Knopf term "hyper-summer," which I define as periods when the nighttime low temperatures don't drop below 80 degrees (with a few nights when lows don't drop below the 90s!). This sort of heat combined with aridity may lead you to believe that this is a ridiculous place to garden. But through perspicacious eyes, a whole new gardening paradigm presents itself: I would argue that the desert regions in this book offer fresh and exciting climes for adventurous spirits. For sculptural form, uniquely adapted plants, and geology, the hot part of the Southwest is endlessly fascinating for gardeners seeking new frontiers. Because many arid plants are well adapted to both the lower and the cooler desert areas, this book will secondarily touch on designing gardens in a few equally warm but slightly wetter arid places such as Prescott and Sedona, Arizona, and Albuquerque's foothills in New Mexico.

As hot as these Southwest deserts are, you might be surprised to learn that cold is usually the more limiting factor when it comes to what will survive in our deserts here. As Jon Weeks of Landscape Cacti in Tucson remarks, "When it is really hot the cacti might shut down and stop growing, but they are generally unfazed by extreme heat as opposed to extreme cold." It is wise to remem-

Conditions at the base of Picacho Peak, Arizona, test even the most rugged plants of the hot-garden region.

The cold side of the hot garden—snow in the desert (Design: Scott Calhoun).

ber that most Southwestern cities are quite high in elevation when compared with the rest of the United States. The Arizona Diamondbacks' downtown Phoenix stadium, at 1,117 feet above sea level, is the second-highest in the country, with only the Colorado Rockies playing at a higher altitude. This is good for home runs but bad for winter nighttime temperatures. Even notoriously hot cities like Phoenix are not reliably frost-free. The winter of 2006–2007 reminded Phoenicians of this fact when nighttime temps sank to the high teens and killed or severely damaged many large Indian laurel figs (not to be confused with Indian fig) that people had mistakenly thought hardy in the area. With the region's low humidity and clear skies, nighttime temperatures can plummet 30–40 degrees overnight. This effect is called "night sky radiation." Cold in many desert cities varies greatly with the topography. In Albuquerque, low areas near the Rio Grande can easily dip into negative territory, while gardens in the foothills areas may be 20 degrees warmer. The same is true for Tucson, where those living in the Tanque Verde Creek drainage experience single digits, while those in the foothills remain significantly warmer.

It seems obvious beyond mentioning, but this region, this sun-baked corner of America, is a dry one. Cities here receive an average of 4–20 inches of rain per year, making xeric plants essential for any garden that is not a water hog and aims to come close to living within a modest and sustainable water budget. Although we receive scant rainfall compared with cities east of the Mississippi, it actually translates into a lot of runoff that can be slowed down and saved when we build our gardens properly. As an example, the roof of my 1,500-square-foot home yields over 9,000 gallons of clean salt-free rainwater each year, most of which is directed to planted areas. If there is one movement that seems to be gaining serious momentum in this region, it is the move toward keeping rainwater from running off our lots and into storm drains, using it instead to water plants. Rainwater harvesting combined with thrifty native plants is the future of gardening here; we might as well find some ways to make it fun and beautiful.

A monsoon storm rolls in over the grasslands of the San Rafael Valley, Arizona.

The Hot-Garden Zone Cities

Here are a few of the vital statistics for the larger towns and cities that fall into what I'm calling "the hot-garden zone" (see pages 17–18 for some data). The population centers in the hot-garden zone are characterized by low rainfall (less than 14 inches annually), hot summers (none of these places is a stranger to the century mark), and relatively warm winters (average January temps at least 32 degrees). To define this region in slightly more technical terms, it is a *mesothermal* arid region, meaning that the average temperature in January is greater than 32 degrees Fahrenheit and the annual precipitation is less than half of the annual evaporation; in other words, hot and dry, without sustained periods of below-freezing temperatures in winter.

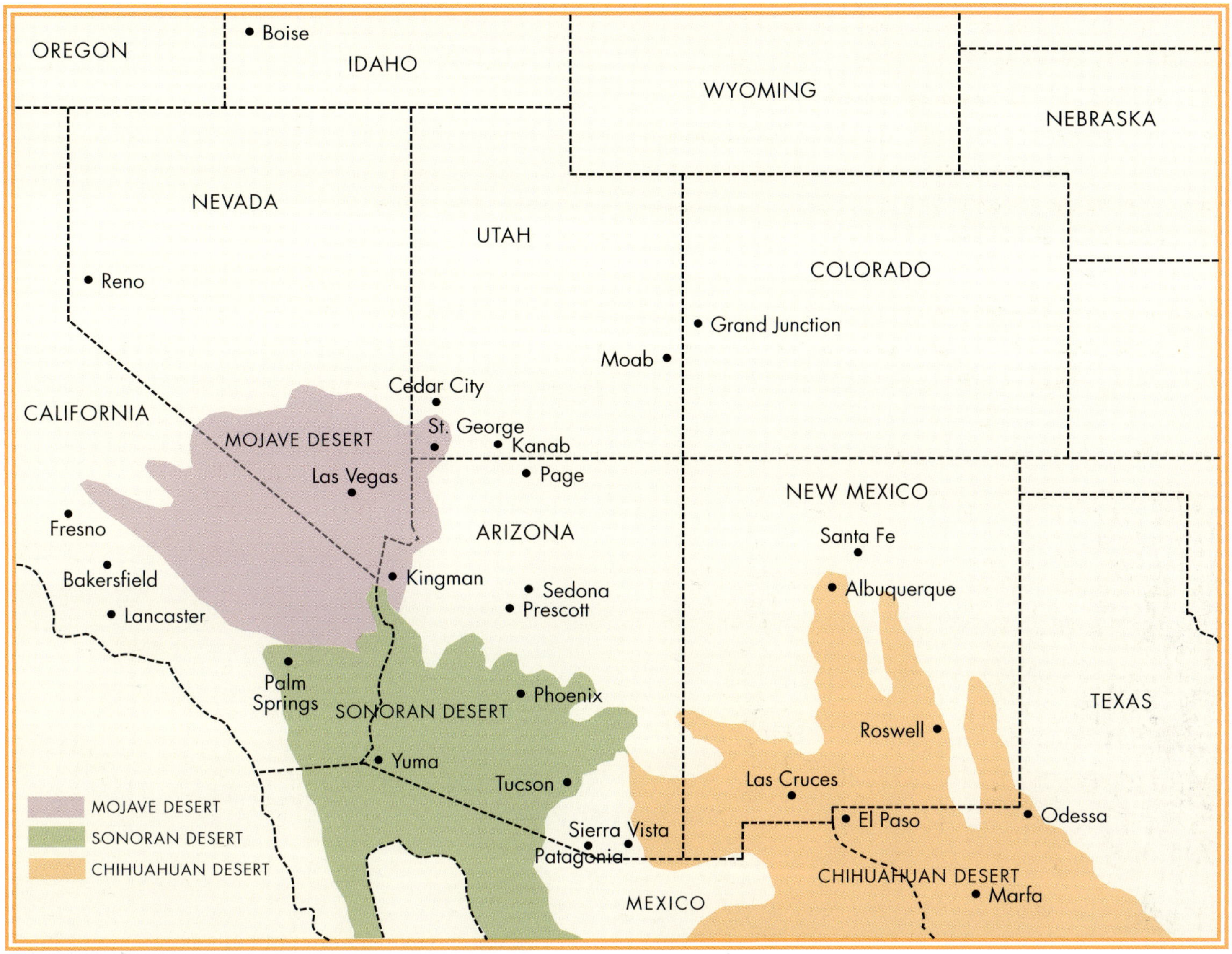

THE WETTER EDGES OF THE HOT-GARDEN ZONE These slightly wetter (receiving over 14 inches of annual precipitation) arid regions have much in common with the hot desert cities just listed, and many plants we will discuss are well adapted to these wetter edges. These areas tend to be desert grasslands at elevations between 3,000 and 6,000 feet above sea level, and they are actually the southern extension of the short-grass prairie. Drainages, also called washes or arroyos, often are studded with oak, juniper, and piñon pine, sometimes transitioning to patches of ocotillo and yucca on the warmer, drier slopes. These areas receive more than 14 inches of annual precipitation.

An ephemeral stream in Brown Canyon, near Arivaca, Arizona.

THE COLDER EDGES OF THE HOT-GARDEN ZONE

While these cities lie outside of the Chihuahuan, Mojave, and Sonoran deserts, their climates are agreeable to growing many of the plants cultivated at lower elevations, so long as said plants are sufficiently cold-hardy. Most of these cities are on the warm fringes of the Great Basin. You will note that while they are colder, they are as dry as or drier than some of the hot-garden cities listed on page 17. As I noted in a lecture I delivered in Boise, Idaho, Tucson is slightly wetter than Boise.

CALIFORNIA'S CENTRAL VALLEY

Although most of the great central valley of California is used for agriculture, it is a warm and relatively arid region in which nearly all of the xeric plants in this book will perform well. These are clearly hot-garden cities worthy of some experimental desert gardens. It should be noted that these California cities are characterized by dry summers, receiving nearly all of their rainfall from fall through spring.

Saguaro National Park East under winter snow.

Hot-Garden Zone Cities

Desert	City	Elevation (in feet)	USDA Hardiness Zone	Record High (degrees F)	Record Low (degrees F)	Mean Annual Temp (degrees F)	Normal Annual Precipitation (in inches)
Chihuahuan (upper colder limit)	Albuquerque, NM	5,312	6b–8a	107	–17	57	8.88
Chihuahuan	Carlsbad, NM	3,295	7b–8a	114	–16	63	12.92
Chihuahuan	Douglas, AZ	4,011	8b	110	–4	63	12.8
Chihuahuan	El Paso, TX	3,740	8–9a	114	–8	64	9.43
Chihuahuan	Las Cruces, NM	3,896	8	110	–4	63	8.35
Chihuahuan	Pecos, TX	2,612	7b	118	–9	64	10.59
Chihuahuan	Roswell, NM	3,650	6b–8a	114	–9	61	13.05
Colorado Plateau (lower warmer limit)	Cottonwood, AZ	3,485	8b	114	5	62	11.84
Colorado Plateau Semidesert (upper colder limit)	Kanab, UT	4,950	6b	108	–20	54	13.49
Colorado Plateau Semidesert (upper colder limit)	Moab, UT	3,965	6a–7b	114	–12	58	9.80
Colorado Plateau Semidesert	Page, AZ	4,270	8a	109	–11	58	6.46
Colorado Plateau Semidesert (upper colder limit)	Tuba City, AZ	4,160	7a	110	–15	55	6.47
Mojave	Bishop, CA	4,147	7a–8a	110	–8	56	5.26
Mojave	Barstow, CA	2,106	9a	116	3	64	4.40
Mojave	Death Valley, CA	–282	10a	134	20	77	2.26
Mojave	Hawthorne, NV	4,330	7a–8a	108	–3	56	4.39
Mojave (upper colder limit)	Kingman, AZ	3,540	8b	110	4	62	10.47
Mojave	Lancaster, CA	2,355	8b	112	2	61	7.75
Mojave	Las Vegas, NV	2,160	9	116	8	68	4.13
Mojave	St. George, UT	2,769	7a–8b	117	–11	61	8.23
Sonoran (lower warmer limit)	Blythe, CA	397	10a	123	20	74	3.60
Sonoran	Inner Grand Canyon (Phantom Ranch), AZ	2,570	9	120	17	69	8.38
Sonoran	Needles, CA	981	10a	125	13	74	4.54
Sonoran	Palm Springs, CA	472	10a	123	19	73	5.47
Sonoran	Phoenix, AZ	1,117	10a	122	17	73	7.66
Sonoran (upper colder limit)	Safford, AZ	2,916	9	116	8	64	8.91
Sonoran	Tucson, AZ	2,389	9b	117	16	69	12.00
Sonoran (lower warmer limit)	Yuma, AZ	138	10a–10b	124	24	74	3.17

City	Elevation (in feet)	USDA Hardiness Zone	Record High (degrees F)	Record Low (degrees F)	Mean Annual Temperature	Annual Normal Precipitation (in inches)
The Wetter Edges of the Hot-Garden Zone						
Albuquerque foothills, NM	6,120	7	102	3	55	15.96
Bisbee, AZ	5,310	8b	106	6	61	18.63
Marfa, TX	4,849	8	106	-2	58	15.49
Nogales, AZ	3,814	8b	106	-3	61	16.57
Odessa, TX	3,002	7b–8a	112	-5	64	14.04
Oracle, AZ	4,250	8b	108	2	62	19.40
Patagonia, AZ	4,062	8b	109	-6	58	18.04
Payson, AZ	4,921	7a	105	-23	53	20.70
Prescott, AZ	5,368	6b–7a	105	-21	53	18.96
Sedona, AZ	4,400	8b	110	0	61	17.95
Sierra Vista, AZ	4,675	8b	108	11	63	14.57
The Colder Edges of the Hot-Garden Zone						
Boise, ID	2,860	6a	111	-25	51	11.72
Cedar City, UT	5,610	6a	105	-26	50	10.60
Grand Junction, CO	4,597	6b	107	-21	53	8.93
Lewiston, ID	1,420	6a	115	-22	53	12.65
Reno, NV	4,400	6a	108	-16	51	7.28
Santa Fe, NM	6,720	6a	99	-17	50	13.81
California's Central Valley						
Bakersfield, CA	490	9a	115	19	65.2	6.20
Fresno, CA	340	9a	113	18	63	8.93
Modesto, CA	90	9a	113	18	62	12.41

Hot-Garden Design

1
Hot-Garden Design: Approaches for Desert Places

The rare moment is not the moment when there is something worth looking at but the moment when we are capable of seeing.

—Joseph Wood Krutch, *The Desert Year*

IN HIS BOOK *The Omnivore's Dilemma,* writer Michael Pollan tells a story about foraging for morel mushrooms in a 17,000-acre stand of burned-out pines and cedar trees in California, a scene he describes as "a graveyard of vertically soaring trunks" both "gorgeous" and "ghastly." Considering the desolate panorama, he writes,

> if you achieved a slightly more aestheticized view of the scene, the same landscape exhibited a tranquil, almost modernist abstraction that was just beautiful. The deadstraight black verticals ordered the hillsides as evenly as bristles on a brush, their steady rhythm varied every so often by a heavy black slash angled weirdly across the grid. The underlying shapes of the land…had the explicitness of a line drawing, everything in view reduced to its formal essentials.

Learning to See: Get Your Desert Eyes On

What does a burned-out pine forest have to do with hot-garden design? In the same way that Pollan learns to appreciate the stark simplicity of the fire-ravaged forest, we need to retrain our eyes to celebrate the powerful minimalism—a style much admired in art—of our deserts. Seeing this way may not come naturally for us, as we seem to be conditioned to associate beauty in gardens with deep green, enclosed, and highly floriferous gardens based on European models. Garden designer Carrie Nimmer once told me that she doesn't think people from the East can see all of the shades of grays and gray-greens we have here in the desert until they have lived here awhile. Perhaps here we are not waiting for the scales to fall off of our eyes, but rather needing to grow some

Visible geology, such as these hoodoos at Bryce Canyon National Park, is a key component of Southwestern landscapes and gardens.

lizard-like scales to put the desert in proper focus. Because so many of our essential desert plants (from all regions of the world) have evolved gray leaves to reflect the sun and conserve water, and thorns to prevent being eaten by animals, making peace with gray and olive greens and thorns is a necessary rite of passage for would-be gardeners here. To eschew all grays and thorns in a desert garden is to unnecessarily limit the already limited (by the climate) number of plants that will thrive here. As Wallace Stegner admonishes, to appreciate nature (and I would add "desert gardens") in the arid West, "you have to get over the color green; you have to quit associating beauty with gardens and lawns." However, getting your desert eyes on is not an impossibility, and for many it comes easily. People travel from all over the world to see our desert plants and highly colored rock formations and canyons; it doesn't take long to become powerfully attached to our American "wastelands." Once you have bought into a desert aesthetic, bringing desert plants and design concepts to a garden becomes not just the easy way but maybe the *only* way to make a garden that feels appropriate here. The extreme summers and relatively cold winters winnow down the plant palette to the essentials, and for those with their desert eyes on, it is an esoteric bounty.

Part of getting your desert eyes on is related to another aspect of mushroom hunting that Pollan describes in the aforementioned book. It has to do with what mushroomers and Pollan call "the pop-out effect," and it is a type of learned visual skill that allows us to "reliably distinguish a given object in a chaotic or monochromatic visual field." For mushroom hunters, this requires picking out small and well-camouflaged fungi from among leaf duff, pine needles, and other tree litter; for desert gardeners, the process involves learning to see different shades of green, leaf patterns, thorn shapes, and structural plants from a given landscape and recognize individuals based on these forms. For the purposes of garden design, I prefer to employ the "pop-out effect" as a tool for recognizing the important accent plants in our gardens. In a given desert, these are usually what I like to call the *charismatic megaflora*, and each desert region has its own: the saguaro in the Sonoran Desert, the Joshua tree in the Mojave, and the soap tree yucca in the Chihuahuan. Thankfully, these big specimens are much easier to spot than morels in pine needles, and once you have a handle on the big "pop-out" plants, you will soon notice legions of smaller ones—all of which may end up on a list of plants to buy for your garden.

In fact, since most of the "pop-out" plants in our deserts are succulents, if you really get your eyes on, it may lead to a condition that cactus expert David Eppele described in a *Tucson Weekly* article as follows: "Whenever man comes in intimate contact with succulent plants, strange changes take place in his mind. These changes are usually of an alarming nature and have at long last been recognized by some authorities as a most insidious disease. When the succulent plants happen to be cacti, the disorder is described as Cactomania and the victim is known as a Cactomaniac." Cactomania, Eppele goes onto explain, has several stages but nearly always culminates with the Cactomaniac amassing a large collection of spiny plants. Not such a bad condition to have when living in a desert…

Design Tips and Tricks

There are no garden design "tricks" or really even "rules," for that matter, that are easily generalized. Garden design is all about context and intuition. For every design rule I can think of, someone could find a garden that breaks that rule. Even if I stuck to what seems like safe territory with a rule of thumb such as "never put a half-dozen junked cars in a front yard as part of a garden" (something the author Jim Harrison calls a "car garden") I would quickly be proved wrong. For example, in the movie *Greenfingers*, a junked car is used as a prop for wildflowers in a display garden at the Chelsea Flower Show. This is largely because humans are endlessly inventive and enjoy challenging established rules. In fact, the entire native-garden and natural-garden design movement is the result of challenging conventional gardening wisdom.

Also, since this is a book about designing gardens in the Southwest, I won't spend too much time rehashing a bunch of general garden-design principles that apply to gardens anywhere. This is not to minimize the importance of principles like balance, proportion, and scale, but these are already addressed at length in many design books. In addition, many of these considerations are intuitive and can be addressed by simply asking yourself: "Does this look good? Does this feel good?" When your design is right, the project will have a recognizable sense of equilibrium and completeness. It will be balanced in a way that is fulfilling but not indulgent: not too little and not too much.

Besides the sharp(!) differences in flora, a number of other factors distinguish our garden-design scene from the rest of the country. Regardless of which North American desert you admire or reside in, here is my personal list of important design considerations, which I will explore further in this chapter: transparency, minimalism, visible geology, naturalistic gardening and ecology, Native Americana, sense of place, architecture, shape, plant numerology, and independent spirit.

TRANSPARENCY Several years ago, I took my first trip to the East Coast. I visited a private woodland garden that grew verdantly—in shades of green that I wasn't sure I had ever seen before—and I was astonished to discover that the garden had never been irrigated. The plants had simply been popped into the ground and left to fend for themselves. Such epiphanies are the likely province of Southwesterners experiencing Eastern gardens for the first time, but to someone who had never ventured east of

Expansive blue skies are the backdrop for desert garden designs. The sense of space, as clearly shown here near Great Sand Dunes National Park, is palpable.

the 100th meridian, the amount of spontaneously occurring greenery was truly remarkable—and then scary.

The layers upon layers of leaves, the teeming broadleaves angling for any bit of sun, the sultry, rococo feeling of it all was disorienting and claustrophobic. This was a landscape of great enclosure and opacity. In a very real way, I could not see the forest for the trees. I recognized that although I could appreciate the lush, Eastern deciduous woodland and quaintly clapboarded Martha Stewartesque villages, this was not my landscape. In the land of restrained Yankee elegance, I was a stranger and tourist; I could visit but it would never be home. It seemed like one of those times when you had to decide one way or another: coyote or cocker spaniel; cactus wren or blue jay; scorpion or deer tick; Mark Twain or Henry David Thoreau; Teva sandals or muck boots; saguaros or maples; rock or loam; transparency or enclosure.

In the Southwest, the big unearthly blue sky and widely spaced flora lay everything bare—the views are utterly transparent. The price we pay for background views of gnarly rock mountains is foreground views of industrial parks, motels, and all manner of industry. I love the clarity of light, the rugged mountains, and the sense of freedom that long vistas afford. In the hot-garden zone the light is bigger, brighter, and stronger—sometimes filtered through as little as 2 percent humidity. This is great for our serotonin levels, but it makes growing traditional garden plants difficult. As Gwen Moore Kelaidis writes in her book *Hardy Succulents*, "The landscapes of the American West may not be luxurious, but they are extraordinarily majestic. They speak to the heart through their sense of sky and space, rock and slope. The challenge of recreating the style of the Southwest is to capture and regenerate this aesthetic sense through the use of the plants. It is no small challenge."

MINIMALISM: THE AESTHETICS OF ASCETICISM Minimalism is one of the defining principles of desert environments; scant precipitation equals more space between perennial plants. The words "verdant" and "lush" infrequently come to mind here, usually only following one of our brief and unpredictable rainy spells. Another way of putting it would be to say that our natural landscapes are monastic in spirit. Perhaps the late Ellen Meloy says it best when she writes, "Epicures of fecund mists will starve here [on the bone-dry sandstone of the Colorado plateau], but ascetics will not." Part of this sort of restraint and ascetic spirit in our gardens involves spacing plants farther apart, allowing them to be more fully appreciated than if they were crowded together. Our sculptural plants become like pieces of art, each on its own plinth, or a modern musical composition with a lot of silence between the notes. In some ways, the negative spaces between the plants are as important as the plants themselves. Minimalist gardens are characterized by stillness and equilibrium between planted and unplanted spaces. In minimalist desert-garden design, the placement of each plant and rock is important. Minimalist desert gardens often rely on long-lived succulent plants for structure; for this reason, they can be more satisfying and enduring than gardens that employ a higher percentage of shorter-lived herbaceous plants. That said, our desert gardens should not be oversimplified—we already have enough yards with one or two cacti sailing in an ocean of gravel. Rather, we should model our garden minimalism and plant spacing on natural examples; the relationship between grasses, annual wildflowers, ferns, trees, and succulent

At the Springs Preserve in Las Vegas, chunky rock mulch and widely spaced Las Vegas buckwheat provide a fall show on scant irrigation.

HOT-GARDEN DESIGN 27

John Fairey's porch steps and containers embody Zen simplicity at Peckerwood Garden, Hempstead, Texas.

plants is exquisite and should be abstracted and replicated whenever possible.

Minimalism and mass planting complement each other. Although it takes a lot of restraint to pare down your plant list and use only a few plant varieties *en masse,* this old landscape architect's trick almost always works: massing and repeating plants adds oomph and rhythm to a design. Is there anything quite as impressive as a grid of 200 lime-green Mexican feather grass clumps or a clutch of half a dozen beaked yuccas cheek-by-jowl? Like most of my design tips, massing and repeating species can be done both formally and informally.

VISIBLE GEOLOGY AND BORROWED LANDSCAPE What we lack in the way of birch trees, we make up for with an abundance of rocks, and rocks piled up into the form of mountains and carved out in the form of canyons. Rocks are as lovely and variously constructed as plants, and many hot-garden plants love nothing more than being placed among them for the fast drainage and water-holding fissures they offer. Since many Western cities are adjacent to mountains with spectacular exposed geology, it makes sense to bring (although not literally) some of that ancient stone into our gardens, thereby tying our gardens to the surrounding landscape. In fact, nearly every significant city in the Southwest has its own backyard mountain range. Consider the following: Phoenix and Mesa, the Superstitions; Albuquerque, the Sandias; Las Cruces, the Organs; Marfa, the Davis Mountains;

ABOVE: In nature, bold geology and distant vistas create drama in arid lands. BELOW: The Humphreys garden in Tucson borrows a view of the Santa Catalina Mountains as the backdrop for the succulent plantings around a pool (Design: Scott Calhoun).

Palm Springs, the San Jacintos; Las Vegas, Mt. Charleston; or Tucson, the Santa Catalinas. Here in the West big rock faces are laid bare, and the large pinnacles and spires appear naked (although vegetation is there) and stand like sculpture against the backdrop of blue sky. Mountains are our best architecture here, and in many ways there is nothing we can do to rival them, so in our yards we simply do our best to complement their stony greatness with our own plants and rocks. As plantsman Panayoti Kelaidis remarked in a lecture I attended at the Denver Botanical Gardens in 2008, "Vista-and-vignette is the secret to gardening with wildflowers—they belong in a context."

Seeing that so many garden settings in our region are graced with dramatic mountain-and-sky views, the Japanese design principle of *Shakei*, or "borrowed landscape," can often be well-employed in Southwestern gardens where Kyoto meets Sedona panache. With Shakei, a picturesque view is preserved and often framed by plantings. In my design practice, I used to be frustrated with clients who to my mind seemed ready to sacrifice everything (particularly shade) for a view. I thought of them as tree-phobic, because at the mere mention of a tree near a view they would begin their mantra of "but we don't want to block the mountains." Now, I see things a little differently; after traveling to regions with squat in the way of mountainous terrain, I understand that some people move to this region to look at rugged mountains every morning. In gardens, I do my best to take a picturesque view and *frame* it with plantings, thus making it a part of the garden—an inexpensive way of bringing massive ancient geology into a yard. I should say that not every garden in the region has this luxury. Many, if not most, urban gardens need more screening and enclosure where million-dollar views are not available.

NATURALISTIC GARDENING AND ECOLOGY Desert dwellers have an uneasy relationship with gardens. Our ambivalence is not due to the difficulty of the task, which is substantial, but rather out of concern for what we are removing when we make a house and garden. Early desert-plant ecologists like Forrest Shreve believed that the desert was a place everyone should "learn to know as untouched by man"—he felt no need to improve the desert around his home on the slope of Tumamoc Hill on the west side of Tucson. In a similar vein, Ed Abbey famously referred to the 33,000 acres of Arches National Park surrounding his forest ranger's trailer as his "garden." Particularly in the Southwest, ideas of wilderness and gardens are complexly commingled. Inventive Western horticulturists and garden designers began happily and enthusiastically dismantling European garden-planting schemes in favor of designs that used native flora to recreate the spirit of the Southwest. I believe that this friction between wilderness and gardens, and our attempts to reconcile them, is a positive and distinguishing force in our gardens. We have become uncomfortable using plants and garden styles that are thirsty and ill-equipped to survive here. Although writers like Abbey would have preferred that our great wastelands remain uninhabited, the people have come and continue to arrive in record numbers—some, we can only hope, out of love for Abbey's sun-baked haunts, an irony that Ed himself would have to acknowledge. So the question becomes, what do we do with all of these new houses, these new dusty blank-slate gardens? What do we plant, how do we enclose and beautify in a way that does minimal harm and intimates the former grandeur of the place? Can we restore and enhance, and is it possible to build a garden that provides better habitat for wildlife and people than what was there before?

As a response to our uneasiness about gardening here, the best Southwestern gardens are closely wedded to surrounding wildlands. These gardens are built by people with hiking boots who travel into canyons and know exactly where a ragged rock flower grows, or what sort of wildflowers will colonize a sandy wash, and how a hedgehog cactus will thrive atop a rocky outcrop. The doyenne of desert garden writing, Mary Irish, puts it this way: "Naturalistic gardening has become the style of choice in much of the country, but it dominates the Southwest… The naturalistic garden employs a casual aspect, as if the plants arose on their own. This style attempts to mimic the surrounding landscape wherever it is used."

You can begin by asking, "Before this house and yard were here, what grew here? Was this agricultural or grazing land? Perhaps a mesquite-tree bosque grew here, or maybe I have sandy soil once colonized by soap tree yucca and desert willow?" In any case, learning what was there before will greatly help you in determining what will thrive there now. This task might be as easy as looking over your back fence to adjacent undeveloped property, or it might require more research using ecological plant atlases and asking experts about plant associations in the area. Native plant and cactus societies are excellent resources for this sort of information. Dryland water-harvesting expert Brad Lancaster suggests that we begin by using plants native to within 25 miles and 500 feet in elevation either above or below your home.

One way of quantifying the ecological success of a garden is to consider what in the garden would endure if you, the gardener, disappeared. If you can imagine that the velvet mesquite tree you planted would continue its twisted growth and the arc of fragrant Texas rangers would still flash purple with the summer monsoon rains, and that all of this would somehow enhance the ever-encroaching wild flora, you can sleep with assurance that you have done little harm.

NATIVE AMERICANA Those of us not of Native American descent sometimes sense that we lack a certain spiritual connection to, and ownership of, these drylands. In her book *Desert Time*, author Diana Kappel-Smith recounts a conversation with a Navajo man who asks, "You got country of your own? Your own land?" to which Kappel-Smith replies, "I have some land I own, where I had a farm once, but it is not my land. In the way that this is your land." Although I like to poke fun at myself and other Anglos, who in our pursuit of the authentic West gussy ourselves up in squash-blossom turquoise necklaces, build modernist adobe homes, and decorate said homes with Navajo rugs, O'odham baskets, Hopi kachinas, and Scandinavian leather furniture, this desire for connection to these places through native peoples and their art is generally a good thing. Americans of European descent who try to understand this place on its own terms are like a tribe of white Westerners—Tohono Honkies, Navahonkies, or Hopihonkies if you will—who, however feebly, seek a deeper relationship to the place they live in through those who have a longer history in these arid climes. We marvel at the O'odham, who count the saguaros as people, and wonder if *we* can experience a relationship like this with plants.

Which brings us back to gardens. I believe that by taking cues from the Native Americans and the Native American landscape, we can begin to claim this land, call it our own, and truly own it in a spiritual rather than chattel-related sense. Besides the rocks, the plants are the longest-running inhabitants of these lands.

We learn from the first native peoples in these drylands that this has always been a tough place to eke out a living growing food, but that it can be done. One only need visit prehistoric Pueblo cliff ruins, complete with elaborate terraced rainwater harvesting, gravel-mulched sunken garden beds, and grid plantings to get an idea of how to grow things in this harsh country. In the river valleys around present-day Phoenix and Tucson, the ancient Hohokam people built ingenious systems of canals to water crops, teaching us that desert horticulture requires hydraulic technology—but that technology can be as simple as contouring the land in our gardens to catch rainwater. There is also evidence that the Hohokam, Sinagua, Rio Grande, Chama, and Mogollon people

Blackfoot daisy planted at the base of a boulder decorated with a petroglyph at the Arizona-Sonora Desert Museum.

all used rainwater-harvesting methods (according to an article by Joel Glanzberg in *Permaculture Drylands Journal*).

A key lesson that the indigenous peoples of the Southwest teach us is that many of our desert plants are edible and surprisingly tasty. To survive in a place with widely spaced plants, you have to know how to extract carbohydrates from a lot of growing things. Many plants that we throw in the trash as "yard waste" or let rot were, and in some places still are, staples of Native Americans. Consider the mesquite bean, the prickly pear (pads and fruit), and the saguaro fruit. As it turns out, things like prickly pear are also extraordinarily healthy for us—evening out the spikes in blood sugar that increasingly cause eaters of modern processed foods to get diabetes. Beyond the health benefits, growing low-water-use native plants you can eat is just plain fun. One of the most exhilarating discoveries you can make in your desert plot is learning that a plant you once considered merely ornamental is indeed quite tasty. In contemporary designs, plants that native peoples used for sustenance can be part of an edible landscape that performs double duty as an ornamental garden. These plants will not only screen out an ugly view of a neighbor's shed or shade a café table from the afternoon sun, they can also be enjoyed in pancakes, salads, and refreshing drinks. Growing tough natives as edibles has the added benefit of not requiring the same level of coddling that we usually associate with traditional vegetable beds.

In terms of contemporary garden design, there is a lot to learn from ancient peoples. Consider the layout of ancient cliff palaces, whose curved kivas, massive walls and solar orientation of gardens (with southern exposure for growing and warmth) can all be translated into new desert yards. Even the ziggurat patterns on ancient black-and-white pottery can be used as a template for pathways and labyrinths. In addition to Native American architecture and art, the first inhabitants of the Southwest are models for harvesting rainwater to irrigate crops, domesticating wild plants, and designing outdoor spaces for human comfort and horticultural success. If you visit the cliffs and alcoves of Mesa Verde in southwest Colorado and don't find it an utterly compelling study of masonry, agriculture, and the integration of indoor/outdoor living spaces, you probably don't have your desert eyes on yet.

SENSE OF PLACE As *Wired* editor-at-large Kevin Kelly comments, "You live in the big here. Wherever you live, your tiny spot is deeply intertwined within a larger place." When we ignore the dynamics of our "here" we end up creating gardens with no sense of place that have to be hooked up to life-support systems to survive. Gardens designed with sense of place at the top of the priority list not only look regionally appropriate, they are genetically programmed to thrive. The following quiz, which I have modified for desert garden-design purposes, is based on one created by naturalist Peter Warshall thirty years ago as a watershed-management exercise. I'm calling it the "Discovering Your 'Big Here' in the Hot-Garden Quiz." The quiz can be completed many ways (by Googling, hiking, visiting museums, sending off soil samples, or through direct observation) but however you complete it, it should form the backbone of your garden-design assumptions.

1. Which direction is north?
2. How many feet above sea level are you?
3. What are the average first and last frost dates here?
4. What are the coldest and hottest temperatures recorded here?
5. From what direction do storms generally come in the winter and summer?
6. What was the total rainfall at your house last year?
7. What percentage of your annual rainfall falls in winter vs. summer?
8. After the rain runs off your roof, where does it go?
9. Trace the water you drink, from rainfall to your tap.
10. Is the soil under your feet more clay, sand, rock, or silt?
11. Is your soil alkaline, acidic, or neutral?
12. What type of rock is found here (volcanic, sedimentary, etc.)?
13. Which geological and archaeological features in your region are, or were, considered sacred or especially respected, now or in the past?
14. What spring wildflower is consistently among the first to bloom in your region?
15. Before the modern population moved here, what did the previous inhabitants eat and how did they sustain themselves?
16. Name five edible native plants in your neighborhood and the season(s) they are available.
17. What are the three most common native species of trees (or succulents) here?
18. What are the three most common cacti or succulents here?
19. Name three invasive exotic plants that you should avoid planting in your garden.
20. Point to where the sun sets on the equinox. How about sunrise on the summer solstice?
21. Name five species each of insects, birds, mammals, and reptiles that live here. Which are migratory and which stay put?
22. Where is the nearest wilderness?

23 What other cities or landscape features on the planet share your latitude?
24 Name two places on different continents that have sunshine/rainfall/wind and temperature patterns similar to here.

ARCHITECTURE: ASK YOUR HOUSE SOME QUESTIONS

Nearly all of our gardens are built around our houses, and those homes, however humble, express some sort of architectural style. In the desert cities, it is not uncommon to find architectural styles that run the gamut from Moroccan, Spanish Colonial, Barrio, Mexican Hacienda, California Ranch, and Arts and Crafts Bungalow to Modern and Postmodern. The reasons for getting a basic understanding of the style of your home have less to do with determining the theme for the garden's plantings than about determining the type of materials you may want to use when building walls and patios in your new garden. For example, it might look funny to enclose a Mexican hacienda–style home with a modern, unadorned concrete block wall and vice versa. Also, if you already have a tumbled-brick patio, introducing multiple new paving materials—such as flagstone or concrete—is often ill-advised. In general, it is best to simplify and pare down the number of materials and textures in the "hardscape" elements of your garden; this will help you avoid having your garden patios look like the demonstration area at a home-improvement store.

Even the plainest tract house can be "read" for design clues. Is the house symmetrical or asymmetrical? Is it one or two stories? Are its walls made of stucco, brick, or concrete? What is the roof material, and what colors is the house painted? Are you willing to change those colors? The first question I suggested that you ask yourself—"Is the house symmetrical or asymmetrical?"—can help you answer one of the basic layout questions about a new garden: will the space be formal or informal? This is not to say formality and symmetry are synonymous, although they are sometimes considered so; one of the untapped frontiers of desert gardening is the organizing of native regional plants into formal yet asymmetrical patterns. The longer I practice design, the more the words of the English design master John Brookes (from his book *Garden Masterclass*) ring true: "I was beginning to discover that formal was not necessarily linear—asymmetry could be as formal as symmetry." The fact is that most desert gardens are asymmetrical and informal, although they don't have to be. I, for one, can certainly imagine an asymetrical alley of saguaro cacti, or a linear grid of fire barrel cacti filling a rectangular courtyard. Formal naturalistic gardens are not oxymoronic—we just don't see many examples.

SHAPE COMES FIRST

Another lesson I've learned from my design practice is that almost everything in garden design is about shape. As John Brookes says in *Garden Masterclass*, "A garden is made up of shapes—ground shape or pattern, water shape, tree shape, leaf shape, and flower shape. All these individual shapes sit within a shaped site, often rectangular, and the biggest shape—the house—sits in the middle of it." Although Brookes's experience is mostly in nondesert climes, his advice about shape holds true in the Southwest. Our gardens are about shape also—perhaps even more so because the shapes we use are often more visible and iconic (particularly the shapes of cacti and succulents).

Brookes's point—that gardens are primarily comprised of shapes—becomes readily apparent when (and is one of the key reasons *for*) drawing your garden design on paper. In classes I teach, I often remark that good conceptual garden designs can be drawn on cocktail napkins. This is because conceptual garden design is about shapes in general, much of which can be experimented within little out-of-scale sketches. Most yards and houses are rectangular, and making a space beautiful and useful begins with arranging shapes within that rectangle in what architects call "plan view" (a bird's-eye view). Whether you sketch a plan on a bartender's napkin, drafting paper, or a computer, drawing is the best way to see how different shapes work within that rectangle and relate to the house and lot perimeters. When drawing like this, you always render the big items first: the house, walls, patios, and walkways before proceeding to the plants, which are also drawn biggest to smallest, with the trees often serving as the pins that hold the design together. Strangely enough, you draw the little flowers last—although flowers may have been the impetus to consider a garden design or makeover in the first place!

Using a labyrinth pattern and small palette of high desert–adapted perennials and grasses, designer Judith Phillips created an Albuquerque garden that is striking for its rhythm and equilibrium.

At this point, some of you might be thinking that you need professional help to create a design—which might be true. I used to be a little uncomfortable designing other people's gardens, thinking that this was something everyone should be able to do on their own. I also could not imagine why someone wouldn't love to design his or her own garden. But as I've become more seasoned at designing gardens, I've come to realize that as a designer I'm often better equipped to articulate ideas spatially—with shapes—than some of my clients. So, with my conflicts of interest clearly stated, it may be money well spent to hire a garden designer or landscape architect to create drawings for your project. They will certainly see your property with different eyes and perhaps will bring a fresh persepective to your project. That said, if you are wired for it you might be perfectly capable of creating your own design with graph paper and pencils, and a stack of good plant and design books.

Once you understand that you are working with shapes, you can begin to decide whether the spaces lend themselves better to rectilinear or curvilinear shapes or a combination of both. On many jobs I find that either will work, depending on the client's preference. In general, rectilinear plans have a more hard-edged contemporary feel, while curvilinear designs are better for creating a softer, meandering look.

PLANT NUMEROLOGY: ODD AND EVEN Unless you are the sort of eclectic plant freak (not that there is anything wrong with this) who doesn't give a damn if you have one of everything, most people want the zing and rhythm that massing adds to a design. Although many desert designers (including me) usually advocate using odd numbers in informal designs, even numbers have their place as well. Of course, a successful outcome is more than just having odd- or even-numbered quantities of the same species of plant—it also depends on how the plants are arranged in the landscape. The talented Chicago-area landscape designer Julie Siegel says it more or less this way (with a few of my own interjections):

1 One plant will visually read as a specimen or unifier. If you're going to use a single plant as a specimen or focal point, be sure its qualities are strong enough that it can stand on its own.

2 The number two conveys formality. Two plants tend to divide the viewer's attention, so this number works best when plants are used like sentries to mark both sides of an entrance or passageway.

3 Three is a charm. Though three can be tricky in human relationships, this number fits expertly into landscapes. Since placing three plants will form a triangle, it is wise to consider the type of triangle you will form in placing the plants; unless your design is formal, acute, obtuse, and isosceles triangles tend to work better than right and equilateral triangles.

4 A good way to use four plants is to put one in each quadrant of a circle or square. Another device that works well is dividing 4 into 3 + 1, positioning three on one side of a path and one on the other.

5 Five is a number that is often used in designs. A classic example is to set up two parallel rows with three in one row and two in the other. The rows can also be staggered for a more infor-

This trio of black pots planted with golden barrel cactus demonstrates the power of the number three in gardens (Design: Urban Organics).

At Lotusland near Santa Barbara, a pair of Mexican fencepost cacti stand guard at an entry way.

mal approach. Along with the number three, five is the stock-in-trade of many desert garden designers.

6 Six works best when it is divided into two groups of three. You can either duplicate the arrangement of threes (in a staggered row or in a triangle) or position them to fill a corner.

7+ With seven plants, you achieve enough mass to start making a strong visual statement. Even numbers higher than seven can be divided into two sets of odd numbers, like 12 divided into 5 + 7. Odd numbers higher than seven can be separated into groups of odd numbers. For example, 3 + 3 + 3 = 9 works, but avoid turning an odd-numbered group of plants into one odd-numbered group and one even-numbered group such as 5 + 4 = 9. At a certain threshold, usually around a dozen depending on the type of plant, the eye can't tell whether you have a mass of 12 or 13. Once you reach a critical mass, you don't need to worry about counting anymore.

BE A NON-CONFORMIST: GO FREE-FORM AND HOT-DOG

If all of the aforementioned tips seem oppressive and bourgeois, I have good news for the anarchist gardeners among you. Unlike New England, with its rock-walled gardens, the desert Southwest is relatively unfettered by garden traditions, and those who like to experiment will find that in desert gardens there is often less (or no) pressure to conform to community standards. I often wonder, as I drive down a Tucson residential street with yards that look as though they haven't been altered (or sometimes weeded) since the 1970s, if we have *any* standards! Mind you, I'm not complaining. When it comes to freedom vs. control, I usually come down on the side of freedom. As noted grassland ecologist Don Gayton writes, "We humans tend naturally to be rather woolly thinkers, forever bringing things in from left field and cobbling them on to the issue at hand… It is our nature to be free-form, hot-dog, and eclectic."

So don't be too intimidated by advice from designers like me. If you have the inclination to go eclectic and buy one of everything, that is okay. It is a way to start gardening. If you fail with a plant, you might feel lucky to have killed only one rather than seven. Don't be intimidated by failure; it happens to everyone. Once you lose a few things and keep a few other things alive, you may find that you want some more of the plant you kept alive—and all of a sudden you have a group of plants, which is the beginning of garden design!

In gardens, this tendency to be "free-form, hot-dog, and eclectic" seems more acceptable here than in other parts of the country. There are gardens here built around strange themes. I know of a garden of saints in shrines, a garden of gems, a garden based on Mexican pop bottles and taco stands (okay, this one is mine), a garden built to attract insects, and a garden with sputnik-shaped propane tanks used as art. If you have a weakness for kitsch in the form of, say, Mexican Day-of-the-Dead skeletons, your hot garden may be the place to indulge.

Keep in mind that newer neighborhoods with homeowners' associations may frown on (or worse, restrict) your funky yard art, so if you live in one, be prepared to fight or have a backup plan. In general, because kitsch is fashion, it is usually best to design your garden around rocks, plants, and pathways, using kitsch as an embellishment rather than the entire focus of the garden. Of course, someone is sure to prove me wrong here by constructing an inspired (no pun intended) garden around graven images of that ubiquitous deity of the touristy Southwest, the humpbacked flutist, Kokopelli.

Designing with Desert Plants

2
Designing with Desert Plants: Toward Southwestern Plant Palettes

Desert denizens…are accustomed to harmonious "emptiness" and therefore find nothing missing.

—Ellen Meloy, *The Last Cheater's Waltz*

SOME PEOPLE ARE DRAWN TO the strange geometry of our local plants right away—like love at first sight—while others take a while to warm up to a landscape of green-trunked trees, star-shaped agaves, zigzag branches, and cacti with pads shaped like Mickey Mouse ears. If you come to the desert Southwest from a part of the country where bluegrass, foundation shrubs, and broad-leaved deciduous shade trees are the norm, our xeric rock-mulched yards may make a rude first impression and take some getting used to. But whether or not you are an instant believer or a recent convert, sooner or later you come to admit that a lot of the magic of the desert Southwest—the sense of place in this place—is contributed by unique desert plants. For this reason (and many others!) they deserve to be celebrated!

The richness of the desert plant palette should be fully exploited in the region's gardens.

As plantsman Panayoti Kelaidis remarked in an American Horticultural Society talk I attended in 2008, "All European perennial borders are the same, but every native garden is different. The perennial border has been done to death!" Some professional garden designers from across the pond—depressing, rainy, green places like Holland—have commented that those of us building gardens in harsh climates will be forced to work with a narrower plant palette and within a narrower range of aesthetic possibilities. This is possibly true—if you compare our plant choices with those of Portland, Oregon, or New Zealand, or you are looking for plant ideas in the *Royal Horticultural Society's Encyclopedia of Plants and Flowers* or in magazines aimed at New England. But if you use another garden tool—your hiking boots—you may be surprised at the riches the Southwest offers up. Consider some planting themes that work splendidly in the Southwest but are hard to pull off elsewhere: Minimalist, Sonoran, Baja, Mexican, Barrio, Hummingbird, Butterfly, Songbird, Chihuahuan, and Found Object gardens are just a few that come to mind. This is just to say, emphatically, that we have no shortage of local plants or interesting ways to use them in the Southwest. Quite the contrary, we have so many intriguing plants and garden styles that we are spoiled by all the choices!

The plant charts at the end of this chapter will help you choose the plants that will fit best in your garden or landscape.

Trees

The whole idea of trees seems somewhat at odds with the idea of arid climates. In deserts perhaps we expect more *Lawrence of Arabia*-style dunes than forests, but in fact all of the North American deserts are home to trees of one sort or another, and the prospect of climate change has made trees increasingly important in desert gardens. The most arboreal desert in the world is the Sonoran, due to its relatively even division of winter and summer rainfall. But even though the Sonoran has a good number of native trees, it will never be mistaken for the temperate forests of the East. We have no birches, no hemlocks, and precious few maples (and only in our high-elevation "sky islands"), but once you get over that—and abandon the idea of having trees that look like lollipops (a single trunk with a big rounded green canopy up top)—it is easy to fall in love with the contorted multiple trunks, spreading forms, and seasonal flower explosions of our desert trees. Landscape designers often call trees the bones, or the pins, of the garden, because trees usually have more impact in a garden than any other plant. Since trees are the largest, longest-lived, and most imposing plants in our gardens, it makes sense that most garden designers place them first.

Because cities like Las Vegas and Phoenix have become "heat islands" in which increased paving and development cause the mean temperature to rise by as much as 10 degrees, we need trees more than ever to cast shade, cool our homes and gardens, and save water. Yes, save water. Research shows that residents of heat-island cities use 550 more gallons of water per person per year than those in non-heat-island cities. Trees can greatly ameliorate the effect of urban heat islands. In our home gardens, we actually grow our own "air conditioning" by planting trees in a solar arc around our homes. A solar arc is a series of trees planted in a U-shape around the north, east, and west sides of our homes, providing shade and cooling during the hottest months of the year while allowing the warming winter sun access to the south side of the house in winter. In-depth information about solar arcs can be found in Brad Lancaster's book *Rainwater Harvesting for Drylands* (volume 1). Work published by the Rocky Mountain Institute indicates that shade trees planted in a solar arc can reduce summer temperatures around a home by 20 degrees!

SMALL TREES Although we consider the Southwest the land of broad vistas and wide-open spaces, our cities are highly urbanized, and as in most urban areas in the United States, new residential lots are shrinking to postage-stamp size. This presents a real dilemma for desert gardeners in that most of our native trees usually spread

The exfoliating bark of the palo blanco is reminiscent of the river birches of the East.

Palo Verde Front: A Sonoran *Sakura Zensen*

This trio of 'Desert Museum' palo verdes in designer Greg Corman's Tucson garden makes for a perfect storm of palo verde blossoms in April.

What desert trees might lack in familiar tree-like shape, many make up for with striking spring flower shows. Consider the blue palo verde (*Parkinsonia florida*), Arizona's state tree, which each April produces a screaming yellow flush of flowers that fall to the ground like a yellow cloak around its trunk. I try to take a little time out each spring to stop and appreciate the blue palo verdes—hiking in Saguaro National Park, or just pausing to admire a nice specimen in the Walgreens parking lot. But my level of passion for palo verde viewing doesn't hold a candle to the national obsession with cherry blossoms in Japan, where families throw flower-viewing parties, picnicking beneath blooming cherry trees and clapping (yes, actually clapping!) when a breeze causes a shower of blossoms to fall. The Japanese follow the *sakura zensen* (cherry-blossom "front") like Americans keep track of the NFL playoffs. The Japanese Meteorological Agency tracks the sakura zensen as it moves from the south to the north of Japan on the nightly television news. So my question is, why don't we have a palo verde blossom festival (or perhaps an ocotillo or desert-willow bloom festival) in the Southwest? I personally plan to pack up a nice lunch and a decent bottle of wine and head out under the yellow umbrella of a green-barked tree with my family this April; and when a nice whack of blossoms falls, you can bet I'll be clapping and encouraging my family to do the same. I might even make a call to a local news channel to see if we can get some coverage. After all, why should cherry blossoms get *all* the attention?

Eat Your Garden: Palo Verde Peas

If you think that after your palo verde tree blooms in spring, the interesting part of its life cycle is finished for another year, think again! All of those flowers that attract lots of buzzing bees turn into one of the more delicious treats in desert gardens: a snack I call palo verde peas. The peas, which are really just young palo verde seeds, are best harvested—much like pea pods—when they are young and tender. The palo verde peas are sweet and have a texture and flavor like peas. Eat them fresh; use them in salads or as a substitute for peas. Since the beans get woody and hard with hot weather, pick them while the outer bean pod is still soft, green, and flexible.

---

out as least as wide as they are tall, making it hard to wedge them into confined spaces. There is, however, a contingent of small water-wise trees for desert gardens. In the warmer desert areas, the bonsai-like elephant tree or wispy-as-a-willow palo blanco can be fine choices, while in the colder deserts, shrubby specimens like the screwbean mesquite and Texas mountain laurel can be shaped into multitrunked specimens to fit the space at hand.

Saving Money with Smaller Trees

When shopping for trees on a budget, smaller is almost always better. As nurseryman Tony Avent remarks, when you decide to have kids you don't usually start out with teenagers, you begin with babies. Unlike nurseries in much colder parts of the country that sell trees balled and burlapped ("B & B"), Southwest nurseries typically sell trees in three container sizes: 5 gallon, 15 gallon,

Due to its manageable size, extreme drought tolerance, and lovely flowers, the foothills palo verde has much to recommend it.

DESIGNING WITH DESERT PLANTS 43

and 24-inch box. Recently, these sizes are labeled as #5, #15, and #24 to satisfy government weights and measures standards (because a 5-gallon pot does not actually hold 5 gallons of soil). This chart illustrates the price differences and potential savings from planting smaller specimens.

Tree Container Size	Typical Retail Nursery Pricing
5 gallon	$15.99–$38.99
15 gallon	$59.99–$99.99
24-inch box	$159.99–$399.99

Depending on the species, a 5-gallon tree can catch up to and surpass a 24-inch-box tree within one to three growing seasons. That said, if you are impatient it might be better to purchase larger sizes for slow-growing trees like ironwoods, Texas ebonies, and foothills palo verdes.

A burgundy-flowered desert willow is a treat in late spring.

Texas mountain laurel mixes well with other desert plantings.

MEDIUM AND LARGE TREES Placing the larger trees in your garden is probably your single most important design task. The key point here is to remember to allow for the mature width of the canopy. A failure to do so often results in time-consuming pruning and undignified misshapen trees. There is a parking lot in Phoenix outside a store where we often shop that has palo brea trees—trees that should spread out into gorgeous 30-plus-foot canopies—planted in narrow spaces and pruned (I use the word loosely here) to within an inch of their lives. Some overzealous grounds crew reduced one of these poor deformed palo breas to a 4-foot-in-

The smooth green bark and big umbrella-like canopy of the palo brea makes it a good choice for large spaces.

Eat Your Garden: The Magic Mesquite Bean

Many desert gardeners are all too familiar with the mesquite bean pod. The fussiest compulsively rake them out from under trees, bag them up, and throw them away like so much trash. But what if the mesquite's bad reputation for litter was actually its best quality? What if you found out you could turn those ubiquitous mesquite bean pods into pancakes? Each fall, that's exactly what one Tucson group does.

Using their $5,000 mobile mesquite-bean mill, which was purchased in 2003 with the help of a Pro-Neighborhood grant, a nonprofit group called Desert Harvesters converts hundreds of pounds of mesquite bean pods into a sweet-tasting flour at sites all over southern Arizona each fall. Then they take that flour and make pancakes, bread, muffins, and energy bars.

For Tucson permaculture expert and founding Desert Harvester Brad Lancaster, making pancakes from mesquite bean pods seemed as natural as getting maple pancake syrup from the maple tree. He told me, "I began to look around at all the untapped resources of the Sonoran Desert, and I focused on foods that were abundant and easy to process, and the lowly mesquite bean pod rose to the top of my list."

As Lancaster was trying to figure out which of the plants in his yard would survive without rainfall and still produce flavorful food and shade, it became obvious to him that the formerly maligned mesquite produced both in ample quantities.

Since most urban mesquite bean pods are usually considered yard waste and end up in our landfills, converting them to flour serves a dual purpose. If you're not enough of a culinary thrill-seeker to eat mesquite-bean-pod baked goods, there are other uses for your bean pods. "Even if you don't want to turn your whole bean pods into flour, they make an

excellent mulch, which fixes nitrogen in your soil and keeps moisture from evaporating."

Historically a staple high-fiber food for southern Arizona's indigenous peoples, mesquite bean pods were traditionally handground; the new mill is much faster and less labor-intensive. According to Lancaster, "While not specifically designed for mesquite pods, it is the best tool for making mesquite flour in large quantities." For example, 10 gallons of mesquite bean pods can be converted into over two gallons of flour in just 10 minutes.

When selecting a mesquite tree from which to harvest your beans, Lancaster suggests a taste test. Sounding like a vintner of fine wines, Lancaster says, "Every tree tastes different. Although you can use either native mesquite beans or Chilean mesquite beans, you should try them first. When you find a tree you like, pick all the beans."

The Desert Harvesters mill is a big, mobile hammer mill on a trailer, so if you live outside the Tucson area you may have to get creative to find a way to grind your own beans.

---

diameter canopy made up of only two scraggly branches. My point is a simple one but one repeatedly overlooked: big desert trees need space to get big. Letting a tree grow to its mature size, or close to it, is the dignified thing to do. If you need to do some selective pruning to walk beneath the tree, that is fine, but remember that in nature many desert trees have branches that sweep the ground.

Shrubs

Desert shrubs provide a cornucopia of shapes, sizes, and flower colors, and are truly the workhorses of most arid gardens. When working with xeric shrubs, consider placing larger, rangier shrubs—such as saltbrush, desert hackberry, and little-leaf cordia—in transition or buffer zones where they can reach their full size without screening out other attractive elements in the garden design. One common mistake that I often encounter in my design practice is ignoring the mature size of shrubs; this often leads to outsized and leggy shrubs that have to be removed prior to rehabbing an older garden. This phase, known as "demolition," can be greatly reduced by choosing the right-sized shrubs the first time around.

ABOVE: Shrubs in the saltbush family (*Atriplex* sp.) are among the best performers in harsh and infrequently irrigated sites. BELOW: The showy red-hot blooms of 'Sierra Starr', a hybrid fairy duster that is bred for flower color and uniform growth.

Getting Your Mesquite Beans Ready for Milling

There are two harvesting seasons for mesquite beans: the dry fore-summer (May–June) and the post-monsoon (late August–September). These are the best times to harvest your bean pods. Lancaster recommends the following steps for harvesting them:

1. As I just mentioned, taste the beans and pick from a tasty tree.
2. Do the snap test. If the pod is dry enough to snap cleanly in half, it is dry enough for milling.
3. If you pick your beans straight from the tree, they do not require washing; simply store them in a dry rodent-free space. If your beans are on the ground, rinse them with water, spread them out, and leave them in a bright, dry, rodent-free area away from dampness.
4. Desert Harvesters encourages fellow bean collectors to pick from the tree rather than off the ground. If you do collect your beans from the ground, make certain they are free from dirt and mold; if the beans are dirty or moldy, use them as mulch around your shrubs and trees or garden beds rather than for milling.

Black dalea provides a blast of purple butterfly-attracting flowers in the fall and looks smart planted with native grasses.

SUBSHRUBS FOR AUTUMN Just because we can't grow big maples with blazing red leaves doesn't mean you can't anticipate some great fall color in your desert garden. Here, our fall color is more the result of flowers than foliage, but it is nonetheless spectacular. Some of the best fall-flowering plants come from the Chihuahuan border region of west Texas and northeastern Mexico, along with smaller shrubs such as the ones of this area, often called subshrubs. The frontier trader Josiah Gregg discovered many of the plants in this region in his travels in the mid-19th century. Many of Gregg's discoveries are now staples in nurseries throughout the Southwest; when you see a plant with the second part of its botanical name listed as "*greggii*" you can bet that Josiah Gregg stumbled onto it first.

One plant that Gregg found has turned out to be an enormously popular perennial plant throughout the Southwest: autumn sage. Autumn sage (*Salvia greggii*) is a semiwoody shrublike plant that explodes with deep magenta flowers in fall as well as in late spring and summer. The flowers are tubular in shape and attract hummingbirds, and the plant's relatively small size makes it perfect for smaller gardens. Because of its popularity, breeders have been constantly developing new autumn sage varieties; these include 'Furman's Red', which has dark red flowers; 'Sierra Linda', which is more heat-tolerant than the straight species; and 'Purple Haze', which has lavender to purple blooms.

Two blue stars in the fall garden are a pair of daleas: Monterey blue dalea (*Dalea bicolor bicolor*) and the so-called black dalea (*Dalea frutescens*). Blue dalea is a feathery plant whose evergreen leaves and six-foot-high habit make it a good candidate for a

> ### Eat Your Garden: Chuperosa
>
>
>
> Ask your dinner guests what the little red flowers on their salad taste like, and after seeing a puzzled look on their faces, watch them exclaim, "Cucumber!" That's right, not only is chuperosa one of the best winter-blooming food plants for hummingbirds, it is also excellent for garnishing a salad and indeed tastes just like cucumber. In addition to eating chuperosa blossoms, rainwater gardener Brad Lancaster is fond of including heart-shaped chuperosa leaves in a salad.

semitransparent screening plant. It flowers late in the fall, and its flowers are a rare true blue. Black dalea—which, contrary to its name, flowers purple—is much lower-growing than its blue cousin and makes a fine complement to plants with blue-gray foliage such as desert spoon and deer grass. Black dalea will tolerate heavy soil so long as it is not overwatered.

RAGING RANGERS Plants in the Texas ranger family (*Leucophyllum* sp.) have become some of the most important garden plants

The deep purple blossoms of 'Green Cloud' Texas ranger fall in a pretty circle around the plant.

in the Southwest. For bloom intensity, these Chihuahuan Desert natives peak during the summer rainy season and turn the roadsides and medians blue, purple, rose, and white in response to humidity. They are one of the great reasons to stick around for the summer—the most underrated desert gardening season. Texas rangers (particularly *Leucophyllum frutescens*) are among the most widely used native plants in the hot-garden zone. When placed in the proper situation, they make excellent shrubs—one of those cases where a plant is popular because it is so useful and showy that it is hard to resist: to see one in bloom is to want one in your garden.

Unfortunately, Texas rangers are often groomed as ridiculously and severely as AKC show poodles. Somewhere, there must be a landscaping school teaching students to prune Texas rangers into balls and boxes. Not only is this method usually overly formal and undignified-looking for the plant, it greatly reduces the number of blossoms produced. To enjoy your rangers in their full glory, first

Texas ranger and red bird of paradise explode with color following monsoon storms.

Although it is picky about drainage, the Texas ranger 'Thunder Cloud' may be the most handsome in its genus—its silver foliage and deep purple-blue flowers are a devastatingly beautiful combination.

make sure to plant the right-sized species of ranger; don't put a 'Green Cloud' Texas ranger, which is sure to get six to eight feet tall and wide, in a spot where you want something only four feet high. This problem can usually be solved by selecting shorter Leucophyllum species rather than the most commonly planted *Leucophyllum frutescens* and its 'Green Cloud' variation. Also, since all Texas rangers appreciate full sun, avoid placing them where trees will eventually cast shade on them, causing them to get leggy and unsightly reaching for the sun. There are a good number of Texas rangers other than *Leucophyllum frutescens*. Consider the compact blue ranger with lovely cupped silver leaves and blue flowers, or the repeat bloomer 'Lynn's Legacy'. If you do have a large area, consider the fragrant ranger (also sometimes called fragrant sage), whose grape-bubblegum scent can be smelled up to 50 feet away!

PRUNING Because this is primarily a design book rather than a maintenance guide, I won't go into detail about pruning other than to highlight some important pruning differences relating to the shaping of desert plants. Pruning our native plants into balls and boxes—a practice sometimes referred to as "meatballing"—can greatly reduce the aesthetic appeal and wildness of our landscapes. Simply put, most of our desert plants do not make good topiary specimens—they are better left to their wild forms. Some of this means relinquishing a little control over your garden. Not only does bad pruning *look* bad, it also reduces a plant's rainwater-harvesting potential by reducing the dripline (the circle beneath a tree or shrub where rain is slowed down and absorbed into the soil as it drips from leaves and branches), which is reduced severely by bad pruning.

Lollipops Are for the Midwest

There are few varieties of lollipop-style trees (single-trunked trees with a rounded leafy canopy) native to the desert. Most of our trees grow multiple trunks and have branches with a significant spread that sweep the ground in nature. In our gardens, it is perfectly natural to desire a tree that can be walked under, and it is acceptable to prune some desert trees for this purpose. What that means in hot-garden regions is preserving a rugged, multitrunked form while increasing the headroom beneath the canopy. When you are pruning, use sharp, clean tools, don't cut more then 25 percent of the canopy at one time, and go slowly, observing the tree from different sides between cuts.

Resist the Urge to "Poodle" and "Meatball"

There is nothing morally wrong with topiary, just as there is nothing morally wrong with grooming your dog to look like a lion, but when you topiary (aka "poodle" or "meatball") your native desert shrubs (or groom your dog to look like the leader of a pride) they often wind up looking ridiculous. In many cases, this sort of severe shaping will also significantly reduce the bloom of the plant. It is okay to remove dead, damaged, or non-performing stems, but do so selectively, with a pair of bypass pruners rather than hedge shears.

Don't Leave "Antlers"

Antlers are branch stubs that are left on trees and woody plants when they are pruned improperly—that is, pruned halfway down a branch rather than at the union with a more substantial branch. In nature, when a tree sheds a branch it usually drops at the point where it intersects with another major branch. If we emulate this pattern in our pruning we avoid antlers.

Ground Covers

Ground covers are great "bumper" plants for succulents. When planted path-side in front of spiky plants like agaves, they act as a colorful soft barrier to keep garden visitors from casual collisions with barbed plants. Although I've already expressed my inclination to let there be a little space between plants, there are certainly many places in desert landscapes where ground covers with interesting flowers and/or foliage are highly desirable. Ground-cover plants cool and shade patches of bare earth, control dust, and lend a lusher feel to pathside plantings. For our purposes here, I'm mostly listing natives (with a few exotics thrown in), and I'm defining ground covers as plants less than two feet tall. To cover large areas, especially in commercial projects, ground covers are planted en masse, but mass plantings often look very good in residential gardens as well.

In the McDougal garden in Tucson, 'Silver Falls' dichondra fills in around a flagstone walkway punctuated with bear grass and rain lilies (Design: Scott Calhoun).

Moss verbena serves as a nice "bumper" in front of desert spoon outside Civano Nursery (Design: Eric Clark).

Vines

On a recent hike I took with prairie plant ecologist Neil Diboll, Diboll remarked, "You have a *ton* of vines down here, don't you?" At the time we were staring down at one of my favorite petite vines, twining snapdragon, *Maurandya antirrhiniflora*, which was rambling around on a cliffside below some petroglyphs in Arizona's Huachuca Mountains. After more thought, I realized Diboll was dead right: we have a great wealth of vining plants—an abundance of garden designer drapery. For garden-design purposes, vines really fall into two categories: large vines for screening and shade, and smaller vines for layering, texturing, and jewel-like flowers. The petite vines are best used rambling up cholla skeletons, ocotillos, yuccas, agaves, or small trees; in this respect, they

Yellow morning glory vine creeps over a cobalt blue wall in this Carrie Nimmer–designed garden.

are an embellishment like jewelry, rather than the main attraction. Vines are an easy and organic way to jazz up your desert trees. If you have a lackluster palo verde or mesquite tree in your yard, training a vine up the tree trunk is a great way to add color and interest. In fact, even a dead tree can be disguised by growing vines through its branches. During spring, most desert trees don't need any extra adornment—they are putting on their own show of flowers and bright-green new leaves. But as fall approaches and trees begin to show signs of dormancy, a colorful vine weaving through the branches is a definite plus.

VINES IN TREES In general, deciduous vines with large tubers (like a potato has) work best with desert trees. Deciduous vines die back each winter, giving the tree time to put out new leaves before being overtaken by green tendrils. Of course, if the tree is dead, concerns for its health need not apply—go ahead with evergreen vines. The majority of those I list here are deciduous, although some deciduous species may function as evergreen or semi-evergreen, depending on your exact location in the hot-garden zone.

In the lists on pages 101–102, I've included mostly Southwestern natives with a couple of useful exotics like cat's claw and 'Tangerine Beauty' crossvine thrown in. Cat's claw is included for its general toughness and for the beautiful tracery its stems make when climbing chainlink fences. I selected 'Tangerine Beauty' for its evergreen foliage (a characteristic uncommon in most native vines), vigorous habit, and showy flower display. In general, the native vines look their best in summer—another reason to become a full-time

'Tangerine Beauty' crossvine enhances the trunk of a velvet mesquite tree (Design: Eric Clark).

Arizona grape ivy growing along an ocotillo fence (Design: Scott Calhoun).

Eat Your Garden: Native Passion Flower

Not only does native "stinky" passion flower vine grow like crazy without a lot of extra water and produce flowers whose sex parts symbolize the crucifixion, it makes tasty fruits the size of large grapes. The plant and fruit are covered with little silver hairs that keep the leaves cool. When the fruit is ripe, it falls to the ground. To eat it, wash and bite a hole in one end, then suck out the clear flesh and tiny, crunchy black seeds (edible seeds as in kiwifruit). During summer monsoon weather, the native passion vine will produce a little bowl of fruit most mornings. Be quick about picking up fallen fruit, or the crickets will beat you to it.

resident of the Southwest! I've included some of my favorites in both the smaller and larger vine categories (many of which are available for sale at botanical gardens or specialty nurseries).

VINING AND CREEPING CACTI At the Arizona-Sonora Desert Museum, there is a garden built around a venerable ironwood tree in which a vining cactus plays a starring role. A Martin's harrisia cactus snakes through is branches; in places it hangs like a python, adding another layer of textural interest to the tree. In the summer, when the vining cactus blooms, the ironwood becomes festooned with dozens of enormous white flowers. For people who are out in their gardens at night, these harrisias are hard to beat. In colder locations, the Arizona queen of the night is a good choice. In a garden situation, a mature plant can produce several hundred fragrant white flowers in one night.

Wildflowers

Although I'm a proponent of minimalism in desert gardens, I'm also a rabid fan of wildflowers; I don't find these two positions irreconcilable. Consider that many newly landscaped desert yards form a virtual sea of gravel, dotted with a few succulent plants. These big gravel areas form reflective heat sinks that are literally hard on the eyes. Enter annual (and a few perennial) wildflowers grown from seed—flashes of brilliant color that germinate and bloom only when conditions are just right. In my time searching for wildflowers, I have come to believe that they are essential to

Firewheel and Goodding's verbena mingle with Engelmann's prickly pear (Design: Scott Calhoun).

hot gardens, knitting things together. Without them, there is a distinct lack of complexity in our desert gardens, hinting that something is missing. In a good spring it is easy to find wildflowers weaving things together. You'll find Mexican gold poppies next to compass barrel cactus, arroyo lupine sidled up to prickly pear, and blue dicks pushing up through fairy dusters.

Wildflowers are part of the wealth of adapted desert plants that are often forgotten about when designing gardens. Mark Dimmitt of the Arizona-Sonora Desert Museum writes that mass displays of annual wildflowers occur only in climates that have distinct dry seasons and generous spaces between shrubs and trees, and that the more arid the climate, the greater proportion of annual wildflowers. In the Sonoran Desert, half of the native plant species are annuals. In our gardens we could have the same proportions, and during rainy seasons, our gardens would surprise us by knitting themselves together with clumps and arroyos of desert flowers. In dry years, the seeds can patiently wait it out. Accepting wildflowers in your garden means accepting that desert plants go through alternating periods of activity and dormancy. Learning to garden with these mercurial desert annuals helps get a person in sync with the bounty and limits of dry places.

Eat Your Garden: Moon Cactus Fruit

As if its generous white blooms that appear several times each summer weren't enough, the moon cactus produces a Sputnik-like red fruit as big as a baseball. Inside the red peel, the snow-white flesh flecked with black seeds can be sliced and eaten with your favorite vinaigrette. The crunchy flesh is not highly flavored (like jicama but without the hint of sweetness), but it has a nice crisp texture and looks incredibly exotic on a plate. It is a side dish that you can pretty much guarantee your dinner guests haven't seen the likes of.

I find much garden-design inspiration in photographing desert wildflowers, and when there is a widespread blanket-type bloom in the desert—something that might happen only every thirty years—I get so excited that I can't sleep; is it possible that I hear the flowers growing? My wife jokes that she becomes a "wildflower widow" as I slip out the door two hours before dawn on spring mornings with my tripod and hiking boots, but the truth is I can't help myself. A big wildflower bloom is an incredible treat—a surprise, almost a joke that nature plays on us every now and then. For me, a desert wildflower bloom is the ultimate display of the Japanese garden–design principle of introducing a brief dramatic surprise into our gardens.

THE PLEASURE OF SEED AND SEED ECONOMICS

For about the cost of one frou-frou topiary juniper—around $40–$60 (and much cheaper—nigh on free—if you collect the seed yourself)—you can landscape an entire yard with seed. What is more, planting with seed is bound to look more natural and less contrived than a garden that is planned and plotted to the square inch. It takes some of the pressure off of you, the gardener, because you relinquish the illusion of control to the seeds themselves. Of course, you will probably want to plant larger plants—trees and shrubs—from containers to ensure that they are exactly where you want them, but allowing wildflowers to work their magic *sub rosa* is a joy and relief. As the renowned rock gardener and plant explorer Panayoti Kelaidis explains, "I don't design plant combinations, the plants design the combinations themselves."

SEED BASICS

If you consider them much, seeds are crazy things; at first glance and touch, they appear inanimate—dead and lifeless as a dried stick—but this is far from the truth. Each seed is a speck of enormous potential—not dead, but only dormant. Most seeds consist of a tiny embryonic plant, complete with a root and leaf (or leaves), surrounded by an energy-rich endosperm. The embryo and endosperm are encased by a hard coat that protects the seed. Seeds form, of course, after a flower is pollinated, and depending on the plant and conditions, this maturation typically takes from three to eight weeks. When you are harvesting seed, you want to make sure you are taking *mature* seed. Luckily, nature gives us lots of clues about when seed becomes ripe. Immature seed is soft and often light green or chartreuse inside, while ripe and mature seed has a hard coating and is often brown, tan, or black on its exterior. You can almost always tell if seed is ripe by breaking apart a seed pod in your hands. Ripe seed pods will snap open, revealing seeds with a hard coating. It is important that the seeds are dry, because a dried seed has slowed down its metabolism (gone to sleep) and is prepared to wait for future planting.

Buying Seed

Many desert wildflower seeds are available from botanical gardens, garden centers, and mail-order sources. This, and getting seed from friends, is usually the best way to start gardening with seeds.

Mexican gold poppy and arroyo lupine mix excellently in early spring wildflower borders.

Picking Seed to Store

When you want to collect seed from your own garden, the first question you have to answer is whether you want to pick it to store it (for later use) or store it in the ground. If you are picking to store, follow these recommendations:

- Make sure the seed is mature. For spring-blooming flowers in the Sonoran Desert, for example, seeds usually mature in May or June. When seeds are ripe they turn a dark color and become opaque. If the seed is green and wet inside, it is not ready for harvest.
- Separate the seeds from their chaff by straining them through an appropriately sized kitchen sieve, or use the manila folder method described next.
- To separate the seeds from chaff with a manila folder, open the folder and place seeds and chaff inside. Close folder, then hold at an angle and tap. The smaller (and usually rounder) seeds will roll out while the chaff will remain in the folder.
- Store seeds in paper bags or breathable plastic bags. Ziploc-type plastic bags often trap moisture inside, causing seeds to mold.
- If you are planning to sow the seeds the following year, keep

Ornamental in flower and seed, the curved pods of devil's claw are featured here woven into steel grid fencing.

them in "human" conditions; that is, in a temperature range that humans enjoy—not too hot, too wet, or too cold. If you plan to save them for several years, keeping them refrigerated increases their survival by five or ten times. If you refrigerate, keep them at temperatures above 32 degrees F.

Sowing

In the deserts that receive some or all of their annual rainfall in the winter months, specifically the Sonoran and Mojave, spring bloomers should be sown in fall to early winter. In desert areas that receive summer rainfall (as in the Sonoran and Chihuahuan deserts) seed for summer- and fall-blooming flowers should be sown just prior to the monsoon season.

Break up your soil with a hard rake or shovel to a depth of four to six inches. If hardpan soil makes tilling a large area impractical, consider using the pointed side of a digging bar to dimple the ground, creating little craters where seeds can take root. Make sure your planting area is free of weeds, and distribute seed evenly over the soil surface. Since most desert wildflowers thrive in lean alkaline soils, soil amendments are generally not necessary. If your yard is mulched with decomposed granite, rake the seeds into the top $1/4$ inch of soil. If you have a gravel surface with spaces between the rocks, simply scatter the seeds on the surface and water them so they will fall into a germinating niche.

Watering

Timing your watering to coincide with incoming wet winter storms is the best way to ensure good germination and prolonged flowering. If regular fall rains are not forthcoming, you can increase your rate of germination by watering your seeds three times a week for about four to six weeks or until seedlings appear. Once seedlings appear, a weekly watering (if it doesn't rain) will ensure good flowering. If you rely on rainfall alone, some years will be good while other years you could end up with nothing.

Precautions

- Some people are allergic to some wild plant stems and/or seeds. If you are unsure about your tolerance, wear a dust mask and gloves.
- Check local regulations but in general, never pick seed in wilderness areas, national parks, state parks, or trust lands.
- Roadsides and friends' yards (with their permission!) are generally fair game. Exchanging seeds with friends can be a fun way to share your favorite desert plants.

ENEMIES OF WILDFLOWERS: QUAIL, RABBITS, AND HOMEOWNERS' ASSOCIATIONS When growing wildflowers there are three things to consider: keeping the seed from getting eaten, protecting plants from getting eaten, and keeping your homeowners' association from throwing a hissy fit when your raked gravel becomes sprinkled with wildflowers (which your HOA might mistake for weeds).

The main culprit for seed consumption is the bird population. In order to keep your carefully selected and dearly loved wildflower seed from becoming very expensive bird food, you have three options:

- Fence the seedbed and cover with bird netting.
- Use "decoy" birdseed in an area away from the seedbed to keep the avian crowd occupied while your seeds germinate.
- Roll up your seeds in clay balls and bombard the garden with them.

As this sign suggests, sometimes you have to defend your wildflowers against overzealous homeowners' associations and maintenance workers.

After the seeds germinate and tiny plantlets appear (that look oh-so-delicious to rabbits) you have another challenge if you live in a neighborhood where the bunnies roam free. For protecting your seedlings you have a couple of options, both in the realm of fencing:

- Although I've never been a big fan of chicken wire or "wildflower corrals," as I call them, I can't say that they are as ineffective as they are ugly. You can either corral an entire area with chicken wire or, for a slightly less controlled look, you can slip a cylinder of hardware mesh over individual plants such as penstemon species and globemallows (both of which are frequent rabbit-target plants).
- For a more visually pleasing, yet not quite as secure, solution, you can use products like liquid fence, which utilizes some formula that either is, or is meant to imitate, large predator (i.e., coyotes, bobcats, and mountain lions) urine, whose scent scares the devil out of the entire rabbit family. This stuff is not cheap and is applied with a spray bottle. It should be reapplied monthly or more often depending on rainfall, which can wash the scent away. To humans, the scent is also repulsive, like a frat-boy's rotten-egg stink bomb, but again the stuff does work.

The Desert Gardener's Bill of Rights for Homeowners' Associations

1. The right to grow annual and perennial wildflowers in your yard and let the seed on the plants mature before cleaning them up.
2. The right to harvest rainwater to water your garden (including the right to reduce impermeable surfaces, direct rainwater to planted areas by creating contours, and to collect rainwater in above-ground storage tanks that may be visible from adjacent properties).
3. The right to grow any native plants found in the wild within 50 miles and at an elevation of 1,000 feet above or below your lot.
4. The right to maintain your plants in natural forms that are not pruned ("meatballed") into balls and boxes.
5. The right to have a yard that is dormant during cold and dry spells.
6. The right to modify the garden as needed (after all, a garden is a living, changing thing rather than a static creation) and include plants that may not currently be on community "approved" lists.
7. The right to plant trees where you want them for shade.
8. The right to dry your laundry outdoors on a line.

Rise Up Against Silly HOAs' Landscaping Rules!

While I understand the desire for uniformity within a community, most of the homeowners' associations whose gardening guidelines I have become familiar with impose rigid and often nonsensical rules about landscaping on their member homeowners. For this reason, I'm advocating the adjacent bill of rights on behalf of desert gardeners yoked with unreasonable homeowners'-association restrictions.

To give you a couple of examples of these crazy restrictions, one HOA's documents (in Tucson) prohibited residents from planting Douglas fir trees. I could only assume that this was to protect the fir tree from a brief and miserable life in the low desert, since anyone who could really grow one here would deserve an award. Another Tucson area HOA's architectural and landscaping documents require that any plant that dies be replaced with the *exact* same species (how many times do you have to do this?). Also, a lot of HOAs prohibit the keeping of chickens. What is wrong with a few chickens (not roosters, mind you)?

THE TWO-SEASON GARDEN: LEARNING TO LOVE SEASONAL DORMANCY

Garden photographer Charles Mann has called attention to the fact that the best Southwestern gardens have a correlation with classic Zen landscapes in Kyoto, in that flowers are not the main focus of the garden. As Mann says, "Where Western gardens are virtually defined by their displays of ever-changing color, the prominence of organic materials like big stones, sculptural shrubs and trees, streambeds of dry gravel or sand, flagstone pathways and the play of sun and shadow are central to the Japanese garden… But just like the desert in spring, occasionally there is a sudden dramatic surprise. When a particular fruit tree or shrub bursts into bloom, the effect can be startling…" In my mind this is the role of annual desert wildflowers, to startle us in spring and summer with a dramatic floral surprise. However briefly a spring wildflower display lasts or however infrequently it occurs, it rarely fails to remind us of the power of germoplasm (seeds) and wow us with jewel-like color.

It is useful to appreciate the different bloom seasons in the various deserts: in the Sonoran Desert, there are two floriferous seasons provided by Mother Nature—spring, and late summer into fall. Both of these flowering seasons are synchronized with the two rainy seasons and allow us to "frontload" (plant for spring bloom) and "rearload" (plant for late-summer and fall bloom) our gardens. The Chihuahuan Desert, which receives most of its annual rainfall during the summer months, bursts into bloom during the late summer into fall, following monsoon rains. The Mojave Desert, whose precipitation comes via winter Pacific storms, is a spring-blooming desert.

In all of these deserts, some of the same rules of thumb apply: when we have good rainy seasons, we get good blooms; no rain and the seeds sit dormant until the next season. It is an ingenious and simple method that can be adapted to our gardens. If your garden is well structured with succulents, shrubs, and trees, you will have interest even when the plants are out of bloom. This sort of gardening means that your garden will explode with wildflowers on a good year, and then as hot weather arrives those flowers will either set seed and die, or, if they are perennials, they may set seed and then rest until the following season. This sort of planting highlights the fact that while wildflowers are an important part of desert gardens, they cannot hold the design together on their own—they are simply not around long enough. As naturalist Joseph Wood Krutch explained, wildflowers "riot briefly and then lie low."

WILDFLOWER PICKS FOR SPRING

Note: In the following list, species marked with an asterisk (*) will tolerate light shade in the low deserts:

- **Barestem Larkspur** (*Delphinium scaposum*) A true delphinium with blue flowers (with one white petal) displayed on a thin stalk that rises 30 inches. This perennial will sprout only in wet years and will otherwise lie dormant.
- **Brittlebush** (*Encelia farinosa*) Usually considered a shrub, this early-blooming silver-leafed beauty is a harbinger of spring in the Sonoran Desert. Its yellow flowers are held above the foliage on slender chartreuse stems. Cut back hard after blooming for best appearance. Prolific from seed.
- **Canyon Penstemon*** (*Penstemon pseudospectabilis*) Medium-green toothed leaves and hot-pink flower spires attract hummingbirds in the spring.
- **Cardinal Penstemon*** (*Penstemon cardinalis*) Red blooms appear on the thick stem of this New Mexico/Texas native.
- **Chia** (*Salvia columbariae*) This petite but beautiful dark blue salvia has been used as a food source by native peoples throughout the Southwest; quail are extremely fond of the seed as well.
- **Desert Bluebells** (*Phacelia campanularia*) One of the few gentian-blue desert flowers, desert bluebells are always a favorite and are probably the easiest to germinate of all of the spring bloomers—just spread the copper BB-like seeds out, water, and wait. Wear gloves when harvesting the seed, as some people get an itchy rash when handling the hairy leaves and stems.

Gloriously blue desert bluebells.

- **Desert Marigold** (*Baileya multiradiata*) Its ferny sterling-silver foliage topped with screaming yellow daisies makes desert marigold one of the most popular wildflowers for home gardeners. It is simple to grow (it will sprout in the cracks in sidewalks), blooms nearly every month of the year, and is hardy to 10 below zero! This short-lived perennial is available in nursery containers (although it dislikes being in pots and often looks it) but is better started from seed in disturbed soil.
- **Desert Zinnia** (*Zinnia acerosa*) Best from seed. Low-growing white daisies with yellow eyes.

Superb penstemon against a backdrop of tawny deer grass in spring (Design: Scott Calhoun).

- **Firecracker Penstemon** (*Penstemon eatonii*) Beginning its bloom season as early as mid-January in the low deserts, firecracker penstemon has striking green leaves and bright red flowers. Firecracker is more cold-hardy than Parry's and will take cold down to −20 degrees.
- **Firewheel*** (*Gaillardia pulchella*) This tough perennial is native to Arizona's grasslands and is a great choice for evoking a meadow. These foot-high yellow and maroon flowers are easy to germinate and produce an abundance of seed, readily spreading in a garden.
- **Giant Penstemon*** (*Penstemon palmeri*) This pink-flowered penstemon giant (up to six feet tall!) is the most strongly scented of the penstemons, and in the low deserts it will tolerate light shade. It needs very fast drainage to thrive.
- **Globemallow** (*Sphaeralcea ambigua*) Easy to grow, globemallow is responsible for the grand orange displays along many desert roadways. Be careful when handling this plant, as the small hairs on its leaves can irritate your eyes. Look for other colors like red, salmon, and pink and white. In containers, try exceptional cultivars such as 'Louis Hamilton', with red-orange blooms, and 'Papago Pink', which sports exceptionally large pink blooms. Hardy to −10 degrees, globemallow is cold-hardy over a large part of the Southwest and is underused as a garden plant.
- **Goodding's Verbena*** (*Glandularia gooddingii*) A short-lived perennial with lavender flowers that loves colonizing disturbed soil. Will bloom into summer and fall when moisture is available.
- **Lupine** (*Lupinus* sp.) Tough to germinate but rewarding. For better germination, boil water and then pour it into a jar of lupine seed. Soak seed overnight and plant the next day. Lupine is a legume that will fix nitrogen in your soil. **Succulent lupine*** (*Lupinus succulentus*) gets to be a large 36-inch-high plant, while the shorter **arroyo lupine** (*Lupinus sparsiflorus*, also known as Mojave lupine) is usually under 24 inches high.
- **Mexican Gold Poppy** (*Eschscholtzia mexicana*) The more arid-adapted cousin to California poppies, Mexican gold poppy is easy to grow from seed. Gene Joseph and Jane Evans of Plants for the Southwest sow Mexican gold poppy in pots with succulents for surprising dashes of color come spring. When harvesting seed, be careful! These ripe seed heads will explode at the slightest touch.
- **Owl's Clover** (*Orthocarpus purpurascens*) Notoriously finicky about germinating conditions, but worth the effort. The stunning purple flower spikes are one of the main blanket-forming flowers in the Sonoran Desert on wet years. Because owl's clover is considered semiparasitic, try sowing with native grass seed such as blue grama.
- **Parry's Penstemon** (*Penstemon parryi*) One of the showiest penstemons for the low desert. Since Parry's penstemon is a perennial, it will bloom best in its second year. Get longer bloom from your penstemon with supplemental watering in early spring. Treat with baking soda in a surfactant (a surfactant—like insecticidal soap—helps spread the baking soda on the surface of the leaves) to kill powdery mildew, which is sometimes a problem with Parry's penstemon, particularly when it is grown in shade. Harvest seed in late May and early June by snapping off flower spikes and inverting them over newspaper to speed seed-gathering.
- **Purple Mat** (*Nama hispidum*) Purple mat's purple bell-shaped flowers and short stature make it a good choice for growing between flagstone pavers.
- **Superb Penstemon*** (*Penstemon superbus*) This coral-flowered beauty is excellent when planted in and among grasses.

- **Tufted Evening Primrose** (*Oenothera caespitosa*) Its big white- and pink-tinged flowers open in the evening and close in the morning and are pollinated by hawk moths with impossibly long tongues. A great plant for moonlight gardens. Prefers well-drained soil.
- **Western Wall Flower** (*Erysimum asperum*) A short-lived perennial with spires of bright yellow flowers. This mustard-family plant is an exceptional companion for desert bluebells, creating a strong blue-and-yellow composition.

WILDFLOWER PICKS FOR SUMMER/FALL

Note: In the following list, species marked with an asterisk (*) will tolerate light shade in the low deserts:

- **Arizona Poppy** (*Kallstroemia grandiflora*) Looking very much like the summer counterpart of the Mexican gold poppy, this poppy is not actually a poppy at all but is related instead to the creosote bush and times its blooms with the monsoon rains. Prevalent in arid grasslands.
- **Blackfoot Daisy*** (*Melampodium leucanthum*) A wonderful perennial that likes to grow in rocky habitat (like the red rocks around Sedona) and can bloom spring through fall. It can be purchased in containers and transplanted as well as grown from seed.
- **'Bright Lights' Cosmos** (*Cosmos sulphureus* 'Bright Lights') One of the best butterfly attracters for the summer garden, this Mexican native reseeds ambitiously but also provides a long season of orange and gold blooms on tall, slender, green stems.
- **Chocolate Flower*** (*Berlandiera lyrata*) Yes, the yellow daisy-like blooms and cup-shaped seedheads do smell like chocolate! To boot, chocolate flower will take partial shade and is hardy to −30 degrees.
- **Cinch Weed** (*Pectis papposa*) Yes, this is yet another low-growing yellow daisy, but this one is particularly good for sandy sites and makes a good pair with the blue-flowering shrub broom dalea (*Dalea scoparia*). This pair is common in nature in the sandy hummocks around El Paso.
- **Colorado Four O'Clock** (*Mirabilis multiflora*) This long-lived cold-hardy perennial succeeds in both high- and low-elevation desert gardens. Growing from a big tuber, its light purple flowers open en masse in the afternoon, attracting scads of hawk moths. It looks particularly good when planted beneath foothills palo verde trees, where it will seed and colonize large areas.
- **Dakota Verbena** (*Verbena bipinnatifida*) This Arizona and New Mexico native is excellent when its purple low-growing flowers are mixed with yellow flowering natives like snakeweed.
- **Damianita Daisy** (*Chrysactinia mexicana*) Forms a tidy hemisphere of aromatic evergreen foliage that is distasteful to rabbits. In spring and summer the foliage becomes eclipsed by small gold daisies. A truly excellent perennial for the hot garden.
- **Desert Senna** (*Senna covesii*) A prolific reseeder that is easy to grow in nearly any soil. Its gold flowers look phenomenal when set against purple-blooming Texas ranger species (*Leucophyllum* sp.).
- **Devil's Claw*** (*Proboscidea parviflora*) A summer-rainy-season bloomer best known for its wickedly hooked seedheads that are used in Tohono O'odham basketry, devil's claw produces big tropical-looking leaves and tri-colored snapdragon-like (white, purple, and yellow) blooms. Soak seeds in water overnight before sowing, for best germination.

Mexican hat in bloom.

During the summer rainy season, yellow desert senna complements a background of purple Texas ranger flowers.

- **Dogweed** (*Thymophylla pentachaeta*) This scrappy little ground cover is a great and mostly rabbit-proof plant that blooms tiny gold daisies on and off almost year-round. Dogs, for some unknown reason, like to sniff around and roll in it.
- **Mexican Hat,** also called **Coneflower** (*Ratibida columnaris*) The toughest and most drought-tolerant of all of the black-eyed Susan relatives, this coneflower blooms drooping daisy-like flowers with a strong central cone. It blooms, depending on the locale, from April to November and comes in yellow, maroon, and combinations of the two.
- **Mexican Sunflower** (*Tithonia rotundifolia*) Big orange Mexican sunflowers that in the wild are considered "rank," or weedy, growers that reach heights of six feet. In the garden it is best to stick with one of the many compact cultivars. Like 'Bright Lights' cosmos, it needs regular water for best continuous blooming. Looks great mixed in with veggie gardens.
- **Paper Flower** (*Psilostrophe cooperi*) A little (18–24-inch) mound of pure sunshine-yellow flowers. This perennial is extremely drought-tolerant and cold-hardy to 10 degrees. Available in nursery-grown containers or from seed.
- **Prairie Zinnia** (*Zinnia grandiflora*) A tough perennial ground cover that spreads by vigorous underground rhizomes and is covered with small, deep gold flowers throughout the warm season.
- **Purple Aster** (*Aster bigelovii*) This wildflower comprises the purple half of a classic fall wildflower combination: the dwarf rabbitbrush (*Ericameria nauseosus nauseosus*) and purple aster that you see in northern New Mexico and Arizona in the fall. In the lower Sonoran and Mojave desert areas, you can achieve the same fall effect with purple aster and turpentine bush (*Ericameria laricifolia*).
- **Rock Penstemon*** (*Penstemon baccharifolius*) Excellent drought-tolerant shubby perennial from south Texas, with evergreen foliage and red flowers all summer. Best purchased in a pot to ensure the best form.
- **Sacred Datura*** (*Datura wrightii*) Thanks to Georgia O'Keeffe, the sensual trumpet-shaped white blossoms of sacred datura have become icons of the Southwest. Because it is a very large and somewhat unruly plant, it is a good choice for rainwa-

The tall orange heads of Mexican sunflower fit well in veggie or cut-flower gardens.

DESIGNING WITH DESERT PLANTS 61

Penstemon amphorellae's delicate leaves and pale blue flowers make it an attractive complement to yellow-flowering plants like Mexican hat.

ter-collection basins, arroyos, and other low-lying areas away from foot traffic. The white flowers are sweetly fragrant, yet the foliage smells like a shaggy dog that has been out in the rain. All parts of the plant are toxic.

- **Trailing Four O'Clock*** (*Allonia incarnata*) A trailing perennial with hot-pink flowers that is common in gravelly arroyo beds, especially during the summer monsoon season—although it will bloom from spring through fall with adequate moisture.
- **Tropical Sage** (*Salvia coccinea*) A rampant reseeder that will appear along with wet hot summer conditions. Great poking up among grasses.
- **White Trumpet*** (*Telesiphonia brachysiphon*) White jasmine-scented flowers and green foliage are the main glories of this rare but worth-seeking low-growing perennial that is native to rocky grasslands, often found growing beneath ocotillo.
- **Yellow Devil's Claw*** (*Proboscidea altheaefolia*) Unlike its purple cousin, yellow devil's claw is a perennial and grows from a sizable underground tuber. Its blooms range from yellow to orange, while its seeds are the same hooked shape as those of purple devil's claw.

GOT BULBS? A FEW BULBS FOR DESERT GARDENS

Here is a short list of bulbs from the Americas. More bulbs, particularly those from the Cape region of South Africa, are just now being tried out in Southwestern gardens, but this list is an excellent start. All of these bulbs are best planted in the fall.

- **Ajo Lily** (*Hesperocallis undulata*) This tall-statured majestic plant is a maddeningly difficult-to-grow white desert lily. It prefers sandy soils and typically grows in places where sand verbena and birdcage primrose grow. From bulbs, it flowers only after it is a few years old. It is wonderful enough to try growing it.
- **Blue Dicks** (*Dichelostemma pulchellum*) A little cluster of purple-blue flowers on elegant onion-like stems, blue dicks is a great little bulb native to rocky slopes throughout the Southwest. Can be propagated by seed or bulb (the seed will take three years to come into flower).
- **Evening Rain Lily** (*Cooperia drummondii*) This strapping white lily comes up in spring and looks great among grasses and prickly pears from Arizona to Texas.

The elusive beauty of the mariposa lily is sure to give you an orange crush on this desert bulb.

An Ajo lily stands tall beside the road in the Pinacate, Sonora, Mexico.

- **Mariposa Lily** (*Calochortus kennedyi*) Its exquisite deep orange flowers tempt many to try growing this temperamental and beguiling bulb at home. Blooms after most other wildflowers have peaked.
- **Pink Rain Lily** (*Zephranthes grandiflora*) This big hot-pink tropical American showstopper is excellent when planted in numbers below mesquite and ironwood trees.
- **'Prairie Sunset' Rain Lily** (*Zephranthes* x 'Prairie Sunset') A hybrid lily that keeps its evergreen foliage over the hot summer months and repeatedly sends up clusters of apricot flowers.

BRING IN THE THUGS: RUDERAL FLOWERS FOR TOUGH SITES Aggressive pioneer plants that are the first to colonize disturbed soils on construction sites, roadsides, and railroad sidings are called *ruderals*. In the right conditions (freshly disturbed soil, plenty of water, little competition) ruderals will overtake entire garden areas, crowding out other desirable plants. Usually ruderals dominate an area only for a few seasons, gradually giving way to other species as the site conditions stabilize. For this reason, ruderals sometimes have a place in hot gardens. For instance, in very dry, poor soils where few other plants will grow, ruderals may be one of the only choices. Ruderals can be native plants or exotics, but the list beginning on page 102 consists of low-water-use annual and perennial plants native to the Southwest that can be used when all else fails. These are plants that I have appreciated in vacant lots and along highways and have tried (usually with an abundance of success) in garden situations. They all flower and have beauty that belies their profligacy.

Sculptural Plants

So the question becomes, if flowers are not the main focus of Southwest gardens, what is? The answer is twofold: sculptural plants and geological specimens (big rocks, gravel, and stones). Another way of saying this is to note that gardening in the Southwest is all about creating interesting textural differences, and there is perhaps no group of plants that provide as much textural contrast as sculptural succulents. And the wonderful thing is, the Southwest is brimming with sculptural plants. Since, as I mentioned, we do have a winter season in which most plants go dormant, designing gardens for winter interest in the Southwest leans heavily on structural plants. These plants are so central to our gardens that I have begun to object to calling them accent plants, because they seem much more important than the word "accent"—with its finishing-touch interior-decorating connotation—implies. Sculptural plants are not limited to succulents—what is more sculptural than a multitrunked desert tree twisting its branches crazily horizontal? But succulents (including cacti, stem succulents such as ocotillo, and "woody lilies"—which includes the agaves, yuccas, spoons, and beargrass) are the low-water-use superstars of desert gardens. The symmetrical geometry of agaves, the Reddy Kilowatt-topped yuccas, and the planetary aura of barrel cacti enliven our gardens in our two dormant seasons: midwinter and the dry fore-summer.

Although we can't forget that these succulent plants are living things, for garden-design purposes it may be more useful to consider them as architectural elements—spheres, stars, columns, and organ pipes. The idea of having these plants serve as architectural elements is not as strange as it might seem. Just take a look at some of the new public art on the streets of Tucson. You'll find steel saguaros and barrel cactus sculptures in the medians alongside their natural namesakes. If these bold plants inspire artists, why shouldn't we celebrate them in our gardens?

WOODY LILIES Woody lilies, a subgroup of the lily family, are some of the most dramatic choices for hot gardens. This group is composed of agaves, yuccas, desert spoons, and bear grasses, to name a few. Most of these plants have mostly fibrous leaves that grow from a central rosette. Some have trunks and can develop into Dr. Seuss-style trees. Many produce showy flower spikes that range in color from cream to gold, butter-yellow, and red.

The Agave: A Hot-Garden Star

When bold, pointed plants are required, agaves can be the stars of your garden—literally. These New World plants come in an amazing range of sizes and colors. From the diminutive and sophisticated Queen Victoria agave to the giant powder-blue Weber's agave, there is a place in nearly every yard for these important American plants.

When planting the larger species of agaves, make sure to leave plenty of room for growth. Big agaves should be kept well away from outdoor dining areas and pathways—places where your

A pair of muscular blue century plants announce the entrance into the blue garden at Lotusland near Santa Barbara.

The mighty bloom stalks of agaves are pretty in their own right.

woods is excellent for growing agaves. Also, most species do better with occasional watering during dry summer months.

Agaves are such a large group of plants, from a large geographic area, that there are plants for nearly every growing situation, including deep shade. Plants like spider, cow's horn, and twin-flowered agave thrive in low light or brighter conditions—they are switch-hitters, so to speak.

Agaves are sometimes mistaken for their African cousins, aloes. One of the main differences between the two types of plants is that most aloes bloom every year, while agaves bloom only once, usually after many years. This trait, called *semelparity*, means that the plant reproduces only once. In the case of agaves, this reproduction is a spectacular big-bang event in which the mother plant, after years or sometimes decades of growth, sends up a massive pole-like flower-spike that can reach heights of 50 feet, depending on the species. I like to make the case that semelparity should not be viewed as a drawback to planting agaves in your garden. Try to think of the bloom event not as the end of your agave's life but more like the erection (pardon the pun) of a vital new sculpture in your garden. After the plants have bloomed you can saw off the pole-like dried bloom stalks and incorporate them into a rustic fence or ramada.

dinner guests' derrières could meet the business end of the plant. The giants of the agave world grow to six feet high and wide, and if the conditions are right you can end up with a 12-foot-high plant. Thankfully, many small and medium-sized agaves fit nicely into pots and smaller beds, even those adjacent to patios and walkways.

Beginning desert gardeners sometimes use agaves the same way they would use cacti: in full reflected heat without any source of supplemental water. While some agaves will take this sort of situation, most agave species do best with a little shade and supplemental watering. Often, the bright filtered shade provided by desert trees such as mesquites, foothills palo verdes, and iron-

The sharkskin agave is a hybrid of *Agave victoria-reginae* and *Agave scabra*. Here it blends nicely with Mexican feather grass.

The contorted leaves of octopus agave, here featured with a backdrop of yellow bells, makes it hard to resist.

Controlling the Snout-Nosed Agave Weevil

Agaves are considered a relatively pest-free plant for Southwest gardens—except, that is, for one particularly nasty pest: the snout-nosed agave weevil. The female of this hook-nosed weevil sticks her snout in agave leaves to test their sugar content. If she finds the plant acceptable, she lays eggs, which turn into fat white grubs that eat your agave plants from the inside out. By far the most susceptible agave species are the century plants (*Agave americana, A.*

With silver leaves and reddish spines, butterfly agave is one of the most attractive recent introductions to the horticultural trade.

americana marginata, and *A. americana mediopicta*). In fact, Mark Sitter of B & B Cactus Farm in Tucson has had so much trouble with the white stripe agave that he once confided that "I'm wondering whether we are doing a disservice to the agave family by selling this plant since it is so susceptible to the weevil." The news that white stripe agave is the Typhoid Mary of agaves is unfortunate for garden designers, because it is one of the most beautiful of the variegated types.

In my own garden, my large century plants and one Weber's agave have fallen victim to the weevil, while other species have remained undisturbed by the pest. Some general rules of thumb for avoiding the pest are: keep the plant healthy with deep infrequent watering, remove infested plants promptly, and if you use

Radical Agave Propagation

My wife, Deirdre, was watching an episode of the Martha Stewart show when she called to tell me that Martha's guest, Tony Avent, plantsman extraordinaire, was taking a power drill with a long bit and drilling down through the center of the rosette of an agave specimen. Avent was "destroying the central nervous system," as he described it, "to propagate more agaves." "What in the hell?" I thought to myself, but after checking it out, it appears that this is one nearly sure-fire method to spur an agave into making pups, or offsets. I double-checked this fact with an agave guru closer to home—Greg Starr—who informed me that it does indeed work. So, on smaller agave types, use a ¼-inch drill bit; on large agaves, use up to a ½-inch bit. Using a hand saw, cut the top of the central rosette off, then drill straight down. You will sacrifice the mother plant, but with any luck it will produce five or six new pups.

pesticides, use a systemic soil drench in the area where the infested plants were. In my own garden I have not used a pesticide, and I've decided to let my plants battle it out against the insect in hopes that I will find species that are unpalatable to the weevil and, with luck, an equilibrium will be reached. What I have found is that my potted specimens have remained relatively weevil-free, as well as most of my agaves that are native to the Southwest. However, for complete eradication, serious systemic pesticides might be required.

Spoons for Deserts, Grasses for Bears, and Red Yuccas (Dasylirions, Nolinas, *and* Hesperaloes)

In addition to yuccas and agaves, three other genera of plants in the woody lily family are important to the hot garden: *Dasylirions*, *Nolinas*, and *Hesperaloes*, known respectively as desert spoons, bear grasses, and red hesperaloes (also called red yuccas). Many of these plants, with their strong, flexible fibrous leaves, are still important basket-making plants for Native Americans. In the landscape, many of these—particularly desert spoon and red hesperaloe—have become mainstays. Speaking of the red hesperaloe, this is truly a blast-furnace plant—able to withstand reflected heat of street medians and sending up a haze of pinky-red bloom stalks in

At Peckerwood garden, John Fairey mixes agaves, nolinas, and desert spoons with great élan.

The vertical punctuation of a desert spoon bloom stalk is effective when set against walls and sky.

late spring and early summer. Other plants in this group are equally attractive. Toothless spoon is very much like a spherical six-foot-high green fiber-optic sculpture that moves in the wind. Blue nolina becomes a massive yucca-like plant with an interesting plume of flowers and long blue leaves.

Yuccalicious

Out on the far southeast side of Tucson, I live in a transitional zone; to my west, the signature plant of the Sonoran Desert, the mighty saguaro, stakes its claim, but only a few miles to my east the land rises up and the Chihuahuan Desert begins in earnest—a change marked by the lack of saguaros and appearance of New Mexico's state flower, the soap tree yucca. From Tucson to Austin, Texas, plants from the genus *Yucca* (which is distinct from the genus of so-called red yuccas, *Hesperaloe*) supplant the saguaro as the charismatic mega-succulent.

In the Southwest, most yuccas bloom in the late spring or early summer. In great contrast to their sharp and linear leaves, yuccas send up almost girly white or cream-colored flowers on stalks that

At the Newhouse garden, the trunkless pale-leaf yucca is the right scale to place in front of the single-story residence (Design: Scott Calhoun).

At the Humphreys garden, large beaked yuccas stand up to the strong masonry and cast interesting evening shadows (Design: Scott Calhoun).

shoot up from the center of the plant like the feather plume on a marching-band helmet. The effect is somewhat ridiculous-looking, a kind of Seussian surprise, like discovering a shark sporting a feather boa. The purpose of yucca flowers is to attract very specific moths, which pollinate only specific yucca species. For hard-core sculptural-desert-plant lovers, you don't have to worry that these flowers will sissify your yucca, because as soon as the flower petals fall, stark dried flower stalks and seed pods picket the sky like antelope horns. You can hasten this process by eating the yucca flower petals, which can be served up fresh in a salad in much the way you would use radicchio.

The yucca is a seriously misunderstood plant. In the case of the soap tree yucca, its bayonet-shaped, gray-green leaves grow from a central rosette atop a trunk; over time, as the leaves die from the bottom up, these leaves form a sort of "grass skirt" around the trunk. On the larger trunk-forming types, this skirt of dried leaves sometimes gives the yucca a bum rap; about the soap tree yucca, writer Ellen Meloy comments, "The overall effect is of a dumpy-looking palm tree with its finger in a socket, Reddy Kilowatt lost in the Chihuahua." Certainly, soap tree yuccas bristle with a certain electricity, but dumpy? I would prefer to call the more fragile

The jagged branching architecture of the Joshua tree is brilliant against desert skies. In gardens, they can take on a true treelike role over time.

queen palm trees overgrown limp yuccas! The soap tree yucca is a good representative of the genus. It has narrow leaves and tiny filaments that glow when it is backlit. The filaments and big creamy bloom stalks that shoot up from the center of the plant in spring are really the only delicate-looking parts of the soap tree. In fact this yucca has proven to be atomically tough. It is one of the tenacious plants that have moved back into the sterilized ground-zero landscape in New Mexico's Jornada del Muerto (meaning Journey or Trail of Death), the site of the Trinity Project nuclear test. A plant this tough is a force to be reckoned with.

No one can say the yucca has not been useful. As William Dunmire says in his book *Wild Plants and Native People of the Four Corners,* "Yuccas constitute the single most important non-cultivated group of plants for prehistoric and contemporary Indians living the Southwest." Beginning with the Aztecs, yucca fibers were used to make sandals, baskets, rope, belts, bowstrings, and fishing nets, to name just a few. As if those uses were not enough, Native Americans also made a shampoo from the roots and cooked with the flowers and fruit.

One of the best things about yuccas is that a large number of them are quite cold-hardy, more so than agave-family plants, and this allows them to be grown across a much broader region. Here are descriptions of a few of my favorites in gardens:

- Featured in gardens as diverse as the Chihuahuan Desert Gardens in El Paso and Chanticleer in Pennsylvania, the **beaked yucca** (*Yucca rostrata*) earns its keep in the garden. Notable for its blue foliage and slightly weeping leaves, the beaked yucca reaches heights of up to 10 feet. Its stout trunk gives it a vertical tree-like emphasis in the garden. The beaked yucca's modest 4-foot width makes it a great choice for courtyards or entry areas that need a bold plant but are too small for most trees. Like most yuccas, the beaked yucca likes excellent drainage. The beaked yucca sports large creamy-white flower spikes that are very showy.

- If you like the blue foliage of the beaked yucca but need a shorter plant, the diminutive **pale-leaf yucca** (*Yucca pallida*) should fill the bill. *Yucca pallida* is a trunkless species that can form clumps with up to 30 heads. Its pure white lily-like flowers are the perfect complement to its blue leaves. Because this plant is only 1½ feet high and wide, it works to excellent effect in hot sidewalk strips, mingling with tough native perennials such as prairie zinnia (*Zinnia grandiflora*) and firecracker penstemon (*Penstemon eatonii*).

- For those who like to browse their own gardens, the **banana yucca** (*Yucca baccata*) is a fine choice; this tasty, low-growing, clumping species is common in the red-rock areas of the Four Corners states. If you are visiting Sedona for a hot-stone massage and aura realignment, the yucca outside the door of your resort will most likely be the banana yucca, so named for the shape and sweet taste of its green fruit. The flowers of the banana yucca are also edible, taste like lettuce, and are good in salads. The banana yucca is a medium-sized plant that looks good against boulders and finer textured perennial plants. Since it is cold-hardy to −20 degrees F, it is adaptable to a fairly wide swath of American gardening regions.

- The best known of the yuccas, and title of a classic U2 album, is the granddaddy of the yucca family—the **Joshua tree** (*Yucca brevifolia*). So named by Mormon pioneers who thought its form looked like the outstretched arms of the biblical prophet Joshua, this Mojave Desert native grows slowly to heights of up to 30 feet. Although the familiar shaggy profile of the Joshua tree is iconic, its enormous size is an anomaly. If any plant in the yucca family can truly be called a tree, the Joshua tree is it. Around Tucson, Joshua trees planted in the early 1970s are now maturing in residential neighborhoods, and the result is awe-inspiring; these front-yard trees immediately bring to mind bold Seussian landscapes. Even though the young Joshua tree you bring home from the nursery will likely be small, don't crowd it. It will mature into a large and strangely dignified plant. The Joshua tree is hardy to 10 degrees F but, like other Mojave Desert yuccas, it is a cool-season grower and dislikes the extreme heat of low deserts. Deep summer watering will help Joshua trees survive the hyper-summer in cities like Phoenix and Yuma. Las Vegas, on the other hand, is a perfect climate for Joshua trees, and southern Nevada residents would be wise to consider them in lieu of the ubiquitous palm trees that seem to accompany every new home sold there.

- For the coldest pockets of the region, the **soapweed** (*Yucca glauca*) is a logical yucca choice. With a native range that

The creamy bloom stalks of the Mexican blue yucca are dramatic when backed by colored walls.

> ### Eat Your Garden: Spinach and Soap Tree Blossom Salad
>
>
>
> *Serves 4.*
>
> The following beautiful green-and-white salad is best made with fresh young yucca flower petals (do not include the heart of the flower, as it is very bitter). Whisk the balsamic vinegar with the olive oil, pour over the other ingredients, toss, and season with fresh ground pepper to taste.
>
> - 2 cups baby spinach leaves
> - 2 cups soap tree yucca petals (*Yucca elata*)
> - ¼ cup shelled pine nuts
> - ½ cup golden raisins
> - ¼ cup balsamic vinegar
> - ¼ cup extra-virgin olive oil
> - Fresh-ground black pepper

extends from north Texas to Canada, soapweed is cold-hardy to a baffling −40 degrees F! (Arizona gardeners don't *really* believe it gets that cold anywhere.) The soapweed is distinguished by its stiff, narrow leaves with hairy filamentous margins and green-white flowers. The soapweed is tolerant of clay soils, drought, and deluge; so long as there is some decent drainage, the soapweed will persist. It is a fine complement to cliff rose (*Purshia mexicana*) and whitestem rabbitbrush (*Ericameria nauseosa speciosus*) in Great Basin and Rocky Mountain gardens.

Skirted or Skirtless: Should I Trim My Yucca's Skirt?

As some of the larger yucca species grow, a thatch of old leaves, sometimes called a skirt, forms around the trunk. The thatch does not hurt the plant and in cold climates may help insulate it from cold; however, removing excess thatch does give older yuccas a more architectural, "manicured" appearance. The choice is really yours; you have to ask yourself, "How shaggy is too shaggy?" If you decide to remove thatch, try using a sharp curved knife, moving up the trunk and creating a barber-pole spiral.

CONSPIRATORIAL CACTUS

Before I venture too far into the cactus forest, it should be mentioned that the cactus family is a vast and—when it comes to scientific names—murky universe. To treat most of them would mean another book bigger than this one, dedicated solely to the topic. The species I'm listing are cacti that are mostly already in the nursery trade, waiting to be used in gardens. The species featured here are grouped together by shape (barrels, hedgehogs, columnar cacti, prickly pears, chollas, and pincushions) and are species that I find particularly striking and adaptable in landscape-design situations. If your design sensibilities are at all like mine, you will be hooked, hopefully not literally, by these thrifty and handsome Southwest denizens and find yourself populating your garden with lots of them.

Barrels of Barrels

Spherical and symmetrical, barrel cacti are—pardon the pun—worlds unto themselves. The glowing yellow of the golden barrel and the deep red of the fire barrel make these plants very desirable accents. Although we generally think of barrels as spherical in shape, many native Southwestern species such as Coville, fish-

The versatile fishhook barrel is oblivious to heat or cold and adds year-round interest to the hot garden.

hook, and compass barrel can become massive columnar specimens five to six feet high, over 30 inches in diameter, and weighing several hundred pounds. Barrel cacti have become a mainstay of the Tucson Cactus and Succulent Society, which saves them

Hooked on Fishhooks

One of the best ways to get your well-gloved hands around some large and venerable fishhook barrel cacti is to get salvaged specimens saved from the developer's blade. The Tucson Cactus and Succulent Society, for example, has a rescue program in which volunteer crews scour properties slated for development for barrel cacti, saguaros, pincushions, hedgehogs, and other species, and for a small fee volunteers can take home some of the cacti in exchange for their labor. Since 1999, more than 40,000 plants have been saved and replanted in private gardens. The salvaged husky fishhook barrels always strike me as a lot of design bang for the buck. More information is listed at www.tucsoncactus.org. In other cities, you could check with your local chapter of the CSSA (Cactus and Succulent Society of America) for local rescue programs.

In Joshua Tree National Park, these brilliant red- and gold-spined compass barrels need only a minimal foothold to grow on rocky outcrops.

from destruction due to development and then resells them to the public. For moving large barrels, a four-handled canvas sling (picture a sort of gurney for short fat elves) is very useful (see the Resources section in this book for some good tool sources). When replanting salvaged plants, remember to orient the plant with its south side (which should be marked) pointing south. For a contemporary look, mass golden barrels in square or rectangular planting beds. Even in informal plantings, barrels make a more powerful design statement when clustered together. If you are going for a more natural look, consider seeding the wildflower desert bluebells around your golden barrel. The combination of blue and gold is a traffic-stopper in the spring garden.

ABOVE: Claret cup hedgehog in full bloom. RIGHT: Fendler's hedgehog at Denver Botanic Gardens artfully grown in a trough planter.

> ### Eat Your Garden: Hedgehog Fruit = Cactus Caviar
>
>
>
> It is no accident that there are at least two hedgehog cacti with the common name of "strawberry hedgehog"—the fruit does indeed taste like strawberries and is very easy to pick. When the fruit is nice and red, it detaches easily from the plant, and the remaining spines that cling to the fruit can be carefully knocked off with your fingers or tweezers. The fruit is excellent, although cactus growers will go nuts at the sheer cost of the little crunchy seeds you are consuming; one grower I spoke with in New Mexico estimated that each hedgehog fruit contained almost $20 in seeds! Think of it as cactus caviar. Not just strawberry hedgehogs have tasty fruit: all of the cacti in the hedgehog family produce delicious flavors.

Hedgehog Hoedown

Hedgehogs are the unsung cacti of spring desert gardens. With their relatively short stature and spiny furred arms, they can be overlooked until they explode with fuchsia, red, or golden flowers in late spring. They provide a welcome flush of color as early wildflowers, like poppies and lupine, are fading, but late spring flowers, like flattop buckwheat, are coming into bloom. Their rugged, thrifty nature recommends them as no-irrigation garden plants in harsh locations.

Other hedgehog-shaped cacti (though not considered true hedgehogs) include the ever-growing number of torch cactus hybrids, including 'Epic', 'Apricot Glow', 'June Noon', 'Volcano Sunset', and 'Glorious'. These hybrids are bred for their large, showy blooms and have become extremely popular as landscape plants. In a garden, I prefer them clustered together under trees

like palo breas, or if they are a collection of different hybrids, presented in labeled pots where their showy flower displays and fun names can be viewed up close.

Columnar Classics

Consider the saguaro. Its columnar structure recalls Greek architecture. Following rain, it swells in the middle like a Doric column, while its fluted ribs suggest the Corinthian and Ionic orders. Columnar cacti like saguaros provide strong vertical elements in a garden. It is hard to argue that there is any plant that more exemplifies the Sonoran Desert; they are, after all, the signature plants of the region. Iconic saguaros look good planted as single specimens or clustered under desert trees, as is sometimes their habit in the wild. A foothills palo verde will often harbor a handful of young saguaros under its fine canopy, and this pattern can be mimicked in desert gardens. When looking at columnar cactus cold-hardiness numbers, it becomes readily apparent that for the colder cities in the region, there are few choices that will survive in-ground year-round. So for locations like Albuquerque there is little hope of growing a saguaro (or any other columnar cactus, for that matter); gardeners there are better served by substituting a

The white-spined snow pole leaps out in front of red bird of paradise.

Organ pipe and Parry's penstemon.

large yucca for a columnar cactus. If you live in a cold spot and *must* have a columnar cactus, the Argentine giant is your best bet. A big handsome brute with golden spines, the Argentine giant fairly glows in the evening light.

For the warmest corners of the hot garden, a cornucopia of columnar freaks and wonders present themselves. For a more modern, stylized version of a column, the totempole cactus works to excellent effect. With its avocado-green color and multifaceted arms that resemble huge melting candles, the totempole is both bizarre and wonderful. When grouped together and set against a colored wall or rocky backdrop, the totempole serves as a free-standing sculpture that is okay to touch because it is virtually spineless. Because the totempole is a Baja California native, it can be sensitive to cold and should be located in warm microclimates, such as in south- or west-facing courtyards near walls or homes, or beneath overhangs.

Like the totempole, the organ pipe and senita are not fond of temperatures below the upper 20s but are worth growing for their multi-armed beauty. Both occur mostly in Mexico, but their range extends north into Arizona. The fruit of the organ pipe cactus, *pitahaya,* tastes like melon and strawberry, another good reason to have an organ pipe close at hand. Other marginally cold-hardy multi-armed cacti include the Mexican fencepost, which had a cameo appearance in the movie *Frida* as a fence around Frida and Diego's Mexico City studio. The Mexican fencepost, with its deep green color and thin vertical white stripes, is a favorite among home gardeners. It is a civilized plant, the cactus equivalent of a pinstriped suit. As with both the organ pipe and senita, the growing tips of the Mexican fencepost should be protected when temperatures fall below 30 degrees. Placing 32-ounce (or larger) Styrofoam cups on cactus growing tips is an easy way to protect them from frost.

For a hairy multi-armed look, the snow pole, Old Man of Mexico, or Old Man of the Andes are obvious choices. For dramatic sculpture in general, columnar cacti are hard to beat.

Mexican Fencepost Fence

More than just an icon of modernist Mexican gardens, the Mexican fencepost is used to form actual fences. In the warmer parts of the hot-garden zone, this is a good alternative to a masonry fence. An installation at the Desert Botanical Garden in Phoenix used a double layer of Mexican fencepost combined with bright masonry walls as a sort of fence. Mexican fencepost will turn into a fence much faster when provided with extra water during the warm months.

A double-layer Mexican fencepost fence at the Desert Botanical Garden in Phoenix.

Eat Your Garden: Prickly Pear Tuna (Fruit) Processing

The fruit on all prickly pears is edible, although some species taste better than others. Thankfully, our most ubiquitous species, Engelmann's, is one of the yummiest for juicing. When Engelmann's prickly pear are ripe, the fruit will turn a deep red and will separate easily from the pads. If fruit is greenish and hard, find another plant or wait. Prickly pear fruit ripens at different times on each plant, but in southern Arizona it generally is ripe from late July through mid-August. After picking for a few minutes, you will easily be able to tell the ripe from the not-so-ripe.

Do not try to pick the fruit or handle it with your fingers (the fruit has tiny hair-like spines called *glochids* that will be hard to remove from your flesh). Use tongs and a 5-gallon bucket.

Wash the fruit thoroughly. You may use a vegetable scrubber to remove bird droppings and dirt. Discard any fruit with holes in it—the birds beat you to it.

Blend it in a sturdy food processor until there are no large chunks of fruit and the mixture is a magenta puree. (As an alternative, Brad Lancaster suggests the following method: put the washed fruit in a clean old pillowcase, freeze, then thaw and strain the juice through the pillowcase into a pan.)

Strain the pulp-and-juice mixture through a colander lined with two layers of cheesecloth. The cheesecloth will strain out any of the remaining glochids. Let the juice strain for 20–30 minutes. Discard the pulp, seeds, and cheesecloth, taking care not to drop pulp or seeds in the juice. Freeze the magenta-colored juice in ice-cube trays for later use, or use fresh.

Juice can be refrigerated for a few days. Frozen juice will last at least one year.

Prickly Pears

I like to call prickly pears—on account of their ear-shaped pads—Mickey Mouse plants, but the truth is, they are one of the ubiquitous signature plants of our region, and for landscapes they come in a surfeit of sizes and colors. Consider the purple Santa Rita or the tree-like Indian fig. All in all, they make for great low-water-use sculptural plants in gardens, with the added benefit—which should not be pooh-poohed—of having edible fruit and pads.

Santa Rita prickly pear putting out new neon pink pads in spring.

A prickly pear with a backdrop of palo verde blossoms at the Ruth Bancroft Garden in Walnut Creek, California.

Preceding the fruit, nearly all of the prickly pear varieties have showy flowers in various shades of yellow, orange, red, or pink. The list on page 108 is restricted to the more ornamental landscape specimens such as the tuxedo spine, beavertail, and milk-chocolate spine prickly pear. Many of these smaller species are excellent when tucked into a rockery or planted amidst wildflowers; they will fit into even the smallest landscapes.

Brad's Gourmet Indian Figs

In Mexico, the Indian fig cactus is nearly as important as corn and beans as a food crop. The Indian fig is hugely popular as a vegetable *and* fruit crop. The young pads, or *nopales,* are chopped, cooked, and eaten somewhat like green beans (which happen to taste a little like nopales). The fruits, or *tunas,* are also tasty, and as with many food plants, selections of plants with different fruit flavors have been made. Tucson rainwater expert Brad Lancaster has made a habit of collecting these interesting fruiting varieties, and in his garden he grows the following, mostly with names that describe their taste: 'Honeydew Melon', 'Red Slush', 'Sicilian Port Wine', 'Papaya', and 'Orange Slush'. Since Indian fig is easily clonally propagated from pads, I'm hoping that Brad's gourmet Indian fig varieties make it into the wider nursery market (as well as my garden) soon!

> ### Drink Your Garden: Scott's Prickly Pear Lemonade
>
>
>
> *Makes 5 servings.*
>
> 4 cups water
> Juice of 6 lemons
> ½ cup prickly pear juice (or 3–4 frozen prickly pear ice cubes)
> ⅔ cup sugar
> 1 fresh lemon, sliced
> Mint or cilantro leaves, for garnish
>
> Combine the water, lemon juice, prickly pear juice, and sugar. Stir until sugar dissolves. Add the lemon slices. Serve over ice or chill until cold. Garnish with a sprig of mint or cilantro.

Cholla

With cylindrical joints hanging akimbo and flowers that range from yellow to orange, red, and magenta, there is no reason for the cholla to be the red-headed stepchild of the ornamental cactus world, yet somehow it is. Although members of this widely adaptable family of plants grow like gangbusters in all of the Four Corners states, not many growers offer a wide selection of chollas for home gardeners. Perhaps this is because even though newcomers are seduced by the backlit glow of a teddy bear cholla (*Opuntia bigelovii*), intimate contact with the plants (getting stuck by them, that is) surely dissuades many from plopping chollas into their gardens. However, there are some strikingly beautiful, useful, and underutilized species, and in a year when the cholla are blooming full force, they are an incredible sight to see.

Cholla buds, which are typically ready to harvest from late March through May, depending on elevation, are easy to pick and fun to process. The species of cholla that you pick from is not important, but the harvest begins when the first couple of flowers open on a plant. Look for the least-thorny buds, and pick up to 30 percent of the fruit on any one plant, making sure to leave plenty for other desert critters to harvest. As you might expect, removing the thorns is the thorny part of the job. Many people enjoy processing cholla buds like pickles. To do this, boil for twenty minutes, drain, dry, and remove any remaining thorns with tweezers. (Traditionally, the buds were roasted in fire pits.) An alternative method of removing thorns is to fill two saucepans ⅓ full of gravel, add the cholla buds, and pour the gravel and buds from one pan to the

Staghorn cholla puts on a show in May after the first flush of wildflower blooms have faded.

other 4 or 5 times until most of the thorns are gone. Then boil as just described. After boiling, the buds can be frozen, used in recipes such as stews, or preserved by drying in the sun on trays. To freshen the frozen or dried buds, soak in water for 3 hours.

Perfect Pincushions: Mammillarias and Ball-Shaped Cacti for Gardens

In the wild, pincushions (*Mammillaria* and *Coryphantha* sp.) are usually the last succulents that you notice; the small, usually white, densely spined globes hide down among the rocks, and you usually spy them only after you kneel down to photograph some other plant. They are similarly overlooked in gardens, but they shouldn't be. Pincushions are among the very most drought-tolerant of succulents; they fit into a no-irrigation garden nicely, and look wonderful tucked into the fissures and holes of stonework. At the Huntington Botanical Gardens in Los Angeles, you can see an impressive mass display of white pincushions popping out of deep-red volcanic gravel. Most pincushion species flower in the spring and summer. Different species produce a variety of flower colors including cream, pink, yellow, and red. Most display their flowers in crown-like rings around the top portion of the plant. Many species of pincushion have dense white spines that protect the flesh of the plant from sun; some species have white fluff between the tubercles. Many pincushions grow well under the filtered shade of desert trees, particularly at lower elevations.

STEM SUCCULENTS AND WEIRD WOODY SHRUBS The plants in this section are all in the ocotillo family, Fouquieriaceae. These unusual woody plants that *look* like cacti, but are *not*

The spiky character of Mexican tree ocotillo is accentuated in a pot at the Arizona-Sonora Desert Museum.

Eat Your Garden: Spicy Ice-Box Pickled Cholla Buds

- 3 cups de-thorned, washed cholla buds
- ¼ cup oreganillo leaves (*Aloysia wrightii*)
- 2 tablespoons fresh or dried chiltepín peppers
- 1 sliced onion
- 2 cloves of fresh garlic
- 1 teaspoon alum
- 3 quarts water
- 1 quart distilled vinegar
- ½ cup coarse salt (not iodized)

Pack the washed cholla buds in a gallon jar. Add oreganillo, chiltepines, onion, and garlic. Add the alum on top. Pour the water and the vinegar into the jar so all the cholla buds are completely covered with liquid. Set in a cool place for 1 week, then keep refrigerated. Will keep for many months.

cacti, are among the most distinctive specimens for hot gardens. Plants like the ocotillo have an amazing adaptation to summer rains, rapidly producing leaves after rains and shedding them during dry spells. Boojum trees—giant pale green pylons that rise from the desert—are technically stem succulents because of the way they store water in their trunks. They are surely among the most bizarre plants in the world and are worthy of consideration for their unique form.

Ocotilloville

When you see the jagged branches of ocotillo, boldly picketing the desert sky at dusk, you can't help but think: the ocotillo is lightning in plant form! Its thorny branches zigzag and slash their way above the horizon, improving yet not obstructing a view. Like lightning, the ocotillo appears dangerous and unpredictable, although after

Massive and vase-shaped, mature ocotillos can serve as a major sculptural element in hot gardens.

Eat Your Garden: The Pleasures of Pincushion Fruit

After flowering, pincushions produce little club-like red or pink fruit with crunchy black seeds. The fruit is very tasty (with a sweet-tart flavor) and complements salads or meats well. The only trick is beating the birds and antelope squirrels to the fruit. It should be mentioned that, as with eating hedgehog fruit, when you consume pincushion fruit you are eating possibly rare and monetarily valuable (depending on the species) seeds and are sure to annoy any cactus growers who might be among your dinner guests. Pick them from your own, rather than wild, specimens.

you work with ocotillos for a while, you come to see them as rather friendly when compared with, say, a cholla cactus. When I was employed at Civano Nursery, I got to where I would comfortably and glovelessly load large bare-root ocotillo plants with only the occasional forearm scratches and minor puncture wounds.

It is hard to imagine a desert plant more versatile in a home garden. It can be used as a focal point, a fence, or even espaliered on a trellis. The fiery red tips of the plant are hummingbird magnets and markers as the hummers migrate north from Mexico in spring. The only downside to the ocotillo is that transplanting large bare-root specimens can be difficult, especially if they are dried-out Texas imports with few roots, as often sold by dubious roadside vendors. Thankfully, nurseries have recognized the need for containerized ocotillos, and many are growing them in pots that will transplant without a hitch. It's a good thing, because what desert yard doesn't need at least one?

The ocotillo fence, as beautiful as it is, unfortunately presents another ethical gardening dilemma, as they are generally made and harvested in Mexico—most likely by removing the entire plant from the ground, roots and all, to remove the canes. I know that using the fencing is not good for the health of the deserts in Mexico, but I can't exactly think of a replacement for the wiry, living, and semitransparent ocotillo fence—a fence that looks like a million bucks with a little twining snapdragon vine crawling up it or as a backdrop for globemallow. My only hope (or maybe my plea) is that someone will start harvesting only the *canes*, which could be cut from the mother plant without harming her, to make fencing. In the meantime, you could find neighbors with big old mature ocotillos and ask them if you can prune a few canes off, tie them together using baling wire, and make your own sustainable, and living, ocotillo fence. After all, the ocotillo fence is just too beautiful a screen to give up on.

Tips for Planting Ocotillo and Ocotillo Fencing

The first and most important step is to purchase ocotillos grown from seed. These are usually available in sizes from one gallon (one to two feet high) to 24-inch box (six-plus feet) in size. Not only are rooted, seed-grown specimens better for the environment; they are also a wise choice in that they survive transplanting much better than bare-root plants. After digging a hole as deep, and three to five times as wide, as the container, carefully cut the bottom off the container (if it is a plastic container) with a utility knife. Gently place your hand under the container to support the soil on the bottom and slide the plant into the planting hole. Now slit the sides of the container and remove it, then backfill the hole, firming it up against the rootball. For faster growth, Jane Evans of Plants for the Southwest recommends watering two to three times a week during the humid summer season. In July alone, Jane has seen growth of six to eight inches just by doing some extra watering during the monsoon.

Ocotillo fencing with a globemallow backdrop at Chihuahuan Desert Gardens on the University of Texas El Paso campus.

For fencing, dig a six- to eight-inch-deep trench, dip the bottom of the canes in a rooting hormone (to achieve a higher percentage of cane growth), and place fencing in the trench, firming up the soil around it. At either end of the fence, you will need a fence post of some sort; anything from lodgepole-type tree stakes to T-shaped barbed-wire-fence posts will do the trick.

Weird Plants

One of the real draws to gardening in the hot zone is the bizarre plants you can grow—like your own little shop of horrors. Although it could be argued that *all* of our desert plants are weird,

The heart-shaped fruit of slipper plant is enticingly strange.

Curiosity cactus against a lime-green wall at Civano Nursery in Tucson.

Janet Rademacher's witty "bed" of blue grama grass shows how native grasses can be made at home in suburban yards.

these are some of the strangest—plants that would look right at home in the *Star Wars* bar on the planet Tatooine. From gorilla's armpit, whose grass-like foliage emerges from a brown hemispherical caudex, to the landscape designers' darling, slipper plant, whose graceful tentacle-like succulent stems twist like medusa's snaky hair, these strange plants add an eccentric spirit to a garden and are sure to start conversations.

Grasses and Palms

HOT GRASSES Lawns are fun for dogs and children to play on. This is why we have public parks. But in our own hot gardens, why not use ornamental grasses instead of turf? As renowned grass

For high impact, 'Regal Mist' muhlenbergia should be grouped together.

man John Greenlee remarks, "Why would you have a lawn when you can have a meadow?" Ornamental grasses have become an important new trend in desert landscaping. When planted in groups they soften the hard-edged architecture of surrounding desert plants and introduce another sensory element into the garden: sound. In addition to their aesthetic appeal, consider that grasses are relatively low-care plants: they need to be cut back only once a year in late winter/early spring, something grass expert John Greenlee calls "the big chop." After the big chop, you'll be surprised at how fast your grasses come charging back. After you've planted your hot-garden ornamental grasses, put the mower in the classifieds. In the L.A. basin, 22 tons of air pollution are created each day by mowers and blowers, so you can feel even better about converting to ornamental grasses that don't require weekly mowing. The grasses listed on page 111 are species I find particularly useful for adding late summer and fall interest in hot gardens.

HOT PALMS

It has taken me a while to warm up to palm trees in desert landscapes. In general, I was trained in an aesthetic that said if palms are used at all, they should be used sparingly. Part of my bias against palms came from working in the Sonoran Desert uplands, where there are no native palms yet many Mexican fan palms are thrown against the desert skyline. In part, my dissatisfaction with palms as landscape plants was the result of not being exposed to enough varieties; you can drive around many towns and see only Mexican fan palms, Canary Island date palms, Mediterranean fan palms, queen palms, and a few California fan palms. I had begun to think that palms smack of a resort industry bent on convincing newcomers that vast tracts of Arizona are lush oases with plenty of water for all.

In its native habitat in Baja, Mexico, the Mexican blue palm shows it has the chops to handle a rocky situation.

Spiny dioon, purple walls, and vining cacti combine for a bold planting underneath an ironwood tree at the Arizona-Sonora Desert Museum (Design: Mark Sitter).

My feelings about incorporating palms into desert gardens began to change when I saw palms in the wild. The first palms I fell for were the icy-colored Mexican blue palms from Baja California, which grow in close proximity to boojum trees near arroyos and on rocky canyon bottoms. Although the terrain where the Mexican blue palms grew was seemingly dry, I couldn't help but notice that their range, unlike their boojum companions, was restricted to the areas in and around arroyos, where they were no doubt tapping into the water table. Palm trees' love of water was confirmed by my second experience with wild palms near Palm Springs, California, in the Sonoran Desert. The wild California fan palms (*Washingtonia filifera*) here are ghettoized in sand oases and wet canyons in the Coachella Valley, and they occur in dense clumps along the San Andreas fault line, where geologic action pushes groundwater to the surface. I hiked into the Coachella Valley Preserve and into a dark world of rustling fronds. I was amazed at how shady and forest-like the dense clutch of palms was. It was shocking to find these verdant green-topped columns in a desert that typically receives only five inches of rain a year. The other wonderful thing about these palms was that they had full skirts of thatch that hung clear to the ground. A palm with a full skirt, as a horticulturist from Palm Springs's Living Desert explained to me, is called a "virgin" palm. A virgin palm is a palm whose skirt has not been burned off—a practice that Native American tribes in the area traditionally used to increase production of fruit (they look and taste like miniature dates) on California fan palms.

These palm oases don't stretch across the San Andreas in an unbroken line but rather in a connect-the-dots fashion that maps out the fault line. In the Coachella Valley Preserve, I hiked from oasis to oasis. In between oases, nearly barren dunes speckled with saltbrush stretched out before me, blowing plumes of sand in my face. But at the next oasis, I would be sitting at the edge of a clear pool of water with cattails and desert pupfish, in the shadows of palms with their long skirts brushing the ground. The California fan palm is the only palm in the world known to hold onto its fronds indefinitely, creating a massive skirt in which orioles like to nest. Other palms, like the taller and ubiquitous street tree, the Mexican fan palm, require expensive frond cleanup and removal, but the California fan maintains a full ample skirt for years, lending a fat and proportional look to the plant.

So for an oasis area, one or maybe even three or five California fan palms, virgins all, could be a striking luxury around a fountain or pond. I say luxury because it is still true that palms are not drought-tolerant. A few months without water, as the accompanying picture illustrates, and you'll be left with hairless columns deader than telephone poles. On the road from Phoenix to Palm Springs, there are several examples of abandoned palm tree dreams—mostly dead circles or felled stacks of date palms that have had the water turned off. At the former date palm circle

Along I-10 between Arizona and California: an example of what happens to date palms when the water gets turned off.

> ### Eat Your Garden: California Fan Palm Mini Dates
>
>
>
> Like tiny versions of larger Arabian dates, the female California fan palm produces sprays of small, almost black fruit that resembles little olives, but with a high sugar content. These mini-dates (with pits) keep well if kept dry and are great trail food for hiking.

where I took this photo, I found it curious that next to the palm trunks, an ironwood tree had happily sprouted and was growing with gusto. Perhaps, I thought, this is an analogy about gardening's past and future in the arid lands between the Colorado River and California's coastal ranges. The ironwood is a tree that can make it here.

Palms are often accused of painfully slow growth, because they have a two-stage growth habit. First, they produce many leaves and do not increase in height. After the requisite leaves are produced, the plant begins shooting up. The salient point when purchasing a palm is to choose a specimen with a full, round canopy—that will soon head upward. Another important maintenance consideration regards pruning. The old leaves should be completely dead before removal—this allows the palm to transfer energy from the dying leaves toward the production of new leaves.

The list on pages 111–112 contains palms and cycads (which look like palms but are actually unrelated) that are good design choices for oasis areas in some desert gardens. Because of their water-use requirements, if palms are used at all, they should be used judiciously and sited carefully in desert gardens.

Exotic Additions

To make a hot-zone garden with a desert sense of place, native plants from the three North American deserts should form the bulk of your palette (I suggest around 80 percent). For the other 20 percent, consider water-thrifty plants from other dry regions around the globe that can provide additional color and sculpture in seasons when your natives may still be dormant. The following lists, while truncated, contain some of the best exotic plants for hot gardens. You'll notice that these plants are shrubs and accents rather than trees; because trees set the tone for the rest of the landscape plants, I usually prefer to use native trees rather than exotics. One exception to this suggestion applies to fruit-bearing trees: when it comes to citrus, fig, and pomegranates—the triumvirate of edible exotic trees for the desert—there aren't really any native tree substitutes. If you are after a tangelo, a mesquite tree won't quite do. That said, since plants such as citrus are high-water-use evergreens, they should be used sparingly in desert landscapes.

OUTBACK SHRUBS Aussie shrubs provide a welcome punch of color, beginning around Valentine's Day with 'Valentine' emu bush. Most of these plants have small silvery leaves, which helps them blend well with North American natives.

Beneath an ironwood tree at the Arizona-Sonora Desert Museum, a yellow-flowering aloe competes for hummingbird attention.

ALOES OUT OF AFRICA Aloes are perhaps the most important African plant family for desert gardens. Since most aloe species prefer some shade, they are naturals for planting under the lacy canopies of desert trees like mesquites and ironwoods, where their tubular blooms provide food for hummingbirds in late winter and early spring before many native plants are blooming. Because aloes resemble agaves, newcomers tend to get the two confused; aloes bloom every year, agaves only once. Although the list on pages 112–113 contains mostly aloes, it includes a couple of African natives that are not aloes but grow in similar conditions.

The chartreuse flowers of gopher plant complement agaves and prickly pears.

MEDITERRANEAN MISCELLANY Plants like rosemary have been longtime favorites in the Southwest because they are evergreen and fairly tough. Because of their deeper green foliage, the rosemary cultivars are usually better when they are set apart from desert plants in planters or containers. Dwarf rosemary is a particularly attractive trailing plant. In this group, gopher plant, with its silver foliage and eye-popping chartreuse flowers, is the easiest to blend with desert plants.

FRUITFUL EXOTICS All of these fruit trees have been grown successfully in the Southwest since the 1600s and were among the very first plants brought over from the Old World by the Spanish missionaries. These non-native plants were also a great boon to the native people, and today even the dryland Hopi farmers grow apricots and peaches. Although these plants are not native they have a *long* history here!

Citrus

Citrus is so widely used that it is almost a cliché in hot gardens; but even hard-core desert rats have a soft spot in their hearts for citrus. Russ Buhrow, curator of plants at Tohono Chul Park in Tucson, is a case in point. Russ is the sort of guy who is usually found extolling the virtues of an obscure desert plant, but when you ask him about citrus he gets a mischievous gleam in his eye and says, "If you are going to put in something that isn't native, why not have something you can eat? They are the golden apples of the Argonauts! Besides, I don't need an excuse—I just like citrus."

The first thing to consider when choosing citrus trees is not what kind of fruit you like to eat, but where you live. If you live where winter lows infrequently drop into the high teens, kumquats, tangerines, grapefruits, and tangelos can work well if properly sited. If temperatures in your locality regularly drop below 20, you'll have to give up the dream or grow your citrus indoors. Here are a few select varieties from most to least cold-hardy.

- **Dwarf citrus** Gardening in small spaces calls for smaller trees. Citrus trees grafted onto dwarf rootstocks produce trees that mature anywhere from 25 to 75 percent smaller than a full-sized tree of the same variety. The smallest trees are those grafted to 'Flying Dragon' rootstock, which produces a mature tree only four to eight feet high and wide. Their miniature size makes dwarf varieties excellent choices for containers.
- **Grapefruits** Although sold as grapefruit, 'Oro Blanco' and 'Melogold' are technically hybrids between grapefruits and the larger pummelos. Forget what you might have heard about pink grapefruit having the sweetest flavor—'Oro Blanco' and 'Melogold' win the sugar taste-test hands down. They are simply the sweetest grapefruit varieties you can grow, and they have the added benefit of being seedless. If you insist on a pink-fleshed grapefruit, choose 'Rio Star' or 'Ruby Red'.
- **Kumquats** Considered by most experts to be the most cold-hardy citrus tree, kumquats are consumed peel and all. Harvested over a long season (October–April), kumquats make a superb ornamental plant, fun snack food, and killer marmalade. Because of their small size, kumquats perform well in pots. 'Nagami', the most common kumquat in cultivation, produces small oval fruit with a sweet rind and tart flesh, spring through fall. 'Meiwa', a variety that bears fruit with a sweet rind and flesh, is not as commercially available as 'Nagami'.
- **Lemons** Vigorous, productive, fairly cold-tolerant, and producing a good, high-acid lemon, 'Lisbon' lemons thrive here. You'll soon be giving away bags of them to friends, neighbors, and complete strangers—there lies some truth in the old nursery saying that home gardeners "should plant only one lemon tree per city block." Unlike the 'Meyer', which is only mildly tart, the 'Lisbon' yields a real puckering lemon flavor that works well for recipes as diverse as lemonade, lemon bars, and lemon chicken. You won't find a better lemon variety for the desert.
- **Limequats** For the weirdos among us, the limequat makes the perfect citrus choice. A cross between the Mexican lime and

'Oro Blanco' grapefruits ripen on the tree beginning in late November.

DESIGNING WITH DESERT PLANTS 85

'Peter's Honey' fig trees produce two crops of honey-sweet yellow-green fruit during the warm months.

the kumquat, its fruit resembles a small, oblong lemon. Once in your mouth, expect a slightly less acidic flavor than a Mexican lime, mixed with the sweet peel of the kumquat. And, as with the kumquat, you can eat the peel. You'll need to find creative uses for all the numerous limequats that will ripen November through March. Limequats make a fine lime substitute in margaritas.

- **Limes** Limes, especially 'Mexican' or Key limes, are the least cold-hardy of the citrus, but they can be grown in Phoenix, Yuma, and Palm Springs. 'Bearss' limes, which look like green lemons and are sometimes called "supermarket limes," are a little more cold-hardy.

- **Oranges** Most gardeners should choose their oranges from the category known as "Arizona Sweets" rather than 'Valencias' or navels throughout most of the zone where it sometimes freezes hard. Arizona Sweets include such popular varieties as 'Early Hamlin', 'Trovita', 'Marrs', 'Diller', and 'Pineapple'. Arizona Sweets oranges peel and juice well, and depending on the variety, bear fruit over a long period (usually November–March). Since most Arizona Sweets varieties bear fruit as early as October, they are not as likely as 'Valencias' to suffer from frostbite.

- **Tangelos** Tangelos, a cross between a tangerine and a grapefruit, are the most underused citrus. With their large fruit, sweet-tangy flavor, and exceptional ease of peeling, what's not to like? Furthermore, because of their tangerine parentage, tangelos rank among the more cold-hardy types of large-fruited citrus.

- **Tangerines** Generally small trees, tangerines (aka mandarins) produce fruit that is easily peeled and sectioned. Due to their ease in peeling, tangerines have earned the common name of "zipper skins." 'Clementines' (aka Algerian tangerines), as well as 'Kinnow' mandarins, make excellent selections. 'Kinnow' mandarins have the very sweet flavor associated with tangerine-flavored drinks sold in stores. Almost all tangerines bear alternately, meaning that trees bear heavy fruit one year and a light crop the next. Tangerines planted next to other types of citrus will cross-pollinate, resulting in an increased yield, but with more seeds. Although the tangerine tree withstands freezing well, the fruit does not. Thankfully, many tangerines ripen early, beginning in November, avoiding most winter cold snaps.

Citrus Care

- **Location:** Choose a warm, sunny spot, preferably on the south or west side of your home. Check the planting hole for good drainage. In cooler areas of town, plant citrus near walls or buildings with southern exposures. If you cannot plant your trees on the southern side of your home, site the trees near buildings or walls that will build up heat during the day and release it at night. Avoid north-facing areas and low spots, especially near washes, as cold air sinks.

- **Planting:** Dig a hole the same depth and three to five times as wide as the rootball of the tree. Cut the container off the rootball and ease the tree into the planting hole. Don't yank the tree out of the container by its trunk. Citrus roots are fragile.
- **Best planting times:** After last frost in spring.
- **Water:** After establishment, most citrus will survive on one to two good deep soaks per week in summer. In winter, you will need to water only every 10–14 days. Because citrus is a high-water-use evergreen, consider dedicating one rainwater harvesting culvert to a tree.
- **Frost protection:** On nights when frost is predicted, cover your trees with a woven frost cloth or cloth sheets. Do not lay plastic on the leaves of your tree. Young trees are the most susceptible to frost damage, so if a severe freeze is predicted, wrap the trunk of your small tree with pipe insulation or cloth. Limes and lemons are the most frost-tender citrus, so extra precautions, such as wrapping the main trunk with lights, may be needed.
- **Fertilization:** In the warmer regions of the hot-garden zone, fertilize your citrus on Valentine's Day, Memorial Day, and Labor Day. Use a citrus-and-avocado fertilizer and fertilize according to the directions on the package.
- **Pruning:** Citrus needs minimal pruning, since reducing the foliage also reduces the amount of fruit the tree will produce. As to the plant's shape, think of citrus more as a large shrub than a tree. In commercial citrus groves, the trees are left to grow leaves so near the ground they obscure the trunk. Prune after last frost, if necessary. Prune out only dead and crossing branches. Do not to leave exposed bark, as this is susceptible to sunburn.

Pomegranates and Figs

Desert gardeners who want fruit without too much fuss will find success with pomegranate and fig trees.

'Wonderful' pomegranates offer carefree fruit production just in time for Thanksgiving. As shown here, they also have attractive yellow fall foliage.

Take the pomegranate: here is a tree made for the desert. It will live on 14 inches of rainfall a year, produces fruit that has more antioxidants than blueberries or red wine, and can be juiced to yield a deep-red sweet-tart liquid not unlike cranberry juice in taste. A tree with an ancient history, the pomegranate has a sensual past. A symbol of fertility, the shapely pomegranate is compared to a woman's breasts in the Song of Solomon. The Chinese would traditionally roll pomegranates onto the floor of the wedding chamber to bless newlyweds with fertility.

The benchmark pomegranate is the 'Wonderful'. It lives in all soil types, has hot orange-red flowers and bright green glossy foliage. The 'Wonderful' pomegranate is so handsome, some gardeners plant the tree purely as an ornamental and leave the fruit to the birds. In my judgment, this is a mistake. The fruit of the 'Wonderful' pomegranate is bright red and the size of a softball. Once it is cracked open, the hundreds of sweet-tart ruby-like arils are revealed. Their rich, clear color makes a fine addition to salads. The fruit can also be juiced or eaten by the handful. Warning, the juice does stain!

When it comes to figs, 'Black Mission' is the clear favorite in Southwest gardens. A large tree, the 'Black Mission' produces fruit with a purple-black skin and strawberry-colored flesh. Like all figs it can be espaliered in small gardens for aesthetic effect. The 'Black Mission' fig bears heavy crops and lives a long time. Another long-time favorite in the region is 'Brown Turkey' fig. Renowned for its brown fruit with a pink interior, the 'Brown Turkey' is heat- and salt-tolerant.

A relative newcomer, 'Peter's Honey' fig has become my personal favorite. Not only does it produce a yellow-green fruit that tastes, well, just like honey, it has a bold branching structure and interesting winter appearance. The amber interior of the fruit is sweeter than one would think possible and really does recall the flavor of wild honey.

Regional Planting Themes

One of the best ways to ensure that your design has integrity is to find a theme and stick with it. The following themes are based mostly on the local flora in and around the hot-garden cities covered in this book. Each theme was developed by a prominent horticulturist or designer familiar with the best low-water-use native plants in the area. They are a great way to begin seeing what your garden could look like through a local lens.

EXPRESSLY EL PASO Compared with the Sonoran Desert flora, Chihuahuan Desert plants might be considered more low-key. But what they lack in saguaros, they make up for in yuccas. One of my very favorite places to see Chihuahuan Desert plants in a garden setting is at the University of Texas at El Paso's wonderful Chihuahuan Desert Gardens. Every time I travel through, I can't help but exit I-10 and walk through the campus gardens filled with rocky nooks, ramadas, sages, and wild snapdragons. Wynn Anderson, the botanical curator there, recommends the following for his corner of the Chihuahuan Desert. These plants, all of which are found in El Paso County, are certain to lend *mucho* Chihuahuan style to garden spaces in this region. This plant palette also would be entirely at home in Las Cruces, Alamogordo, Truth or Consequences, or Deming (all in New Mexico).

Trees
'Bubba' Desert Willow (*Chilopsis linearis* 'Bubba')
Golden Leadball Tree (*Leucaena retusa*)
Texas Mountain Laurel (*Sophora secundiflora*)
Western Soapberry (*Sapindus saponaria drummondii*)

Shrubs
Evergreen Sumac (*Rhus virens*)
Mexican Buckeye (*Ungnadia speciosa*)
Yellow Bells (*Tecoma stans*)

Perennials
Cardinal Penstemon (*Penstemon cardinalis*)
'Raspberry Fuzzies' Copperleaf (*Acalypha monostachya* 'Raspberry Fuzzies')
Skeletonleaf Goldeneye (*Viguiera stenoloba*)
Sundrops (*Calylophus hartwegii*)
Texas Violet Sage (*Salvia farinacea* 'Texas Violet')
Trailing Indigo Bush (*Dalea greggii*)

Accents

Desert Spoon (*Dasylirion wheeleri*)
New Mexico Agave (*Agave neomexicana*)

TOTALLY TUCSON   Greg Corman has made a name for himself by landscaping his garden totally with Tucson Basin native plants, a concept that he has dubbed "Totally Tucson." About the plants in the upper Sonoran Desert list here, Corman says, "I'd be happy with [these plants] if someone told me I could use no others. I think it includes the barest bones for full sun and part shade with lots of interesting form and color. I trust them all to live un-irrigated in a swaled yard."

Trees

Blue Palo Verde (*Parkinsonia florida*)
Velvet Mesquite (*Prosopis juliflora*)

Shrubs

Creosote Bush (*Larrea tridentata*)
Flattop Buckwheat (*Eriogonum fasciculatum poliofolium*)
Limber Bush (*Jatropha cardiophylla*)
Pine-leaf Milkweed (*Asclepias linaria*)

The elephant tree's fat gnarled branches are peerless among desert trees. If you garden in a frost-free region, be sure to try one in the ground; if not, grow one in a pot.

Shrubby Senna (*Senna wislizenii*)

Trixis (*Trixis californica*)

Vines

Arizona Grape Ivy (*Cissus trifoliata*)

Cacti

Fishhook Barrel (*Ferocactus wislizeni*)

Santa Rita Prickly Pear (*Opuntia violacea santa-rita*)

Accents

Banana Yucca (*Yucca baccata*)

Bear Grass (*Nolina microcarpa*)

Golden-flowered Agave (*Agave chrysantha*)

Ocotillo (*Fouquieria splendens*)

Perennial Wildflowers

Dogweed (*Thymophylla pentachaeta*)

Parry's Penstemon (*Penstemon parryi*)

Tufted Evening Primrose (*Oenothera caespitosa*)

POSITIVELY PALM SPRINGS As a longtime oasis for wealthy and famous Angelinos seeking desert sun, Palm Springs has suffered from a malady common to Scottsdale and other winter escapes: "resort landscaping." By resort landscaping, I mean an overabundant use of turf grass, annual bedding plants, and exotic plants, at the expense of their own beguiling native palette. Thankfully, a new crop of designers has moved in, celebrating the joys of their local flora. Palm Springs has almost unrivaled potential for desert landscaping on account of the bevy of modernist architecture, with yards ripe for conversion into spectacular xeric gardens. This, coupled with the advantage of being a nearly frost-free zone, bodes well for the future of this desert city with hyper-summers. Because of the mild winter lows, plants like elephant tree that come from the warmest parts of the Sonoran Desert can be planted in the ground in Palm Springs—a rarity and treat. I compiled the following list on a trip to Palm Springs that opened my eyes to the garden possibilities that large smoke trees and California fan palms present:

Trees

California Fan Palm (*Washingtonia filifera*)

Elephant Tree (*Bursera microphylla*)

Ironwood (*Olneya tesota*)

Screwbean Mesquite (*Prosopis pubescens*)

Smoke Tree (*Psorothamnus spinosus*)

Shrubs

Brittlebush (*Encelia farinosa*)

Creosote Bush (*Larrea tridentata*)

Desert Lavender (*Hyptis emoryi*)

Perennials

Chuperosa (*Justicia californica*)

Desert Marigold (*Baileya multiradiata*)

Hummingbird Trumpet (*Zauschneria californica*)

PLANTS OF ENCHANTMENT: MADE IN CENTRAL NEW MEXICO This list from New Mexico landscape architect David Cristiani is for the Albuquerque area and the central New Mexico valleys and foothills below 7,500 feet, from Socorro to Tent Rocks. Cristiani points out that Albuquerque gardeners sometimes forget they are in the dry part of the state and mistakenly select plants such as aspen that fail to thrive in the unforgiving arid climate. Although a few of the plants here (such as gray oak) are not yet in wide production, this list is populated with smart natives that are genetically programmed to succeed in central New Mexico.

Trees

Gray Oak (*Quercus grisea*)

Netleaf Hackberry (*Celtis laevigata reticulata*)

Texas Honey Mesquite (*Prosopis glandulosa*)

Shrubs

Mariola (*Parthenium incanum*)

Mormon Tea (*Ephedra viridis*)

Accents

    Comanche Prickly Pear (*Opuntia comanchica*)
    Engelmann's Prickly Pear (*Opuntia engelmannii*)
    Green Desert Spoon (*Dasylirion texanum*)
    Havard Agave (*Agave havardiana*)
    Sacahuista (*Nolina texana*)
    Soap Tree Yucca (*Yucca elata*)

Perennials and Grasses

    Blackfoot Daisy (*Melampodium leucanthum*)
    Bush Muhly (*Muhlenbergia porteri*)
    Dakota Verbena (*Verbena bipinnatifida*)
    Damianita Daisy (*Chrysactinia mexicana*)

LAS VEGAS REDISCOVERED I'll admit it: I've never found Las Vegas a particularly inspired desert-gardening town. Perhaps they have been so busy fashioning their fantasy versions of other places that they have forgotten what is special about their own corner of the Mojave Desert? This list is meant to remedy that. It will work not only in Las Vegas but is also appropriate for St. George, Utah, and Kingman, Arizona. Created by the well-respected plantsman Dennis Swartzell, this list is perfect for bringing the essence of the Mojave Desert into gardens. According to Swartzell, not very many native plants have made their way into Las Vegas landscapes yet. This may be because not many Las Vegans venture out into the surrounding desert. As writer Dianna Kappel-Smith remarks, "what I've learned in Vegas is that no one there goes out to the desert much; they're far more likely to hop a plane to Boston than to drive an hour and a half." This I predict will change, and with it more desert plants will make it into landscapes, if for no other reason than that pressures on southern Nevada's water supply make the turf and palm approach untenable. One example of the new type of thinking is the Las Vegas Springs preserve, an ambitious and elegantly executed new garden focused on the area's native flora and fauna. The following list, supplied by Dennis Swartzell, is a sort of "wish list" and includes plants that Dennis would like to see more of, both in nurseries and—especially—in Las Vegas gardens. Plants like Mojave aster could provide a swath of lavender in gardens, and as Swartzell remarks, plants like silk tassel tree "are just begging for nursery production."

Trees

    'Art's Seedless' Desert Willow (*Chilopsis linearis* 'Art's Seedless')
    Joshua Tree (*Yucca brevifolia jageriana*—a variety specific to the Las Vegas area)
    Scrub Oak (*Quercus turbinella*)

Accents

    Beavertail Prickly Pear (*Opuntia basilaris*)
    Claret Cup Cactus (*Echinocereus triglochidiatus*)
    Compass Barrel Cactus (*Ferocactus cylindraceus*)
    Cotton-Top Cactus (*Echinocereus polycephalus*)
    Mojave Yucca (*Yucca schidigera*)
    Utah Agave (*Agave utahensis*)

Shrubs

    Apache Plume (*Fallugia paradoxa*)
    Desert Holly (*Atriplex hymenelytra*)
    Mormon Tea (*Ephedra nevadensis*)
    Silk Tassel Tree (*Garrya flavescens*)
    Yerba Santa (*Eriodictyon angustifolium*)

Perennials

    Desert Sage (*Salvia dorrii dorrii*)
    Las Vegas Bear Paw Poppy (*Arctomecon californica*)
    Las Vegas Buckwheat (*Eriogonum corymbosum nilesii*)
    Mojave Aster (*Xylorhiza tortifolia*)
    Sunray (*Enceliopsis argophylla*)

TAKE ME HIGHER: SANTA FE AND BEYOND Plantsman David Salman, xeric plant pioneer and founder of Santa Fe Greenhouses and creator of the *High Country Gardens* catalog, has a knack for matching tough native plants with appropriate exotics. His list, which will also work in Boise or Prescott, features an excellent mix of natives and introduced plants for colder regions adjacent to hot-garden zones:

DESIGNING WITH DESERT PLANTS

Trees and Accents
- Algerita (*Berberis fremontii*)
- Faxon's Yucca (*Yucca faxoniana*)
- Piñon Pine (*Pinus edulis*)
- Rio Grande Cottonwood (*Populus deltoides wislizenii*)

Shrubs
- 'Dark Knight' Bluebeard (*Caryopteris* x *clandonensis* 'Dark Knight')
- Prostrate Three Leaf Sumac (*Rhus trilobata* 'Autumn Amber')
- Rabbitbrush (*Ericameria nauseosus*)
- Russian Sage (*Perovskia atriplicifolia*)

Perennials and Grasses
- Blue Catmint (*Nepeta* x *faassenii* 'Select Blue')
- Blue Grama Grass (*Bouteloua gracilis*)
- 'Desert Sunrise' Hummingbird Mint (*Agastache* x 'Desert Sunrise')
- Maximilian's Sunflower (*Helianthus maximiliana*)
- Rocky Mountain Penstemon (*Penstemon strictus*)
- Sacred Datura (*Datura wrightii*)

Soil Preparation and the Design Process

Whether you do it before or after you've completed your design, at some point you need to get out the shovel (or pick!) to see if what you have designed will be compatible with the soil you've got. The type of soil we plant in greatly affects the range of what we can plant and the vigor of our gardens in desert environs. Much of the soil in our region is alkaline and very low in organic matter. I often remark, and not completely in jest, that gardening in the Southwest is more like *mining* than gardening. This largely stems from the different soils we have west of the Mississippi. East of the Mississippi, they have *pedalfer* soils—very porous and organically rich soils with a resemblence to fluffy chocolate

Sharkskin agave rising from Mexican feather grass and fronted by Sierra sundrops makes for a nice spring combination.

cake—whereas here in the West, *pedocal* soils are common. Pedocals are rich in minerals and low in organic matter—in layman's terms, more like rock than soil. In some areas, you may encounter a hard chalky material called *caliche* (some say that the word "caliche" is Texan for "cement")—a layer of calcium carbonate that can be as hard as concrete (which it resembles) and can range in depth from a few inches to several feet. Compounding the challenge of gardening in these soils are modern construction methods, which through the use of very heavy equipment often achieve 95 percent compaction in soils around new homes. These soils are basically devoid of air, organic matter, and microbial activity. Although you can improve the tilth (crumbliness), organic matter, and microbial activity in the soil, the basic composition of the soil (either alkaline, neutral, or acidic) is impossible to alter permanently. For this reason, it is much wiser to select plants adapted to the kind of soil you have rather than trying (futilely) to change the makeup of your soil.

There are two schools of thinking regarding soil amendments in the region, and I will do my best to summarize both: through the work of the late Jimmy Tipton, we have learned that native trees root in better and grow more quickly if they are planted in native (un-amended) soil that has been dug up to increase its tilth. The planting method that Tipton suggests to achieve tilth is digging a hole the same depth as your container and three to five times as wide, planting the tree, and backfilling the hole with the native soil that you dug out. By breaking up the soil in this diameter around the tree, oxygen and tree roots can more easily penetrate surrounding soils. I have found Tipton's method to be excellent for planting native trees—it both increases their growth rate and reduces incidents of root lodge (blowing over because of root failure). Tipton's method is also effective for many desert-adapted shrubs and perennials.

The other option for planting is to amend your native soils (the planting hole should still be the same size whether you amend or not). Since the great majority of the plants mentioned in this book will thrive without extra fluff and feed, consider amending soils a last resort—only for the most degraded and compacted soils. Amending is intended to improve the soil's fertility and

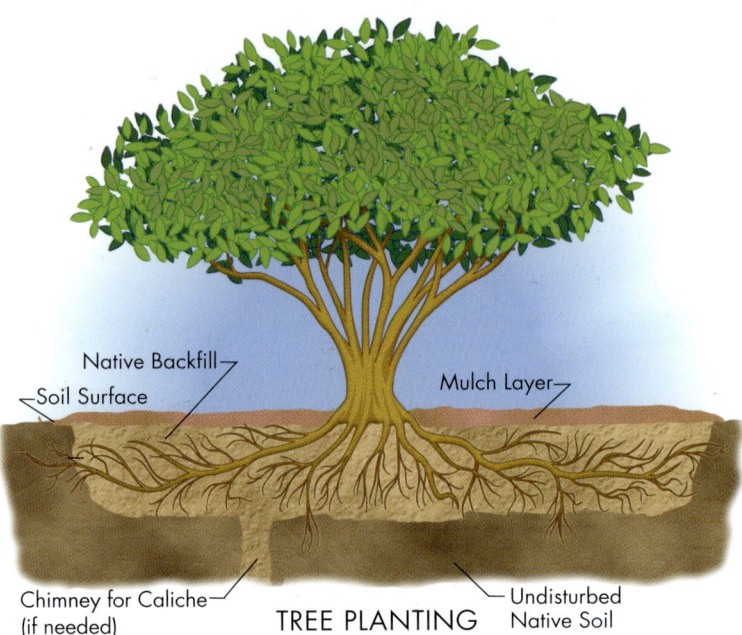

TREE PLANTING

sometimes its water-holding capacity. You can mix equal amounts of compost and sand, then dig that blend into your native soil for growing native plants that like sharp ("fast draining") soil. In my own garden projects, I have experimented and had success with both methods. If you do plan on amending your soil, I encourage you to amend the entire planting area rather than amending only the backfill soil in the planting hole. The logic behind this is that plant roots don't like crossing soil barriers, and just amending a planting hole may restrict the roots to a smaller area. Since most ground covers and perennials root to a depth of 1–2 feet, this is how deeply the new organic material should be incorporated.

So do you amend or not? The answer is: it depends. In normal uncompacted soils, when you are planting native trees, cacti and succulents, and tough regional shrubs, you are usually fine simply breaking up the soil to improve its tilth. On the other hand, if you are working with highly compacted soils and planting perennials or food-producing plants that like more fertile soils (especially in compacted clay around new construction), adding compost and other composted organic material may produce larger, more robust plants that will produce more flowers and fruit.

A blooming foothills palo verde adds a wild touch to an otherwise overly pruned and controlled desert landscape.

Plant Charts

Plant Name	Mature Height x Width	Cold Hardiness (degrees F)	Water Use (*see pages 165–166)	Scott's Notes
Small Trees				
Blackbrush Acacia (*Acacia rigidula*)	15' x 15'	15	2	Underused small patio tree with semi-evergreen leaves. Chihuahuan Desert limestone lover.
Brazilwood (*Haematoxylum brasiletto*)	10–20' x 10–20'	24	2*	Only for the warmest parts of the hot garden—spectacular deeply fluted bark with showy yellow and red flowers.
'Bubba' Desert Willow (*Chilopsis linearis* 'Bubba')	20' x 20'	−10	3	Larger leaves and flowers than the straight species. Deep purple blooms.
Cascalote (*Caesalpinia cacalaco*)	15–18' x 15–18'	20	3	Cool trunk with giant stud-like thorns. Yellow flowers in winter that smell like Ivory soap.
Catclaw Acacia (*Acacia greggii*)	15' x 20'	0	1	Super-tough small tree for nonirrigated gardens. Very thorny.
Chihuahuan Orchid Shrub (*Bauhinia lunarioides*)	12' x 10'	10	3	Blooms white (most common) or pink flowers in spring. Interesting leaves.
Curl-leaf Mountain Mahogany (*Cercocarpus ledifolius*)	15–18' x 12–15'	−30	2*	Dense gray trunk with leathery green leaves. Best at cooler, higher elevations.
Elephant Tree (*Bursera microphylla*)	12–18' x 12–18'	28	1	Needs heat and a nearly frost-free area. Spectacularly fat branches.
Foothills Palo Verde (*Parkinsonia microphyllum*)	10–20' x 10–20'	15	1	Good size for small gardens; slow grower.
Golden Leadball Tree (*Leucaena retusa*)	20' x 15'	0	2	Big (1½") yellow puffball flowers in summer.
Guajillo or Berlandier Acacia (*Acacia berlandieri*)	12' x 12'	15	3	Feathery foliage and fragrant flowers.
Kidneywood (*Eysenhardtia orthocarpa*)	18' x 15'	0	2	Nice overstory plant for wildflowers and agaves.
'Lucretia Hamilton' Desert Willow (*Chilopsis linearis* 'Lucretia Hamilton')	18' x 18'	−10	3	Small desert willow selection with deep burgundy flowers.
Mexican Bird of Paradise (*Caesalpinia mexicana*)	15' x 15'	15	2	Bright green foliage and gold flowers.
Mexican Elderberry (*Sambucus nigra cerulea*)	10–20' x 15–25'	0	3	A great small tree with cream-colored clusters of flowers followed by blue-black fruit and, with age, a gnarled trunk.
Mexican Orchid Tree (*Bauhinia mexicana*)	10–18' x 15–26'	15	3*	Blooms more frequently than the Chihuahuan orchid tree.
Mexican Redbud (*Cercis canadensis mexicana*)	15–25' x 15–25'	0	3	Pink flowers followed by heart-shaped leaves with undulated margins.
Netleaf Hackberry (*Celtis laevigata reticulata*)	30' x 30'	−20	3	Good underused shady tree. Gawky in youth, distinguished knobby bark at maturity.

Plant Name	Mature Height x Width	Cold Hardiness (degrees F)	Water Use (*see pages 165–166)	Scott's Notes
Palo Blanco (*Acacia willardiana*)	20' x 15'	variable, 19–28	2	The river birch of the desert. Needs heat and frost protection in cool areas.
Piñon Pine (*Pinus edulis*)	10–25' x 10–25'	−20	2	A charismatic pine for the higher, cooler areas of the region.
Screwbean Mesquite (*Prosopis pubescens*)	15' x 20'	0	2	Spiral bean pods and a great form for small gardens.
Scrub Oak (*Quercus turbinella*)	8' x 12'	−10	2	Great heat tolerance, even at lower elevations.
'Sierra Sun' Hybrid Bird of Paradise (*Caesalpinia* x 'Sierra Sun')	15' x 15'	15	2	Vase-shaped with orange-centered flowers.
'Silver Peso' Texas Mountain Laurel (*Sophora secundiflora* 'Silver Peso')	8–15' x 8–15'	10	2	Silver leaves and deep purple flowers.
Smoke Tree (*Psorothamnus spinosus*)	10–20' x 10–15'	20	1*	Fine silvery foliage with purple-blue flowers. Exceptional drought tolerance.
Sweet Acacia (*Acacia farnesiana*)	15–25' x 15–25'	10	3	Exceptionally fragrant blooms. A bit messy, with seedpods that look like sun-baked dog turds.
Tenaza (*Harvardia pallens*)	25–30' x 15–20'	15	2	Fragrant white puffball flowers that attract scads of pollinators.
Texas Mountain Laurel (*Sophora secundiflora*)	8–15' x 8–15'	10	2	Like 'Silver Peso' but with green leaves.
Texas Olive (*Cordia boissieri*)	15–25' x 15–25'	20	2	Hairy leaves with white crinkled flowers in spring.
Texas Persimmon (*Diospyros texana*)	20' x 10'	10	3*	Handsome ornamental with wonderful mottled bark and tasty black fruit.
Tranquility Tree (*Caesalpinia paraguariensis*)	15–30' x 15–30'	18	3*	Mottled bark, thornless with yellow flowers. South American.
Whitethorn Acacia (*Acacia constricta*)	10' x 15'	−10	1	Underused and good for no-irrigation gardens.

Medium and Large Trees

Plant Name	Mature Height x Width	Cold Hardiness (degrees F)	Water Use	Scott's Notes
'Art's Seedless' Desert Willow (*Chilopsis linearis* 'Art's Seedless')	25' x 25'	−10	3	Great for attracting hummingbirds and pollinators. Can be planted next to paving.
Blue Palo Verde (*Parkinsonia florida*)	30' x 30'	15	2	The Arizona state tree. Luminous yellow flowers in April.
Chinquapin Oak (*Quercus muehlenbergii*)	30' x 30'	−20	3	A majestic large Texas oak adapted to alkaline soils.
Desert Museum Hybrid Palo Verde (*Parkinsonia* x 'Desert Museum')	25' x 25'	15	2	Thornless hybrid with enhanced flowering.
Emory Oak (*Quercus emoryi*)	25' x 25'	−10	3	Grassland favorite.

Plant Name	Mature Height x Width	Cold Hardiness (degrees F)	Water Use (*see pages 165–166)	Scott's Notes
(Medium and Large Trees, continued)				
Escarpment Live Oak (*Quercus fusiformis*)	35–50' x 35–50'	–10	3	Another Texas oak good for desert areas.
Gray Oak (*Quercus grisea*)	15–30' x 15–25'	0	3	Leathery leaves and a great gnarled form make this hard-to-find oak worth seeking.
Ironwood (*Olneya tesota*)	30' x 30'	20	1	The granddaddy of Sonoran evergreen shade trees.
Netleaf Hackberry (*Celtis laevigata reticulata*)	30' x 30'	–20	3	Underused, interesting gnarly bark with age.
Palo Brea (*Parkinsonia praecox*)	25–35' x 25–35'	20	2	Muscular branching, lime-green bark.
'Phoenix' Hybrid Mesquite (*Prosopis* x 'Phoenix')	35' x 35'	15	2	Velvet mesquite rootstock grafted to a South American top for sturdy roots and fast growth.
Rio Grande Cottonwood (*Populus deltoides wislizenii*)	20–30' x 30–60'	–20	3+*	Although it is only for riparian areas, this cottonwood has beautiful bark and fall color.
Texas Ebony (*Ebenopsis ebano*)	15–40' x 15–30'	10	2	Dense, deep green, and thorny.
Texas Honey Mesquite (*Prosopis glandulosa*)	35' x 35'	0	2	Weeping leaves and good hardiness.
Tree Catclaw (*Acacia occidentalis*)	20–40' x 20–40'	18	2*	Highly fragrant flowers that smell like orange blossoms. Real tree-like (modified lollipop) shape and dense canopy.
Velvet Mesquite (*Prosopis juliflora*)	30' x 30'	0	2	Twisted and picturesque trunk with age. Good bird habitat.
'Warren Jones' Desert Willow (*Chilopsis linearis* 'Warren Jones')	25' x 30'	0	3	An exceptionally large, fast-growing, pink-flowered desert willow selection.
Western Soapberry (*Sapindus saponaria drummondii*)	25–40' x 15–30'	0	2	Underused and hard-to-find single-trunked shade tree.

Hot-Garden Shrubs

Plant Name	Mature Height x Width	Cold Hardiness (degrees F)	Water Use	Scott's Notes
Algerita (*Berberis trifoliata*)	6–8' x 6–8'	15	2	The most striking silver-blue foliage of all the Berberis species. Not to be confused with *Berberis fremontii*, which also has the common name "algerita."
Arizona Rosewood (*Vaquelinia californica*)	15' x 10'	–10	2	Underused barrier plant. Good oleander substitute.
Autumn Sage (*Salvia greggii*)	3' x 3'	15	3	Popular with hummingbirds, unpopular with rabbits.
Baja Fairy Duster (*Calliandra californica*)	4' x 4'	26	2	The North American answer to the bottlebrush.
Black Dalea (*Dalea frutescens*)	4' x 5'	0	3	Awesome purple flowers in autumn. Good with desert spoon.

Plant Name	Mature Height x Width	Cold Hardiness (degrees F)	Water Use (*see pages 165–166)	Scott's Notes
Chiltepin (*Capsicum annuum*)	2' x 4'	15	3*	Good landscape shrub with small globe-shaped hot peppers that birds and humans can enjoy.
Chuperosa (*Justicia californica*)	4' x 4'	26	2	Winter hummingbird food. Edible blossoms.
Cleveland Sage (*Salvia clevelandii*)	3' x 5'	15	2	Über-aromatic foliage.
Creosote Bush (*Larrea tridentata*)	6' x 8'	0	1	Underused in residential landscapes. Can be pruned to bonsai-like forms.
Desert Holly (*Atriplex hymenelytra*)	1–3' x 1–3'	20	1*	Tolerates the hottest, driest sites in Death Valley. Its silver holly-shaped leaves are highly reflective and handsome.
Desert Sage (*Salvia dorrii dorrii*)	2' x 2'	−20	2	Silver with blue flowers; rabbit-resistant.
Evergreen Sumac (*Rhus virens*)	8' x 10'	5	2	Waxy leaves and showy red berries.
Flattop Buckwheat (*Eriogonum fasciculatum poliofolium*)	1.5' x 2'	15	2	Umbel-shaped cream and pink flowers.
Four Wing Saltbush (*Atriplex canescens*)	3–6' x 4–8'	−30	1	Unspeakably tough. Salt-tolerant.
Giant Flowered Purple Sage (*Salvia pachyphylla*)	3' x 30"	−20	2*	Huge purple flower spikes with silvery foliage.
'Gold Star' Yellow Bells (*Tecoma stans* 'Gold Star')	4–6' x 4–6'	20	2*	A very floriferous version of Arizona yellow bells.
Goldeneye (*Viguiera parishii*)	2–4' x 2–4'	15	3	Good late-winter and spring color. Can bloom as early as January.
Guayacan (*Guaiacum coulteri*)	10' x 10'	25	3	Sonoran shrub with electric blue flowers in the monsoon. Needs winter protection.
Hop Bush (*Dodonaea viscosa*)	12' x 10'	15	2	Shiny leaves, evergreen, and fairly dense habit.
Indigo Bush (*Dalea pulchra*)	5' x 5'	15	2	Underused for late winter and early spring color.
Jojoba (*Simmondsia chinensis*)	6' x 6'	22	1	Tough and evergreen; underappreciated.
Las Vegas Buckwheat (*Eriogonum corymbosum nilesii*)	2' x 2'	15	1*	A glowing haze of neon-yellow flowers presented above airy foliage in fall. Native only around Vegas.
Lavender Spice Mexican Oregano (*Poliomintha maderensis*)	3' x 3'	10	3	Edible foliage with light purple flowers.
Limber Bush (*Jatropha cardiophylla*)	3' x 3'	20	1	Mahogany-colored stems in winter, tropical foliage in summer.
Little-leaf Cordia (*Cordia parvifolia*)	6' x 8'	15	2	Tissue-paper-like white flowers on rangy stems.

Plant Name	Mature Height x Width	Cold Hardiness (degrees F)	Water Use (*see pages 165–166)	Scott's Notes
(Hot-Garden Shrubs, continued)				
Little-leaf Sumac (*Rhus microphylla*)	6' x 8'	–10	2	Red leaves in autumn.
Mexican Blue Sage (*Salvia chamaedryoides*)	2' x 2'	15	2	Small and silver with blue flowers. Excellent in Albuquerque.
Mexican Buckeye (*Ungnadia speciosa*)	10–15' x 10–15'	0	3	Dramatic golden fall leaf color.
Mexican Flame (*Anisacanthus wrightii*)	5' x 5'	0	2	Orange-red flowers summer through fall.
Mexican Orange (*Choisya dumosa*)	3–6' x 3'	17	2*	Rare (in cultivation) Chihuahuan shrub.
Monterey Blue Dalea (*Dalea bicolor bicolor*)	6–8' x 5–6'	10	2	Tiny true-blue flowers on a fine-textured plant.
Mormon Tea (*Ephedra nevadensis*)	3' x 3'	0	1	Spiky, leafless, straw-like jointed foliage. Tough as nails.
Mountain Delight Dalea (*Dalea versicolor sessilis*)	4' x 4'	10	3	Mounding habit; blooms from fall to early spring.
Oreganillo (*Aloysia wrightii*)	5' x 5'	15	2	Edible foliage; heady fragrance from white flower spikelets.
'Phoenix' Bird of Paradise (*Caesalpinia pulcherrima* 'Phoenix')	6–10' x 6–10'	28	2	Yellow version of the popular red bird.
Pink Fairy Duster (*Calliandra eriophylla*)	3' x 3'	15	1	Nice pink flowers, beautiful when backlit. Great with ocotillo.
Prostrate Three Leaf Sumac (*Rhus trilobata* 'Autumn Amber')	2–3' x 6–8'	–40	2	Yellow and red fall color. Small form and good heat tolerance.
Ragged Rockflower (*Crossosoma bigelovii*)	3–6' x 3–6'	0	2*	Fragrant white flowers; early spring bloomer.
Red Bird of Paradise (*Caesalpinia pulcherrima*)	6–10' x 6–10'	28	2	Overused but graced with pretty flowers in the hottest months. Good with Texas rangers.
Red Justicia (*Justicia candicans*)	3' x 3'	26	2	Hummingbird plant for part shade.
Shadscale Saltbush (*Atriplex confertifolia*)	1–3' x 1–3'	–20	1*	Compact, with folded silver leaves that are edible and salty tasting. Extra salt tolerant.
Shrubby Senna (*Senna wislizenii*)	4–6' x 6–8'	10	2	Native senna as a replacement for overused Aussie sennas.
Silk Tassel Tree (*Garrya flavescens*)	4–6' x 6–8'	5	3	Wonderful native shrub begging to be grown commercially.
Sonoran Justicia (*Justicia sonorae*)	1.5' x 1'	17	2*	Slender straw-like stems with violet blooms.
Sugar Bush (*Rhus ovata*)	8–15' x 8–15'	10	2	Big evergreen screening plant.

Plant Name	Mature Height x Width	Cold Hardiness (degrees F)	Water Use (*see pages 165–166)	Scott's Notes
'Sunrise' Bells (*Tecoma* x 'Sunrise')	6–8' x 6–8'	10	3*	Two-tone copper-yellow flowers.
Superstition Mallow (*Abutilon palmeri*)	5' x 5'	25	2*	Velvety silver leaves with orange mallow flowers.
Texas Firecracker Bush (*Hamelia patens*)	3' x 5'	10	3	Summer tubular orange flowers; red autumn foliage.
'Trident' Sage (*Salvia* x 'Trident')	3' x 3'	0	2	Three-way cross that makes a compact, fragrant plant with purple-blue flowers.
Turpentine Bush (*Ericameria laricifolia*)	2–3' x 2–3'	–10	2	A great mounding fall blast of yellow.
Valesia (*Valesia glabra*)	5' x 5'	25	2*	Evergreen foliage and highly fragrant flowers. Best in warmer (nearly frost-free) areas.
Warnock Condalia (*Condalia warnockii*)	6–8' x 4–6'	18	1	Fine green leaves and fragrant flowers. Excellent bird-habitat plant.
White Ball Acacia (*Acacia angustissima*)	5' x 5'	20	2	Open lacey foliage—superb butterfly attractor.
White Bursage (*Ambrosia dumosa*)	2' x 2'	10	1	Small silver shrub with butter-colored flowers. Well suited to hyper-desert conditions.
Wolfberry (*Lycium freemontii*)	3–5' x 3–5'	0	1	Good bird-habitat screening plant.
Wooly Butterfly Bush (*Buddleia marrubifolia*)	5' x 5'	15	1	Silver with orange pompom blooms.
Yerba Santa (*Eriodictyon angustifolium*)	3–5' x 3–5'	15	1*	Nice deep green evergreen leaves with white flowers in summer. Great substitute for dwarf oleander.

Rangers

Plant Name	Mature Height x Width	Cold Hardiness (degrees F)	Water Use	Scott's Notes
Chihuahuan Sage (*Leucophyllum laevigatum*)	4' x 5'	10	2	Thin architectural branching and lavender flowers.
Cimarron Sage (*Leucophyllum zygophyllum*)	3' x 3'	10	2	Silver cupped leaves and true-blue flowers.
Compact Ranger (*Leucophyllum frutescens* 'Compacta')	5' x 5'	10	2	Smaller version of the standard Texas ranger.
Fragrant Ranger (*Leucophyllum pruinosum*)	6–8' x 6–8'	10	2	Silver leaves with grape bubblegum–scented dark violet flowers.
'Green Cloud' Texas Ranger (*Leucophyllum frutescens* 'Green Cloud')	6–8' x 6–8'	10	2	Green-leafed version of the standard Texas ranger.
'Houdini' Sage (*Leucophyllum revolutum* 'Houdini')	4' x 4–5'	10	2	The most underused ranger. Unique whorl-like leaves.

Plant Name	Mature Height x Width	Cold Hardiness (degrees F)	Water Use (*see pages 165–166)	Scott's Notes
(Rangers, continued)				
'Lynn's Legacy' Ranger (*Leucophyllum langmaniae* 'Lynn's Legacy')	5' x 5'	10	2	Not as dependent on humidity for blooming. More repeat blooms.
Rio Bravo Sage (*Leucophyllum langmaniae*)	5' x 5'	10	2	Rounded form with medium green leaves and lavender flowers.
'Thunder Cloud' Texas Ranger (*Leucophyllum candidum*)	3' x 3'	10	2	The shortest, most silver ranger; needs excellent drainage.
'White Cloud' Texas Ranger (*Leucophyllum frutescens* 'White Cloud')	6–8' x 6–8'	10	2	White-flowered version of the standard Texas ranger.

Ground Covers

Plant Name	Mature Height x Width	Cold Hardiness (degrees F)	Water Use (*see pages 165–166)	Scott's Notes
Buffalo Gourd (*Cucurbita foetidissima*)	1' x 20'	root hardy to 0	3*	Wild, stinky, and rambling, with interesting leaves.
Chihuahuan Primrose (*Oenothera stubbei*)	1' x 4–6'	10	2	Yellow flowers and lance-shaped leaves.
Clover Fern (*Marsilea macropoda*)	8–10" x 2'	0	3+*	Good in between paving stones in damp areas. Good for riparian areas.
Frogfruit (*Phylla nodiflora*)	3–6" x 4–6'	14	3+*	Larval food plant for Phaon crescent butterfly.
Mexican Evening Primrose (*Oenothera speciosa*)	1' x 3'	5	2	Often besieged by flea beetles, but with water can be aggressive. Good for shady spots.
Moss Verbena (*Glandularia pulchella*)	1' x 2'	15	3	Good in front of silvery-toned agaves. South American.
Prairie Zinnia (*Zinnia grandiflora*)	6" x 1–1.5'	−30	2	Awesome gold ground cover; dislikes having its roots disturbed during transplanting.
Raspberry Fuzzies Copperleaf (*Acalypha monostachya* 'Raspberry Fuzzies')	6" x 3–4'	10	2*	Underused burgundy-flowered plant with hairy foliage.
'Sierra Gold' Dalea (*Dalea capitata* 'Sierra Gold')	6" x 3'	0	3	Fine, delicate texture.
'Silver Falls' Dichondra (*Dichondra argentea* 'Silver Falls')	4" x 3–6'	root hardy to 15	3	Good for shady enclosures with extra water. Selection of plant native to AZ, TX.
Sundrops (*Calylophus hartwegii*)	8" x 2'	−20	3	Giant petunia-like yellow blooms frequented by hawk moths. Good with Parry's penstemon.
Thompson Hybrid Desert Broom (*Baccharis* x 'Starn')	18–24" x 2–4'	15	2	Sturdy evergreen ground cover. Good en masse and mixed with agaves.
Trailing Indigo Bush (*Dalea greggii*)	1–2' x 4–6'	10	2	Vigorous silver spreader with violet flowers.

DESIGNING WITH DESERT PLANTS 101

Plant Name	Mature Height x Width	Cold Hardiness (degrees F)	Water Use (*see pages 165–166)	Scott's Notes
Small Vines				
Arizona Grape Ivy (*Cissus trifoliata*)	to 15'	10	2	Succulent leaves; nice tracery in winter.
Canyon Morning Glory (*Ipomoea barbatisepala*)	to 15'	5	3*	Good trained on native mesquite trees.
Climbing Janusia (*Janusia gracilis*)	to 10', often smaller	18	2*	Svelte little vine—nice on wire fencing.
Mexican Flame Vine (*Senecio confusus*)	to 10'	18	3*	Tropical and unusual exotic-looking vine, good for butterflies. Semi-evergreen where lows stay over 30 degrees F.
Milkweed Vine (*Sarcostemma cynanchoides*)	to 15'	15	2*	Available only from seed. Vastly underused.
Native Passion Flower (*Passiflora foetida*)	to 10–15'	20	2	Excellent larval butterfly plant with edible fruit.
Scarlet Creeper (*Ipomoea coccinea hederifolia*)	to 10'	10	2*	Little red fireworks on thin tendrils.
Southwestern Pipevine (*Aristolochia watsonii*)	to 3'	15	2*	Great butterfly-attracting native.
Twining Snapdragon Vine (*Maurandya antirrhiniflora*)	to 10', often smaller	18	2*	Delicate and tough. Great trained on ocotillo.
Virgin's Bower (*Clematis drummondii*)	to 25'	0	3*	Glows when backlit.
Larger Vines				
'Barbara Karst' Bougainvillea (*Bougainvillea* 'Barbara Karst')	30' or more	20	2	South American native. Technically, bougainvillea is a woody plant rather than a vine, but is often used as a vine. Plant in hot microclimates in cold areas (south- or west-facing walls). Semi-evergreen in protected microclimates where low temps stay above 30 degrees F.
Cat's Claw Vine (*Macfadyena unguis-cati*)	25'–40'	22	2	Vigorous, good for chainlink and blazing-hot exposures. Semi-evergreen.
'Hacienda Creeper' (*Parthenocissus* sp. 'Hacienda Creeper')	25'	0	2*	Red foliage with cold weather. Smaller than Virginia creeper.
Purple Orchid Vine (*Callaeum lilacaena*)	to 20'	15	2	Lilac flowers from tuberous root. Evergreen where lows stay above 25 degrees F.
Queen's Wreath (*Antigonon leptopus*)	25'	root-hardy to 15	2*	Sprays of magenta-red blooms in late summer and fall.
'Roger's Red' California Grape (*Vitis californica* 'Roger's Red')	25'	0	3*	Bright red foliage in fall and winter. Unlike the 'Mission' grape, this one is a Southwest native.
'Tangerine Beauty' Crossvine (*Bignonia capreolata* 'Tangerine Beauty')	to 30'	−10	3*	An explosion of orange trumpets on this exotic evergreen.

Plant Name	Mature Height x Width	Cold Hardiness (degrees F)	Water Use (*see pages 165–166)	Scott's Notes
(Larger Vines, continued)				
Yellow Morning Glory (*Merremia aurea*)	to 25'	root-hardy to 17	2	Giant bright yellow blooms in summer.
Yellow Orchid Vine (*Callaeum macropterum*)	to 20'	20	2	Tough with small yellow orchid-like flowers. Evergreen where lows stay above 25 degrees F.
Vining and Creeping Cacti				
Alichoche (*Echinocereus pantalophus*)	10" x 4'	20	1*	Sprawling understory creeper available from Tohono Chul Park in Tucson.
Arizona Queen of the Night (*Peniocereus greggii*)	3–6' x 3–6'	10	1	Good trained through foothills palo verde.
Creeping Devil (*Stenocereus eruca*)	10" x 10'	28	1*	Baja native that forms ganglia of spiky stems. Will take the light shade of desert trees.
Martin's Harrisia (*Harrisia martini*)	8–20' x 2–20' (depending on support)	20	1*	Good under ironwood trees.
Moon Cactus (*Harrisia bonplandii*)	8–20' x 2–20' (depending on support)	19	1*	Good on trellises.
Ruderals				
Bahia (*Bahia absinthifolia*)	1' x 1'	15	1	Like a small desert marigold.
Blazing Star (*Metzelia involucrata*)	2' x 2'	N/A (annual)	1*	Good with snakeweed.
Desert Sunflower (*Geraea canescens*)	3' x 1–2'	N/A (annual)	1*	Likes sandy soils.
Prickly Poppy (*Argemone platyceras*)	2–3' x 2–3'	0	1*	Fried-egg-like flowers.
Sacred Datura (*Datura wrightii*)	3' x 3–6'	0	2	Easy to grow, attracts hornworms.
Sonoran Nightshade (*Solanum tridynamum*)	2–3' x 2–3'	26, root hardy to 20	2*	True-blue, and sometimes white, flowers.
Spreading Fleabane (*Erigeron divergens*)	1' x 1'	−10	2	Seed everywhere.
Wild Poinsettia (*Euphorbia heterophylla*)	8–16" x 8–16"	N/A (annual, except in frost-free zones)	2*	Likes wet areas.

Plant Name	Mature Height x Width	Cold Hardiness (degrees F)	Water Use (*see pages 165–166)	Scott's Notes
Small to Medium-sized Agaves				
Artichoke Agave (*Agave parryi truncata*)	3' x 3'	10	2	Tight symmetrical rosette.
Butterfly Agave (*Agave potatorum*)	2' x 2'	25	2	Exceptionally handsome silver plant with twisted spiny points along the leaf margins.
Cerro Guiengola Agave (*Agave guiengola*)	3' x 4'	25	2	Unique widely spaced silver leaves; needs shade and frost protection. Will grow in significant shade.
Desert Agave (*Agave deserti*)	1.5' x 2'	15	2	A nice small underused agave.
'Durango Delight' Agave (*Agave schidigera* 'Durango Delight')	2' x 2'	15	2	Handsome white-streaked leaves with white filaments.
Golden-flowered Agave (*Agave chrysantha*)	2' x 4'	10	2	An Arizona native.
Huachuca Agave (*Agave parryi huachucensis*)	2' x 3'	0	2	Great oak-grassland specimen.
'Jaws' Agave (*Agave gentryi* 'Jaws')	2–3' x 2–3'	10	2*	Huge serrated shark-like teeth on a deep green plant.
Jet-tipped Agave (*Agave macroacantha*)	2' x 2'	25	2	Silver leaves with black terminal spines. This agave produces a lot of offsets.
Mescal Ceniza (*Agave colorata*)	3–4' x 3–4'	15	2	Looks like it was dusted with powdered sugar.
Mescal Pelon (*Agave pelona*)	2' x 3'	15	2	Deep green with yellow streaks, very ornamental.
Murphy's Agave (*Agave murpheyi*)	3' x 3'	15	2	Nice small form.
New Mexico Agave (*Agave neomexicana*)	1.5' x 2'	−20	2	Striking twisted mahogany-to-black terminal and marginal spines.
Ocahui (*Agave ocahui*)	2' x 3'	15	2	Deep green solitary rosette, takes reflected heat.
Octopus Agave (*Agave vilmoriniana*)	3' x 3'	20	2	Nice recurving form. Short-lived, but produces babies on bloom stalk.
Palmer's Agave (*Agave palmeri*)	3' x 4'	5	2	Used to make mescal in Mexico.
Parry's Agave (*Agave parryi*)	2' x 3'	−20	2	Über cold-hardy and handsome.
Queen Victoria Agave (*Agave victoriae-reginae*)	18" x 18"	10	2	Highly sought-after; great in pots.

Plant Name	Mature Height x Width	Cold Hardiness (degrees F)	Water Use (*see pages 165–166)	Scott's Notes
(Small to Medium-sized Agaves, continued)				
Santa Cruz Striped Agave (*Agave parviflora*)	6" x 6"	10	2	Tough and tiny; deep green with white markings; grows with Santa Rita prickly pear.
Spider Agave (*Agave bracteosa*)	1–2' x 1–2'	10	2	Switch-hitter: grows in sun or shade (prefers shade in deserts with hyper summers). Nice recurving leaves. Will grow in significant shade.
Sharkskin Agave (*Agave 'Sharkskin'*)	2–3' x 3–4'	15	2*	Sharkskin agave's sturdy dark green leaves look magical when planted among ornamental grasses.
Twin-flowered Agave (*Agave geminiflora*)	3' x 3'	15	2	Also a switch-hitter (see previous entry); prefers shade in deserts with hyper summers. Will grow in significant shade.
Utah Agave (*Agave utahensis*)	1' x 1'	–10	2*	Likes to grow in tiny rock fissures.
Whale's Tongue Agave (*Agave ovatifolia*)	3' x 4'	0	2	Huge wide leaves, nice form.
White Stripe Agave (*Agave americana mediopicta*)	3' x 3'	15	2	Beautiful form, though extra-susceptible to weevil damage.
Large Agaves				
Cow's Horn Agave (*Agave bovicornuta*)	4' x 4–5'	20	2	Dark green with mahogany edges, good under ironwood trees. Will grow in significant shade.
'Green Goblet' Hardy Century Plant (*Agave salmiana ferox* 'Green Goblet')	4' x 4'	10	2	Dark green and urn-shaped inward-curving leaves.
Havard Agave (*Agave havardiana*)	3' x 4'	–20	2	Perhaps the most cold-hardy agave.
Variegated Century Plant (*Agave americana marginata*)	10' x 13'	15	1	Yellow and blue-gray.
Weber's Agave (*Agave weberi*)	5' x 10'	15	2	Huge, with handsome blue-gray leaves.
Dasylirions, Nolinas, and Hesperaloes				
Bear Grass (*Nolina microcarpa*)	5' x 7'	–10	1	Switch-hitter: part shade or full sun. Curlicue leaf tips.
Bell-flowered Hesperaloe (*Hesperaloe campanulata*)	3' x 3'	10	2	Light pink hummingbird-attracting flowers.
Bigelow Nolina (*Nolina bigelovii*)	6' x 6'	10	1	Handsome symmetrical silver plant.
Blue Nolina (*Nolina nelsoni*)	10–12' x 4–5'	0	1	Trunk-forming, with a huge flower plume.
Desert Spoon, or Sotol (*Dasylirion wheeleri*)	5' x 5'	0	2	Architectural bloom stalks that picket the sky.

Plant Name	Mature Height x Width	Cold Hardiness (degrees F)	Water Use (*see pages 165–166)	Scott's Notes
Giant Hesperaloe (*Hesperaloe funifera*)	6' x 6'	–10	2	Big deep-green sword-like leaves.
Green Desert Spoon (*Dasylirion texanum*)	6' x 5'	15	2	Green version of desert spoon.
Night-blooming Hesperaloe (*Hesperaloe nocturna*)	5' x 6'	0	2	Switch-hitter: part shade or full sun. Interesting greenish flowers that open at night.
Red Hesperaloe (*Hesperaloe parviflora*)	3' x 3'	–20	2	Stalwart and oft used, with showy red-pink bloom stalks.
Sacahuista (*Nolina texana*)	3' x 3'	–20	1	Leathery dark green leaves.
Toothless Spoon (*Dasylirion quadrangulatum*)	10' x 6–8'	15	2	Switch-hitter: part shade or full sun. Looks like giant green fiber-optic grass. No lethal thorns.
Tree Bear Grass (*Nolina matapensis*)	12–15' x 6'	15	1	Switch-hitter: part shade or full sun. Trunk-forming with recurving leaves.
Yellow Hesperaloe (*Hesperaloe parviflora* 'Yellow')	3' x 3'	–20	2	Nice creamy yellow bloom stalks.

Yuccas

Plant Name	Mature Height x Width	Cold Hardiness (degrees F)	Water Use	Scott's Notes
Banana Yucca (*Yucca baccata*)	4' x 6'	–20	1	Tasty fruit on a very cold-hardy plant.
Beaked Yucca (*Yucca rostrata*)	10' x 4'	–20	2	Dramatic blue trunk-forming yucca.
'Dusky Blue' Yucca (*Yucca linearifolia* 'Dusky Blue')	5–7' x 2–3'	–10	2*	Related to beaked yucca. Looks like a blue-tinted smooth spoon with a trunk.
Faxon's Yucca (*Yucca faxoniana*)	7–20' x 4–8'	0	2	Giant stiff green leaves, trunk-forming.
Harriman's Yucca (*Yucca harrimaniae*)	18–24" x 1'	–20	2	Tiny, trunkless, and cold-hardy.
Joshua Tree (*Yucca brevifolia*)	15–40' x 10–30'	0	1	Use it like a small tree; over time it will provide shade.
Mexican Blue Yucca (*Yucca rigida*)	12' x 4–6'	0	2	Stiff powder-blue leaves, great with autumn sage.
Mottled Yucca (*Yucca endlichiana*)	6" x 6"	10	2	Silver-blue leaves mottled with purple spots, growing from caudexes. Good for bonsai-type plantings. From Sonora.
Mountain Yucca (*Yucca harrimaniae*)	6–20' x 4'	–10	2	Good under oaks.
Our Lord's Candle (*Yucca whipplei*)	3' x 6'	0	1	Forms low colonies.
Pale-leaf Yucca (*Yucca endlichiana*)	1–2' x 1–3'	–10	2	Non-trunk-forming with silver laeves; looks good with sundrops.
'Sapphire Skies' Yucca (*Yucca rostrata* 'Sapphire Skies')	10' x 4'	–20	2	A bluer selection of beaked yucca.

Plant Name	Mature Height x Width	Cold Hardiness (degrees F)	Water Use (*see pages 165–166)	Scott's Notes
(Yuccas, continued) Soap Tree Yucca (*Yucca elata*)	6–20' x 3–10'	–10	2	New Mexico's state flower.
Thompson Yucca (*Yucca thompsoniana*)	6' x 6'	–20	2	Similar to Beaked Yucca but with shorter leaves.
Twisted Yucca (*Yucca rupicola*)	2' x 2–3'	–10	2*	Trunkless with medium green corkscrew leaves.

Barrels

Plant Name	Mature Height x Width	Cold Hardiness (degrees F)	Water Use	Scott's Notes
Baja Fire Barrel (*Ferocactus gracilis coloratus*)	3' x 1'	15	1	Deep red gracefully curved spines and red flowers.
Baja "Punk Rock Hairdo" Barrel Cactus (*Ferocactus rectispinus*)	3' x 1'	15	1	Extremely long, elegant red spines.
Blue Barrel (*Ferocactus glaucescens*)	18" x 18"	20	1	Gray-blue color with light yellow spines.
Compass Barrel (*Ferocactus cylindraceus*)	5' x 1'	0	1	Red and yellow spines, yellow flowers.
Coville Barrel (*Ferocactus emoryi*)	6' x 2'	15	1	Red ring of flowers.
Devil's Tongue (*Ferocactus latispinus*)	1' x 2'	20	1	Wide, curved red spines.
Fire Barrel (*Ferocactus pringlei*)	3' x 1'	15	1	Very red spines and red flesh in winter's colder temps.
Fishhook Barrel (*Ferocactus wislizeni*)	5' x 2'	10	1	Sculptural with a crown of orange flowers followed by yellow fruit.
Golden Barrel (*Echinocactus grusonii*)	3' x 4'	10	1	Ubiquitous and handsome en masse.
Mexican Hairy Barrel (*Ferocactus stainsii*)	3' x 1'	18	1	Red spines with a mesh of white hairs beneath.

Hedgehogs

Plant Name	Mature Height x Width	Cold Hardiness (degrees F)	Water Use	Scott's Notes
Arizona Rainbow Hedgehog Cactus (*Echinocereus rigidissimus*)	8" x 3"	10	1	Striking red stripes.
Claret Cup Cactus (*Echinocereus triglochidiatus*)	1' x 3'	0	1	Deep red flowers on an attractive cold-hardy plant.
Cotton-Top Cactus (*Echinocereus polycephalus*)	2–4' x 2–4'	10	1*	Mounding multiple heads covered by thick white spines that turn red after rain. Found in the harshest desert climates.
Fendler's Hedgehog (*Echinocereus fendleri*)	6" x 2'	0	1	Violet-purple flowers, great hardiness.
Golden Hedgehog (*Echinocereus nicholii*)	2' x 3'	15	1	Glowing yellow spines.

Plant Name	Mature Height x Width	Cold Hardiness (degrees F)	Water Use (*see pages 165–166)	Scott's Notes
Leding Hedgehog (*Echinocereus ledingii*)	1' x 2'	0	1	Golden spines and magenta flowers. Great in rockery.
Strawberry Hedgehog (*Echinocereus engelmannii*)	1' x 2'	10	1	Great form, magenta flowers, and yummy fruit.
Strawberry Hedgehog (*Echinocereus stramineus*)	30" x 5'	0	1	Ditto the above.
Torch Cactus Hybrids (*Trichocereus* hybrids)	2' x 5'	10	1	Impossibly big showy flowers. Try the Mark Dimmitt hybrids from B & B Cactus Farm, based in Tucson. Not really hedgehogs but similarly shaped.
'White Sands' Claret Cup (*Echinocereus triglochidiatus* 'White Sands')	1–2' x 3–5'	0	1	Largest and fastest-growing claret cup variety.

Columnar Cacti

Plant Name	Mature Height x Width	Cold Hardiness (degrees F)	Water Use (*see pages 165–166)	Scott's Notes
Argentine Giant (*Trichocereus terscheckii*)	20' x 10'	5	1	Branches sooner and lower than a saguaro. Gold spines.
Mexican Fencepost (*Pachycereus marginatus*)	15' x 4'	25	1 (or 2 or 3*)	Classic deep-green column with white pinstripes. Likes extra water.
Night-blooming Cereus (*Cereus hildmannianus*)	15' x 6'	15	1	This is the most common species referred to as "night-blooming cereus," although there are others as well. Often misidentified as Peruvian cereus.
Old Man of Mexico (*Cephalocereus senilis*)	20' x 6'	20	1	Snowy long hair.
Old Man of the Andes (*Oreocereus celsianus*)	6' x 6"	15	1	Another long-haired old dude.
Old Man of the Mountain (*Oreocereus trollii*)	2' x 3'	20	1	White hair bristling with gold spines.
Organ Pipe Cactus (*Stenocereus thurberi*)	10' x 10'	25	1	Sublime fruit, wonderful form.
Saguaro Cactus (*Carnegiea gigantea*)	30' x 10'	15	1	Signature plant of the Sonoran Desert.
San Pedro (*Echinopsis pachanoi*)	6' x 6'	20	1	Medium green candelabra form without prominent spines.
Senita (*Lophocereus schottii*)	10' x 10'	20	1	Spectacular mop-top hairiness.
Snow Pole (*Cleistocactus strausii*)	8' x 3'	19	1	Pure-white spines with red flowers on the sides.
Totempole Cactus (*Pachycereus schottii monstrosus*)	10' x 10'	20	1	Angular melted-candle form without spines.

Plant Name	Mature Height x Width	Cold Hardiness (degrees F)	Water Use (*see pages 165–166)	Scott's Notes
Prickly Pears				
Beavertail Prickly Pear (*Opuntia basilaris*)	1' x 3'	10	1	Good size for small gardens. Hot-pink flowers.
Comanche Prickly Pear (*Opuntia comanchica*)	18" x 3'	0	1	Flame-like orange-yellow flowers.
Cow Tongue Prickly Pear (*Opuntia engelmannii linguiformis*)	4–6' x 4–6'	0	1	Unusual pad shape that adds a different texture to plant combinations.
Dinner Plate Prickly Pear (*Opuntia robusta*)	10' x 10'	15	1	Huge sculptural pads.
Engelmann's Prickly Pear (*Opuntia engelmannii*)	6' x 10–15'	5	1	Bulletproof, with tasty fruit.
Grizzly Bear Prickly Pear (*Opuntia erinacea*)	1' x 3'	0	1	Interesting hairy spines.
Indian Fig (*Opuntia ficus-indica*)	15' x 10'	22	1–3*	Edible pads and fruit; can be grown as a hedge. Needs more water if you want better fruit production.
Milk-chocolate Spine Prickly Pear (*Opuntia violacea gosseliniana*)	1–2' x 24–30"	10	1	A miniature Santa Rita with chocolate-colored spines.
Red-flowered Prickly Pear (*Opuntia engelmannii lindheimeri*)	3' x 3–4'	5	1	Unusual prolific red flowers.
Santa Rita Prickly Pear (*Opuntia violacea santa-rita*)	4' x 4'	10	1	Purple winter color.
Tuxedo Spine Prickly Pear (*Opuntia violacea macrocentra*)	1' x 5'	0	1	Yellow and red flowers, small stature, purple pads.
Cholla				
Buckthorn Cholla (*Cylindropuntia acanthocarpa*)	4' x 4'	10	1	Yellow, orange, bronze, or magenta flowers.
Cane Cholla (*Cylindropuntia spinosior*)	6–10' x 6'	0	1	White through magenta flowers.
Desert Christmas Cholla (*Cylindropuntia leptocaulis*)	3–6' x 3–4'	0	1	Pretty red fruit for winter color.
Paper-spined Cholla (*Cylindropuntia papyracantha*)	6" x 2'	15	1	Weird curving spines like long fingernails.
Pencil Cholla (*Cylindropuntia arbuscula*)	4' x 4'	15	1	Yellow-green to red-brown flowers.
Silver Cholla (*Cylindropuntia echinocarpa*)	2' x 2'	0	1	Handsome white spines, yellow flowers.
Spruce Cone Cholla (*Cylindropuntia articulata inermis*)	1' x 3'	15	1	Pinecone-like segments.
Staghorn Cholla (*Cylindropuntia versicolor*)	5' x 5'	10	1	Tree-like with showy flowers.

DESIGNING WITH DESERT PLANTS 109

Plant Name	Mature Height x Width	Cold Hardiness (degrees F)	Water Use (*see pages 165–166)	Scott's Notes
Tree Cholla (*Cylindropuntia imbricata*)	8' x 6'	0	1	Native to grasslands.

Pincushions

Plant Name	Mature Height x Width	Cold Hardiness (degrees F)	Water Use	Scott's Notes
Corky Seed Pincushion (*Mammillaria tetrancistra*)	6" x 4–12"	10	1	Attractive hot-pink to purple flowers.
Cream Cactus (*Mammillaria macdougalii*)	2–12" x 12"	5	1	Yellow-green flowers.
Fishhook Pincushion (*Mammillaria grahamii*)	6" x 4–12"	5	1	Bicolored pink flowers and tasty fruit.
Golden Beehive Cactus (*Coryphantha recurvata*)	10" x 3'	5	1	The largest pincushion-type cactus in Arizona.
Green-flowered Pincushion (*Mammillaria viridiflora*)	4" x 2–6"	1	1	Distinctive green flowers.
Old Man Pincushion (*Mamillopsis senilis*)	2" x 2–6"	5	1	Huge pink to red flowers.
Owl's Eyes (*Mammillaria parkinsonii*)	6" x 6–12"	25	1	Resembles a barn owl's face.
Pancake Cactus (*Mammillaria heyderi*)	2" x 6–10"	5	1	Interesting flat species.
Snowball Cactus (*Mammillaria candida*)	6" x 6"	20	1	One of the whitest pincushions.
Spiny Star (*Coryphantha vivipara*)	4" x 6–10"	–10	1	Large magenta flowers.

Ocotillos

Plant Name	Mature Height x Width	Cold Hardiness (degrees F)	Water Use	Scott's Notes
Adam's Tree (*Fouquieria diguetii*)	6–15' x 3–6'	25	1	Rare in cultivation, nice for containers.
Boojum Tree (*Fouquieria columnaris*)	60' x 5'	15	1	Plant in the fall; very slow-growing.
Mexican Tree Ocotillo (*Fouquieria macdougalii*)	8' x 6' (potted)	26	1	Beefy trunks, good in pots.
Ocotillo (*Fouquieria splendens*)	12–18' x 6–10'	10	1	An indispensable hot-garden plant. May be able to sustain colder temperatures, depending on provenance.

Weird Plants

Plant Name	Mature Height x Width	Cold Hardiness (degrees F)	Water Use	Scott's Notes
Candelilla (*Euphorbia antisyphilitica*)	1' x 2–3'	15	1	Used for wax; very tough and pretty little silver straw-like stems.
Curiosity Cactus (*Cereus peruvianus* f. 'Monstrose')	4–6' x 6–10'	20	1	Striking form and blue color.

Plant Name	Mature Height x Width	Cold Hardiness (degrees F)	Water Use (*see pages 165–166)	Scott's Notes
(Wierd Plants, continued)				
Gorilla's Armpit (*Calibanus hookeri*)	2–3' x 2–3'	10	2	Grows from a woody caudex, evergreen.
Limber Bush (*Jatropha cardiophylla*)	3' x 6'	15	1	Handsome red twigs in winter, glossy heart-shaped leaves in monsoon.
'Macho Mocha' Mangave (*Manfreda* x 'Macho Mocha')	18" x 3'	15	2*	Fleshy leaves with chocolate-purple spots.
Rock Fig (*Ficus petiolaris*)	10–30' x 10–30'	30	2	Great as a bonsai with roots over rocks.
Silver Leopard Tuberose (*Manfreda* x 'Silver Leopard')	18" x 30"	15	2*	Simular to 'Macho Mocha', but with narrower silver leaves spotted with burgundy.
Slipper Plant (*Pedilanthus macrocarpus*)	3–4' x 3–4'	25	1	Switch-hitter: part shade or full sun. Snake-like succulent stems and red flowers.
Southwest Coral Bean (*Erythrina flabelliformis*)	3–6' x 3–6'	15	2	Lipstick-red flowers in late spring, early summer.
Texas Tuberose (*Manfreda maculosa*)	1' x 1–2'	0	2*	A tuberous plant that looks like a little yucca with purple spots. Plant on 2-foot centers for a weird ground cover.
Twisted Cereus (*Cereus hildmannianus* f. tortuosus)	10–15' x 6'	18	1	Its ribs form a nice spiral.

Grasses

Plant Name	Mature Height x Width	Cold Hardiness (degrees F)	Water Use	Scott's Notes
Autumn Glow (*Muhlenbergia lindheimeri*)	5' x 5'	–10	3	Strong upright form with tall flower spikes.
Bamboo Muhly (*Muhlenbergia dumosa*)	4–5' x 4–5'	10	3	Zigzagging mini-bamboo-like stems. Good in Zen gardens.
Big Sacaton (*Sporobolus wrightii*)	4–5' x 4–5'	–30	3	Big, stiff, picturesque seed heads; grows in heavy soils.
Blue Grama Grass (*Bouteloua gracilis*)	2' x 2'	–30	2	Eyelash seedheads; can be grown as a drought-tolerant lawn in Albuquerque.
Bush Muhly (*Muhlenbergia porteri*)	2–3' x 2–3'	–10	1	Airy pink bloom—a dwarf water-wise 'Regal Mist'.
Cane Beardgrass (*Bothriochloa barbinodis*)	2–4' x 2–4'	–10	2	Silvery seedheads glow when backlit.
Deer Grass (*Muhlenbergia rigens*)	4–5' x 4–5'	–10	2	Stiff 5-foot-high flower spikes.
'El Toro' Bull Grass (*Muhlenbergia emersleyi* 'El Toro')	3' x 3'	–10	2	Plumy flower spikes.
Indian Rice Grass (*Achnatherum hymenoides*)	2' x 2'	–30	3	Bunch grass with airy seedheads.
Mexican Feather Grass (*Nassella tenuissima*)	2' x 2'	–10	2	Lime-green leaves; frequently used; the "blonde of grasses."

Plant Name	Mature Height x Width	Cold Hardiness (degrees F)	Water Use (*see pages 165–166)	Scott's Notes
Nashville Muhly (*Muhlenbergia rigida*)	2' x 2'	−10	3	Compact size with purple-tan spikes. Southwest native.
Purple Three Awn (*Aristida purpurea*)	2' x 2'	−10	2	Purple-tinged stems on a compact plant.
'Regal Mist' Muhlenbergia (*Muhlenbergia capillaris* 'Regal Mist')	2' x 3'	0	3	Brilliant haze of mauve flowers in fall. Native to the Gulf Coast.
Sideoats Grama (*Bouteloua curtipendula*)	2' x 2'	−30	2	Pretty bloom stalks with seeds that dangle like pendants.
Sprucetop Grama (*Bouteloua chondrosioides*)	18" x 18"	0	2	Seedheads that resemble little Christmas trees.

Palms

Plant Name	Mature Height x Width	Cold Hardiness (degrees F)	Water Use	Scott's Notes
California Fan Palm (*Washingtonia filifera*)	60' x 15'	15	3	Leave the skirts on!
Guadalupe Palm (*Brahea edulis*)	10' x 8'	20	3	Great with deer grass beneath.
Mexican Blue Palm (*Brahea armata*)	25' x 8'	15	3	Icy blue foliage.
Palma de la Virgen (*Dioon edule*)	2' x 4'	15	3	Good underneath desert trees.
Sonoran Palmetto (*Sabal uresana*)	30' x 18'	15	3	Blue-green fronds.
Spiny Dioon (*Dioon spinulosum*)	6' x 8'	32	2	Stunning potted plant.

Outback Shrubs

Plant Name	Mature Height x Width	Cold Hardiness (degrees F)	Water Use	Scott's Notes
Aussie Ranger (*Eremophila hyrgrophana*)	2–3' x 3'	17	2*	Striking silver foliage with lavender flowers and compact size.
Bluebush (*Maireana sedifolia*)	4' x 4'	25	1	Silver-white teardrop-shaped leaves. Salt-tolerant.
Old Man Saltbush (*Atriplex nummularia*)	6–9' x 10–15'	14	1	Large very silver shrub—good quail habitat.
Outback Cassia (*Senna oliogophylla*)	5' x 5'	25	2*	Eye-catching red stems; needs warm locations. May be toxic to North American butterflies.
'Summertime Blue' Emu Bush (*Eremophila* x 'Summertime Blue')	6' x 10'	25	2	Bell-shaped lilac-blue flowers throughout the spring and summer.
'Valentine' Emu Bush (*Eremophila maculata* 'Valentine')	4–5' x 5–6'	15	2	Pink to red flowers mid-February.

Plant Name	Mature Height x Width	Cold Hardiness (degrees F)	Water Use (*see pages 165–166)	Scott's Notes
African Aloes				
'Blue Elf' Aloe (*Aloe* x 'Blue Elf')	1' x 2'	15	2	Petite with striking blue foliage and coral flowers.
Bulbine (*Bulbine frutescens*)	1' x 2'	15	3	'Hallmark' is a compact selection with orange flowers.
Cape Aloe (*Aloe ferox*)	12' x 5'	25	2	Big orange-red flower candelabra in late winter, early spring. Protect from afternoon sun.
Coral Aloe (*Aloe striata*)	2–3' x 1–2'	25	2*	Good underneath desert trees like ironwood.
Elephant's Food (*Portulacaria afra*)	3' x 4'	25	3	Switch-hitter: Full sun to shade. Like a mini-jade plant.
Kokerbom (*Aloe dichotoma*)	30' x 20'	23	2*	Can be a big, treelike plant; trunk-forming with interesting foliage pattern. Protect from afternoon sun.
Medicinal Aloe (*Aloe barbadensis*)	2' x 3'	25	1	Fleshy leaves and yellow flowers; used to treat burns. Protect from afternoon sun.
Partridge Breast Aloe (*Aloe variegata*)	1' x 1'	15	2	Relatively cold-hardy with dark green leaves with white markings.
Mediterranean Miscellany				
Dwarf Rosemary (*Rosmarinus officinalis* 'Irene')	1–2' x 4'	0	2	Dwarf selection with excellent cold tolerance.
Gopher Plant (*Euphorbia rigida*)	3' x 3'	−20	2	Chartreuse flowers, blends well with succulents.
Gray Creeping Germander (*Teucrium aroanium*)	3" x 18–24"	−20	2*	Good silver-gray ground cover for Albuquerque. Lavender-pink flowers.
Olive (*Olea europaea*)	15–30' x 15–30'	15	2	'Mission' and 'Manzanillo' are good fruiting selections. 'Swan Hill' and 'Hills of Santa Cruz' are good non-fruiting varieties. One of the few exotic trees that blend with desert landscapes (the silver leaves and twisted trunks help) while producing fruit. Fruiting olives are prohibited in some municipalities. Green olives are damaged at 28° F.
Prostrate Germander (*Teucrium chamaedrys* 'Prostratum')	1' x 2–3'	−10	2	Evergreen ground cover with lavender flowers.
Shrubby Germander (*Teucrium fruticans* 'Azurea')	4' x 5'	20	2	Eversilver (silver in color, with leaves that stay on in winter) leaves and blue flowers.
'Tuscan Blue' Rosemary (*Rosmarinus officinalis* 'Tuscan Blue')	3–6' x 3–4'	10	2	Vertical habit, good for culinary use.

Columnar cacti make fine scaffolding for vining plants with similar water needs (Design: Arizona-Sonora Desert Museum).

Outdoor Life

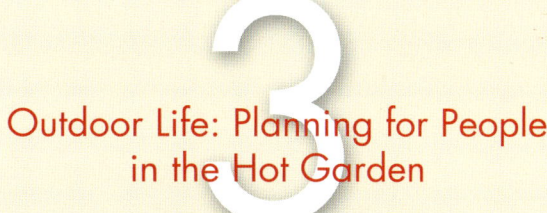

Outdoor Life: Planning for People in the Hot Garden

I love to go out on summer nights and watch the stones grow. I think that they grow better here in the desert, where it is warm and dry, than almost anywhere.

—Richard Shelton, *The Other Side of the Story*

IN THE NOT-TOO-DISTANT past, it seemed as though the business of garden design had been taken over by interior designers intent on remaking (and usually repaving) yards into lavishly furnished outdoor rooms. Some of these spaces featured $50,000 Roman-style pavilions next to pools with swim-up bars and gas-plumbed fire urns—the sort of mini-resort gardens that Albuquerque designer David Cristiani says "look like they were designed for overgrown teenagers." Considering cost to the environment (not to mention the homeowner!), building this sort of conspicuously consumptive garden now seems as ill-advised as buying a Hummer H2 with those shiny chrome spinning hubcaps. Still, having a life in your garden is important, so how can we build outdoor living spaces that are both lively and responsible in desert climates? In this chapter, I hope to show you how to enclose and color, shade and furnish, get creative with junk, and attract interesting visitors both human and animal. It's all part of the program for outdoor life in the desert.

Hill country penstemon (*Penstemon triflorus*) and an "Arabian Red" wall make a powerful vignette in the Boertjens garden.

Colored Walls + Native Plants = Garden Magic

When photographers focus on one plant, they often choose a wide lens opening (aperture) that will blur the background and bring the subject into sharp relief. In desert gardens, colored walls accomplish the same artistic effect for native plants—causing them to "pop" into high relief. It's the equivalent of putting a dancer in a neon-pink leotard in front of a black velvet theater curtain. Since planting in front of a colored wall puts your plants center stage, you want to make sure your best and most interesting specimens are featured.

Colored walls also provide a less-advertised benefit: reduced need for water-wasting annual carpet bedding plants. Because people want year-round garden color they often feel compelled to buy annual bedding plants (that must be replaced at least twice annually in the desert Southwest), which require intensive watering and fertilizing. In harsh climates, colored walls provide a better low-water-use alternative to the sort of throwaway annuals purchased at "big box" stores. It seems needless to say, but paint counts as color in a garden! With year-round strong color provided by paint, gardeners are freed up to play with thrifty and sculptural native plants.

Why more innovative and vivacious walls are not installed in more desert gardens is hard to fathom. When I drive through new planned developments, I am dumbstruck not only by the monotonous architecture—variations of flat-roofed pueblo-style or red-tile-roofed Mediterranean homes lined up in rows with prominent garages—but also by the monochromatic colors of these newly minted communities. I was beginning to think that to have a colorfully painted home and garden, you have to be very rich or very poor, because in new middle-class communities earth tones like beige are often enforced by covenant. I recently worked in one new upscale neighborhood whose governing documents flatly stated, "No bright colors will be permitted." I have written, with no shortage of religious zeal (yet still no monetary compensation from the National Paint and Coatings Association?), that we can encourage Gen X, Gen Y, and the masses of retiring Boomers to take up a new sort of gardening if we can get their attention with innovative gardens that are easily cared for and do not waste resources. I can see no other garden-design concepts that accomplish these objectives quite as strongly as the combination of sculptural succulent plants and boldly colored walls.

Although the Southwest is one of the best places to install colored garden walls, I'm sorry to report that just-plain-ugly and uninspiring walls are still the status quo across much of the region.

Botanical Design Color Wheel

In a color wheel—a circle of the primary colors (red, yellow, and blue) with the secondary colors in between (orange, green, and violet)—it is interesting to note a few things about how colors interact with each other. Colors next to each other on the wheel (such as yellow and orange) are called "related colors," while colors on opposite sides of the Botanical Design Color Wheel (like yellowy-green and reddish purple) are called "complementary colors." Complementary colors provide maximum contrast and impact when pairing plants and colored walls. For example, a new chartreuse pad of Engelmann's prickly pear against a deep purple wall (Dunn-Edwards Purple Passage) creates exhilarating contrast. This is not to say that related colors cannot be just as successful. Consider this example of a lime-colored wall (Dunn-Edwards Lime Sorbet) combined with a blue-green curiosity cactus.

If a conventional home builder erected your home, you may have had no choice but to accept a sturdy yet stark concrete-block wall—as lifeless, generic, and foreboding a surface as was ever used in the construction of a prison cellblock (although regular concrete block can be used to excellent effect, as I will recount shortly)—as the perimeter enclosure for your backyard. If you purchased an older home, it may be surrounded by a brittle and arthritic cedar fence ready to splinter at your touch or blow flat in a microburst. The good news is that we have a long history of exemplary enclosure in designing walls in the Southwest, and with a little thought—and perhaps some stucco and paint—dull backyard walls are often easily remedied.

Colored walls can be constructed of many materials, but standard 8 x 8 x 16-inch concrete masonry units, which are readily available throughout much of the country, provide a long-lasting base for cement stucco and paint, and a solid backdrop for plants. If you are demolishing an old fence and replacing it with a new one, be sure to check with your local municipality to see if a permit is needed. In some cities walls with a height of less than six feet don't need a permit.

Once your wall is constructed and ready for paint, the truly sexy part of the job begins: pairing the plants with the wall colors. If you have a garden plan or sketch and know some of the plants that will be included in the garden beds in front of the wall, it can be helpful to have them on site in movable pots while you play with paint colors. Most important, don't forget to have fun! I find playing with vibrant-colored walls and architectural native plants to be some of the most creative and satisfying work that I do outdoors. A tip to remember when working with vibrant-colored walls: use lots of plants with silver foliage, which tends to pop out against saturated colors and works as a neutral tone that is compatible with any wall color. The following general suggestions are followed by more specific plant-and-paint color pairings that have proven successful in my garden-design practice.

THE EVOLUTION OF COLORED WALLS IN HOT GARDENS

Predictably, landscape architects and garden designers often argue about whether the built elements or the plants are more important when designing a garden. The truth is, the very best gardens marry inspiring hardcapes with sophisticated and wisely chosen plants. Nowhere is this illustrated more obviously than in the vigorously colored walled gardens in the hot-garden zone.

Moroccan Blues

Although the European tradition of enclosed gardens really came on strong in 14th-century Spain, a walled garden constructed in the 1920s in Marrakech, Morocco, may be the closest ancestor to the modern Southwestern colored-walled garden. To compete with the fierce Moroccan sun, the French painter Jacques Majorelle created a garden whose plaster walls and masonry fountains were painted a deep saturated blue that became known as "Majorelle Blue"—a blue so potent that Moroccans believe it wards off evil spirits. Not only was Majorelle's use of color innovative, his garden was among the first to use cacti and sculptural succulents in front of brightly colored walls, which worked to excellent effect under a blazing Moroccan sun.

A recipe for garden zing? Engelmann's prickly pear against a purple wall.

Selecting Wall Colors

In desert regions, even a weak, light tan is blown into the realm of blinding white in the midday sun and becomes difficult to look at without sunglasses. Darker, richer colors absorb more light and can better hold their own against the intensity of the big sun. In the right situation, almost any high-key (intensely saturated) color will work—from hot pinks to deep burnt reds and velvety purples—so long as they are saturated tones. That said, you don't want to create a situation where it looks like a 13-year-old girl got into the makeup cabinet. One or two high-key colors, rather than five or six, is usually plenty.

Albuquerque architect Chris Calott gets his wall color inspiration from nature, using leaf and flower colors to inform his paint color decisions. One of his walls is the color of young cottonwood leaves and another is the color of lavender blossoms. With modern color-matching technology, you can bring an actual leaf or flower into the paint store and have its color matched exactly. Before committing to painting an entire wall, you may want to buy a few quarts of paint to experiment with by painting color swatches on a wall. Make sure to observe the color swatches at different times of day to see how the hue looks in different light conditions. Of course, if you do make a mistake, remember that it is just paint and can always be painted over!

When selecting paint, check the chips for manufacturer codes or information that will help you determine the compatibility of the colors with your wall material. For example, some colors are alkali-sensitive, which means that they are more likely to fade on highly alkaline surfaces such as new masonry. Some very bright (almost Day-Glo) colors are for interior use only and have a low resistance to the sun's UV rays and will fade early if used outdoors. Other bright colors are "low hide" and may require multiple coats to achieve uniform coverage.

¡Viva Barragán!

The use of high-key blue at Majorelle's Moroccan garden was not lost on a young Mexican architect, Luis Barragán. If you are a designer using bright-colored walls in the Southwest, you are a child of Barragán whether you know it or not. Barragán's courtyards sought to "bewitch" the user through his brio with color and strong lines. He is said to have taken up to a year to choose the right color for walls. Although his early color palette was limited, by the 1940s Barragán's use of color was deliberate and fearless. Sometimes he used color as a metaphor—suggesting the sky with a blue or sunlight through a yellow—while other times his vivid purples, pinks, and reds were taken from traditional Mexican clothing and festivals. Like many good designers, he took inspiration from local vernacular materials, preferring adobe and plaster to fancier, more manufactured products. Although the architectural lines that Barragán used were pared down to modern sensibilities, he managed to evoke the spirit of Mexican haciendas and ranchos in many of his projects. In addition, Barragán was one of the first designers to incorporate existing geology into a design and to juxtapose native plants (such as coral bean trees, *Erythrina* sp.) against brightly colored walls. The reciprocal relationship between the house and its garden walls became an obsession for Barragán, and his massive single-planed garden walls created great volumes of color to set plants against. I find Barragán's vibrant pink and orange walls and rectilinear fountains great touchstones for Southwest garden design. Deservedly, Barragán's influence is pervasive among the best designers in dry regions, and it is hard to argue that he is not the father of the colored wall in New World gardens.

Colored Wall Garden Gallery

My ongoing obsession with walls and "weeds" has drawn me to gardens with colored walls throughout the Southwest. Here are a few of my favorites:

STEVE MARTINO: KING OF THE CONTEMPORARY COLORED WALL Phoenix-based landscape architect Steve Martino could be described as the contemporary American Barragán. In designing walls as sculptural pieces that include shark-fin shapes, wave walls, giant radius curves, and offset planes, Steve Martino has taken the colored wall to an artful new level, although he modestly describes his work with screening and native plants as "just walls and weeds." An example of Martino's mastery in matching wall color with native plants is an undulating acid-yellow wall he designed for Civano Nursery in Tucson, which runs through the middle of a native-plant demonstration garden marking the entrance to the nursery. Throughout the seasons, the

The fruit, flowers, and flesh of the fishhook barrel are expertly matched against this "Imperial Palace Yellow" wall at Civano Nursery (Design: Steve Martino).

Silver and green yuccas and agaves contrast nicely with the "Imperial Palace Yellow" wall.

natives play out their dramas against that yellow canvas (Frazee Imperial Palace Yellow). In winter, a blue beaked yucca stands in sharp relief. Later in summer, fishhook barrel cactus blossoms and fruit add their orange and yellow colors to the composition. Other plants along the wall include: fishhook barrel (*Ferocactus wislizeni*), 'Radiation' lantana (*Lantana camera* 'Radiation'), curiosity cactus (*Cereus peruvianus* f. 'Monstrose'), and senita (*Lophocereus schottii*). The Martino-designed wall at Civano has recently undergone a makeover. It is now a glowing green (Dunn-Edwards Lime Sorbet), which contrasts nicely with the blue of the curiosity cactus and damianita daisies (*Chrysactinia mexicana*) in front of it.

THE GRAY AREAS OF JIM MARTINEZ Taking cues from the artist Donald Judd, designer Jim Martinez proves that gray—the natural color of concrete—is an honest color worthy of garden walls and patios. As an added bonus, gray-colored stucco walls don't require painting. Martinez, a gifted designer and plantsman, brings minimalism and plant savvy together on a residential scale in the small and arty west Texas town of Marfa. In backyards and courtyards, Martinez demonstrates that gray and white walls are a fitting backdrop for Chihuahuan Desert plants and short-grass prairie natives. When compared with the brightly colored walls of Barragán, Martinez's wall colors are decidedly understated, yet plants like 'Regal Mist' muhlenbergia still "pop" out from the gray

In this Jim Martinez–designed Marfa garden, Thompson yucca plays off unadorned gray stucco.

background, while more gray-leafed plants, like beaked yucca, use light and shadow and subtle color differences to distinguish themselves from wall planes. Before I saw Jim Martinez's work in Marfa, I would have thought that gray plants on gray walls would have been a non-starter, but after visiting Marfa and seeing the magic of a gray-walled garden planted with sophisticated grids of grasses and rows of yuccas, I became a convert—a man of the gray cloth, so to speak. I began to understand that a gray color scheme was a way to reduce the intensity and reflectivity of bright white light. Although I don't think I'm anywhere near giving up my more vividly colored projects, Jim Martinez's deft restraint has added the color gray to my arsenal of wall treatments. I no longer think of the color gray as drab or lifeless—just a color waiting to be enlivened by plants, light, and shadows.

ALBUQUERQUE BARRAGÁNESQUE Architect Chris Calott is deliberate about his color choices in his projects around Albuquerque. Rather than pluck the color du jour from the latest style magazine, he uses colors that specifically relate to the context of the site to adorn his mostly minimalist desert gardens. Calott learned the importance of color from firsthand experience with Luis Barragán's projects, when Calott taught college courses in Mexico City inside Barragán's studio. In a project near a cottonwood gallery along the Rio Grande River, Calott selected a color (a custom-mixed color that is close to Dunn-Edwards Citrus Leaf) that matches a newly emerging cottonwood leaf as the backdrop for a garden wall. Although the backdrop is derived from the leaf color of a riparian plant, the actual plantings are much more xeric: Parry's agave (*Agave parryi*), Mexican feather grass (*Nassella tenuissima*), and ocotillo (*Fouquieria splendens*) are the pop-out plants. In small urban yards, Calott relies on the richness and depth of color to convey the feeling of a garden. Calott's garden walls are variously colored to match chile peppers, lavender blooms, and cabernet wine. To increase the play of light and shadow on his walls, Calott employs rusted-steel botanical-themed windows that resemble the branching patterns of tree limbs.

Against a wall the color of newly emerged cottonwood leaves, Mexican feather grass and Parry's agave are enlivened and brought into focus in this Chris Calott–designed entry garden.

FRIDA KAHLO AT PECKERWOOD GARDEN A garden that uses deep-saturated-colored walls and bold native plants with élan is plantsman John Fairey's Peckerwood Garden in Hempstead, Texas. Inspired by Frida Kahlo's bright blue house in Coyoacán outside Mexico City, Fairey returned home to Texas to construct his first colored garden wall—a waist-high vibrant blue wall that

Whale's tongue agave hops into sharp relief against a burnt-orange wall at Peckerwood Garden.

denotes the entry into the dry portion of his garden. Against that blue wall, Fairey planted a rhythmic collection of silver-leafed yuccas, palms, and red and yellow hesperaloes. The red and yellow hesperaloes work so well against the blue wall that their bloom stalks almost appear to bounce off it. Fairey's first wall, which was painted with the Mexican paint brand Comex's color Colonial Blue, was so successful that he built another one, this time in a burnt-orange color (Dunn-Edwards Colorado Peach). In front of the burnt-orange wall Fairey planted an appropriately bold whale's tongue agave (*Agave ovatifolia*), whose wide silver leaves seem the perfect complement for orange. "The geometry of the wall and the agave work wonderfully," says Fairey. The orange wall is taller than his first low wall, and its presence created two small courtyards. These courtyard walls have been so satisfying that Fairey says, "I wish I could afford a lot more walls."

ARIZONA-SONORA DESERT MUSEUM PURPLE WALL Powerful architecture and powerful desert plants make for a potent garden—and this divine pink (Dunn-Edwards Lipstick) and purple (Dunn-Edwards Bossa Nova Blue) courtyard at the Arizona-Sonora Desert Museum in Tucson, designed by cactus master Mark Sitter, is proof. With its central ironwood draped with snake-like Martin's harrisia, this is one of the most memorable desert gardens I have ever visited. I have spent hours photographing this garden, and I never tire of being in the center of its pink and purple heart. In addition to the ironwood (*Olneya tesota*) and Martin's harrisia (*Harrisia martini*), the plants in this intricate garden include: totempole cactus (*Pachycereus schottii monstrosus*), *Dioon edule*, Baja "Punk Rock Hairdo" barrel cacti (*Ferocactus rectispinus*), desert marigold (*Baileya multiradiata*), and canyon penstemon (*Penstemon pseudospectabilis*).

In this Mark Sitter–designed garden at the Arizona-Sonora Desert Museum, massed totempole cacti dance against a purple wall.

Pink walls and totempole cactus make a bold statement.

SONORAN-MOROCCAN BLUE GARDEN
Borrowing an idea or two from the Jardín Majorelle in Marrakech, Morocco, I designed this central Phoenix courtyard with silvery plants, hairy white cacti, and flashes of strong red, orange, and yellow, all of which bounce off the blue walls—along with the homeowner's collection of rusty sculptures to make a design statement. Although the wall color is Moroccan-influenced, the major plants are Sonoran Desert species. Plants adjacent to the wall include: palo blanco (*Acacia willardiana*), sweet acacia (*Acacia farnesiana*), Mexican blue palm (*Brahea armata*), white stripe agave (*Agave americana mediopicta*), old man of Mexico (*Cephalocereus senilis*), snow pole (*Cleistocactus strausii*), 'Dallas Red' lantana (*Lantana camera* 'Dallas Red'), coral aloe (*Aloe striata*), 'Silver Falls' dichondra (*Dichondra argentea* 'Silver Falls'), 'Gold Star' yellow bells (*Tecoma stans* 'Gold Star'), and beaked yucca (*Yucca rostrata*).

A Marrakech-inspired blue wall works as a backdrop for Sonoran Desert plants like palo blanco trees (Design: Scott Calhoun).

NEW MEXICO PURPLE PRIDE
When landscape architect David Cristiani moved into his Albuquerque foothills neighborhood, his home looked pretty much like all of the others on his street—a newer pueblo-style affair with a flat roof and tan stucco. After considering his landscaping options and negotiating with his wife, Cristiani surrounded the front of his home with a bold purple wall (Dunn-Edwards Purple Pride) that initially shocked one neighbor: "It looks like Mexico." Cristiani was undeterred and loved the way the new wall differentiated his house on the otherwise monotonous streetscape. Around the wall he planted Chihuahuan Desert native plants like damianita daisy, rock penstemon, and prickly pear cactus. In addition to the color it provided, the new purple wall created expanded outdoor living areas, including a dining spot, a fire pit, and a water feature. Now the couple could enjoy al fresco dinners in their own private purple room. As nice as the outdoor living space is, Cristiani believes that his wall's highest purpose is to show off his native plant collection—a function it performs particularly well, especially when the damianita daisy is blooming and its gold flowers resonate against the purple wall.

The plantings in the Cristiani garden survive without supplemental irrigation, except in times of severe drought, and provide a long bloom season. They include damianita daisy (*Chrysactinia mexicana*), Engelmann's prickly pear (*Opuntia engelmannii*), rock penstemon (*Penstemon baccharifolius*), claret cup cactus (*Echinocereus triglochidiatus*), Maximilian's sunflower (*Helianthus maximiliana*), Mormon tea (*Ephedra viridis*), Colorado four o'clock (*Mirabilis multiflora*), cow tongue prickly pear (*Opuntia engelmannii linguiformis*), and Texas honey mesquite (*Prosopis glandulosa*), among others.

David Cristiani's exuberant xeric plantings and purple wall turn up the volume to 11 in this suburban front yard.

BIG CHERRY SUN Designer Selena Souders (also proprietor of Big Red Sun Nursery) chose a bright cherry-pink (Dunn-Edwards Cherry Hill) for her updated Austin bungalow. This profoundly cheery color, especially when combined with the green chair (Dunn-Edwards Palm Tree) of equal saturation, creates a pleasing vignette. The mounding potted pincushion cactus (*Mammillaria* sp.) on the table is yet another example of how well white hairy cactus works against saturated, even loud, colors.

THE COLORS OF TOHONO CHUL PARK In the Desert Living Courtyard at Tohono Chul Park in Tucson, landscape designer Jeffrey Trent made good use of color in 10 distinct garden vignettes designed to give homeowners ideas about different garden themes for their yards. Three of these gardens, the Barrio Garden, the Moorish Garden, and Meditation Garden, have particularly striking colored walls and plant combinations.

Austin designer Selena Souders' super-saturated pink house makes the perfect backdrop for pincushion cactus (potted on the table).

Barrio Garden

In this barrio-style garden, Trent juxtaposes a red miniature climbing rose (*Rosa* hybrid) against a tangerine-colored (Dunn-Edwards Tangerine Tango) masonry wall with an arch of 'Mission' grape (*Vitis vinifera* 'Mission') growing over the top. This very bright combination is near-neon but is nonetheless effective.

Moorish Garden

The Moorish garden uses two highly contrasting colors—inky cobalt blue (Dunn-Edwards Cobalt) and cool white (Dunn-Edwards Whisper)—on the walls that surround the garden. The cobalt is mirrored in the glaze of an urn fountain that is the centerpiece of the garden. The plants in the garden are composed mostly of butter-yellow and white specimens that play well against the wall and include golden columbine (*Aquilegia chrysantha*), coral bells (*Heuchera sanguinea*), white autumn sage (*Salvia greggii* 'White'), and white rain lily (*Zephranthes candida*).

Meditation Garden

The meditation garden at Tohono Chul takes advantage of a lavender purple wall (Dunn-Edwards Lavender Sweater) as a backdrop for the tough little vine 'Hacienda Creeper' (*Parthenocissus* 'Hacienda Creeper'). The red leaf edges and stems of 'Hacienda Creeper' look unexpectedly smart against the wall. Below the 'Hacienda Creeper' the tawny bloom stalks of big sacaton (*Sporobolus wrightii*) splay out against the wall.

Uncommon paint colors like "Lavender Sweater" make for interesting contrast with vines like this 'Hacienda Creeper' (Design: Jeffrey Trent).

A rustic mesquite arch supports 'Mission' grape at the barrio garden at Tohono Chul Park.

Portal windows in this El Paso garden's walls provide sneak previews of the fearlessly colored rooms that make up the garden (Design: Martha Schwartz).

TUCSON BOTANICAL GARDENS VEGGIE-BED SEAT WALL A curved raised veggie bed in Tucson Botanical Gardens' children's garden not only provides a home for spinach, Merlot lettuce, and Egyptian walking onion, it also is a *visual* feast. The wall is decorated with handmade tiles that are stylized versions of strawberries, peas, beans, and pomegranates, with a focal point that is a corona of a cantaloupe surrounded by rays of chiles. As pretty as the tiles are, they are really just decoration—the true star of this wall is color: opulent orange (Dunn-Edwards Orangeville) and velvety salmon (Dunn-Edwards Valley of Fire) stand on their own sans tile. The strength of the wall colors complements the deep red of the lettuce and fertile green of the onions to make for an altogether satisfying garden, with the salmon portion of the wall doubling as a convenient garden seat.

THE BRIGHT BARRIO Although the gentrification of Tucson's historic barrios has led some to dub one freshly restored and newly affluent neighborhood "Barrio Volvo," what has persisted in the barrio is the intrepid use of color. Most of the homes in Tucson's barrios are very close to the street, leaving a very small planting strip along the streetscape. Because of the restricted planting area, designers and homeowners have chosen a handful of plants—often Indian fig prickly pear—to stand statuesque against rich wall colors. You can find everything, including hot-pink walls (Dunn-

128 THE HOT GARDEN

In Tucson's historic barrios, hot pinks and ocotillos feel right at home.

Indian fig prickly pears are common in barrio neighborhoods and are well paired with high-key colored walls like this one.

Edwards Real Raspberry) with a singular ocotillo (*Fouquieria splendens*) rising up to the sky forming a hypnotic pink, green, and blue composition. In other gardens you will find a vivid aqua wall (Dunn-Edwards Faded Jeans) fronted with Engelmann's prickly pear (*Opuntia engelmannii*) and Indian fig (*Opuntia ficus-indica*). A variation on that theme is a simple but glowing planting of Indian fig in front of an orange-pink wall (Dunn-Edwards Rose Fusion).

PAINT AND SHADOW Sometimes a wall can be used to excellent effect with just the shadow of a tree branch or light fixture. On an acid-yellow wall at downtown Tucson's venerable El Charro restaurant, the elongated flying-saucer shadow of a light-fixture hood makes for afternoon interest. In the southwestern extreme of the Sonoran Desert, the Resort at the Villages of Loreto Bay at Loreto, Baja California, uses a Barragánesque color scheme with square and rectangular portals to wash the space with alternating bands of shadow and light. Because of the long shadows and ethereal morning and evening light in North American deserts, walls that play with light can be extremely effective.

CIVANO CELEBRATES COLOR Color can be a good antidote for monotony in new subdivisions, a fact borne out in the community of Civano in Tucson, a sustainable community known for its bright colors and energy and water efficiency. These four examples show how a neighborhood with flexible design restrictions when it

A cantilevered commercial light fixture creates dynamic shadows on this acid-yellow wall outside El Charro Café, Tucson, Arizona.

comes to paint can end up with a diverse range of colors that sets it apart from developments with row after row of beige houses.

Ocotillo Wall

This example at the Wheeler residence in the community of Civano is an example of placing sculptural plants against a good backdrop and letting nature take care of the rest. This combination in front of a cornflower-blue wall (Dunn-Edwards Cornflower) is composed of two varieties of prickly pear and a fully leafed-out ocotillo that were propagated with cuttings from other specimens on the homeowner's property. The Santa Rita prickly pear pads echo the color of the wall. The plants are ocotillo, Santa Rita prickly pear, and Engelmann's prickly pear.

Sonoran Painted Lady

Poet and editor Simmons Buntin went beyond just painting a garden wall an intense color. Inspired by the use of high-key color in Mexico and enthusiastic literature on the subject by a Tucson writer (me), he painted his entire Civano home three bold shades of purple (Dunn-Edwards Ode to Purple, Dunn-Edwards Concord Jam, and Dunn-Edwards Putman Plum). The result exceeded my expectations. When I visited the home in late summer, it was a riot of purple Rio Bravo sage and Engelmann's prickly pear fruit thrown up against the wall and then in spring the hot-pink Parry's penstemon bounced off the purple. Who would have guessed that throwing pink and purple flowers at purple walls would be so effective? The plants in the Buntin garden include Weber's agave (*Agave weberi*), Engelmann's prickly pear (*Opuntia engelmannii*), palo blanco (*Acacia willardiana*), and Rio Bravo sage (*Leucophyllum langmaniae*).

At the Buntin garden, a hulking Weber's agave pops off a background composed of three shades of purple.

Hot Penstemon Wall

Civano resident Alan Boertjens is no coward when it comes to bold paint. When he planted two different Southwestern penstemons—superb penstemon (*Penstemon superbus*) and Hill Country penstemon (*P. triflorus*)—against a deeply saturated red-orange garage (Dunn-Edwards Arabian Red), it certainly caught my eye.

Superb penstemon and "Arabian Red" paint make for an unexpected but successful color combination in the Boertjens garden.

Green Spear Cloud

A late-summer combo shows off the purple blooms of a 'Green Cloud' Texas ranger against the backdrop of John and Shelly Lauer's two-tone green home (Dunn-Edwards Linden Spear and Velvet Clover).

BEESWAX COLUMNS FOR GRAPES A central feature in Janet Rademacher's Phoenix garden is a crescent of earthy orange columns (Dunn-Edwards Beeswax) topped by a crown of 'Roger's Red' California grape (*Vitis californica* 'Roger's Red'). In winter, the leaves of 'Roger's Red' turn a full red, which mimics the color of a pair of weathered red vintage metal motel chairs next to the columns.

OTHER WALL OPTIONS Steel and stonework also make excellent and long-lasting walls in hot gardens. In Jill Nokes's Austin, Texas garden, she uses local limestone mixed with tumbled red glass and salvaged horned toad figurines, among other found objects. Margaret Joplin used steel strips for her gate in Tucson.

ABOVE: An arch of 'Roger's Red' grapes climbs up orange columns in the Rademacher garden. BELOW: A wall of local limestone and found objects surrounds Austin garden designer Jill Nokes's garden.

Tucson landscape architect Margaret Joplin wove together these steel strips to create a modern basketweave effect for her backyard gate.

The Garden Floor: Paving and Mulching

When we choose interior flooring, we bring home endless samples of wood, tile, and carpet to make sure that the colors and textures work with walls and furniture. But what about our garden floors? Perhaps our outdoor rooms deserve a little bit of the attention that we squander on Berber carpet. Since paving is often the most expensive single line item in a landscape budget, it is wise to consider the options. Here, from least to most expensive, are a few popular patio-paving ideas for Southwest gardens.

The least expensive way to cover, or pave, a bare patch of dirt in your yard is with decomposed granite, or dg, which is a rock product. Although inexpensive, dg is often more subtle and handsome than harder impermeable surfaces such as concrete and brick, especially in a garden aiming for a natural look. It has a satisfying crunch underfoot, looks clean and casual, allows seamless transitions from pathways and patios to planting areas, and works with any style of home from Santa Fe to ranch to French country. Decomposed granite comes in a range of earth tones from tan to red. For a surface you will be able to walk on easily, you will want to use a relatively fine granite size, like $1/4$-inch minus (minus means that the pieces smaller than $1/4$ inch are left in the mix). To create a firm walking surface, decomposed granite should be tamped or rolled with a water-filled drum while wetting it down with a hose.

Next to decomposed granite, bricks or cement pavers set in sand offer the next-least-expensive option. Economical bricks can be laid in beautiful herringbone and basketweave patterns; the downside is that the sand can settle under heavy pots, and tree roots can heave the bricks. Depending on your point of view, using bricks or pavers in sand has the advantage—or problem—of being able to grow wildflowers—and weeds—between the cracks. Some gardeners will spread wildflower seeds, like Mexican gold poppy, around the perimeter of the brick or paver patios for spring blooming because, as anyone who has ever pulled up a brick off the dirt knows, the soil under bricks stays cool and moist. For a more rustic look, consider tumbled or recycled bricks, which are often available at salvage yards at bargain prices. A slightly more expensive option is tumbled concrete pavers set in sand. These tumbled concrete pavers resemble Old World stone. Some manufacturers produce tumbled pavers in shapes designed to be laid in circles—which to my sensibilities looks quite smart.

Regular old gray concrete is a good option when you already have gray concrete patios adjacent to the area(s) you want to pave. For concrete tinted with integral color or finishes like exposed aggregate, the installed price rises, with the benefits of added textures and color.

ABOVE: In the Tumarkin garden, a rectilinear pattern of colored concrete pavers provides a path that is minimal and permeable (Design: Scott Calhoun). BELOW: The Huxman garden employs circular patterns, including a patio constructed of tumbled concrete pavers (Design: Scott Calhoun).

Tiles or bricks laid in concrete make for long-lasting surfaces. Laying tile or brick on concrete ensures that the patio won't settle. When choosing tile, make sure that it is high-fired and will be able to withstand sun, heat, and moisture outdoors.

The most expensive outdoor paving is flagstone set in concrete. Unfortunately, it is also beautiful. Because the flagstone must be cut and shaped with blades that cost over $50 each, the installed price rises accordingly. The installed price also varies depending on the thickness and color of the stone selected.

In Jason Isenberg's garden, simple scored concrete paving complements the straightforward block walls (Design: Urban Organics).

MULCHING In my wildflower-chasing trips, I have often observed that many wildflowers seem to prefer growing among rather large rocks. Some of the thickest and best displays are on hillsides cobbled with 4- to 6-inch rocks scattered over the soil surface. Poppies, blue dicks, and lupine grow in areas of scattered rocks smaller than shoeboxes, whereas brittlebush seems to like volcanic hillsides covered in rocks bigger than shoeboxes. Either situation illustrates the point that larger rocks can slow down

This expertly constructed flagstone patio at Tohono Chul Park in Tucson is expensive but beautiful (Design: Jeffrey Trent).

water. Rocks that are not packed down and have air space around them are excellent for slowing down water and allowing it to percolate into the soil. If you are using decomposed granite as a mulch where you want to grow wildflower seeds, it is helpful to incorporate larger rocks, which have more damp and shadowy nooks and crannies for seeds to fall into and germinate. Incorporating slightly larger rock into your design also helps reduce the chances of your gravel silting over and clogging up after periodic flooding. Not only is rock excellent for growing wildflowers, it is also a regionally appropriate, permeable water-harvesting material. The noted Southwest plantsman David Salman says, "If I had to choose only one mulch, it would be gravel."

When selecting rock mulches, you will be faced with a wide array of colors, sizes, and textural choices. Colors range from neutral tans to roses, golds, and dark reds. In contrast to my feelings about paint colors, I generally lean toward the more natural earth-tone colors rather than darker colors (especially if you have a brightly colored garden wall or house). Remember that dark colors absorb heat, and like paint, gravel colors may look different when you spread them out over a large area. For this reason, it is wise to bring color samples home in 5-gallon buckets to spread over an area for consideration.

Gravel

Gravel, also known as "decorative rock," comes in a variety of sizes such as $3/8$, $1/2$, $5/8$, $3/4$, and 1-inch pieces. Gravel is typically a "screened rock" product, meaning that if you order $5/8$-inch gravel you get a smaller portion (typically 30–40 percent) of rocks smaller than $5/8$ of an inch, which are also known as fines (powdery dirt-like crushed-rock material).

Decomposed Granite

Decomposed granite, also known as "minus material" or simply "dg," is usually sold as $1/4$, $1/2$, and $3/4$-inch minus, and has more fines (70–80 percent) when compared with screened gravel. You can use $1/4$-inch minus to make patios and even driveways inexpensively by simply spreading it, wetting it, and rolling it with a water-filled drum roller. If the area doesn't have a border, you may want to use steel edging to retain the dg.

When choosing the size of your dg (and this applies to gravel as well), consider how much foot traffic it will get. Larger gravel or dg is harder to walk on, while a rolled $1/4$ minus dg patio can be walked on with bare feet. Although it's more comfortable to walk on, smaller gravel or dg is also more easily tracked into homes.

Decomposed granite is a common but extremely useful mulch and pathway material for hot-garden zones.

Riprap

Riprap is larger, angular, and chunky rock material. Like gravel, it comes in a variety of colors. Its sizes range from 1–3-inch pieces to 4–8-inch pieces. It can be used to stabilize soil along water-harvesting berms, the banks of raised pathways, and along the edges of rainwater-catchment basins. In general wildflowers will seed well in riprap. It is not good to walk on and doesn't look natural when used as a dry streambed material (although it might in an abstracted contemporary version of an arroyo). Also, it is often badly used on banks for erosion control.

Organic Mulches

Although I generally prefer rock mulches, organic mulches also have their place. Resource-efficient gardeners like Tucson's Brad Lancaster prefer to do their plantings in basins mulched with organic materials, such as mesquite bean pods and tree branches. In fact, Brad simply throws his pruned tree branches beneath the tree, where they act as mulch and slowly decompose. By reusing your pruning and leaf litter on site, you sequester carbon rather than shipping it off to the landfill. The difficulty with this sort of wild mulching is in maintaining a tidy appearance in your yard. One solution to this issue involves circumscribing specific areas (under the canopy of mesquite trees for example) with a border. Within that border we allow bean pods, leaf litter, and other organic materials to collect and serve as mulch. Outside of this border, a more manicured appearance is maintained—perhaps using gravel.

Coverage

For rock mulches to be effective in suppressing weeds and reducing soil evaporation, rock should be spread between two and three inches thick. One ton of rock mulch usually covers 120 square feet. Do not put black plastic beneath your gravel, as it dries out and becomes ugly, and it prevents air and water from reaching plant roots.

Fertilizing over Rock Mulches

Once gravel is put down, it is not easy to dig up and amend the soil. For this reason, David Salman recommends broadcasting a fine-grained organic fertilizer (like Yum Yum Mix) over the top of rock mulches. If you are spreading a fine fertilizer during dry or windy weather, it should be watered in with a hose to keep it in place.

LABYRINTHS FOR DESERT LANDSCAPES When you think of garden mazes and labyrinths, you might conjure up the great green clipped hedges of England or cornfield mazes in the Midwest. On its face, the idea of building a maze or labyrinth in the Southwest might seem daunting—giant dark-green hedges are alien to desert landscapes. However, if your vision includes rock, native plants, and gravel, a labyrinth can be a central design element—even in the arid West. In fact, labyrinths should feel right at home in our gardens, as Native American tribes have used them for hundreds of years. The most famous religious symbol of the Tohono O'odham, the "Man in the Maze," is actually a seven-circuit labyrinth.

Mazes and labyrinths are totally different landscape elements. The maze, with its dead ends, cul-de-sacs, tricks, and intersecting paths, is meant to elicit fear and a sense of danger. Like an amusement-park hall of mirrors, it thrills us with illusions. Solving a garden maze is a right-brain activity that requires memorizing the twists and turns. Mazes are about riddle-solving and choice-making.

Patio Design Hints

- A 12 x 12-foot patio is the minimum size for six people to sit comfortably.
- A 25 x 25-foot patio will accommodate 12–18 people.
- Flagstone has an informal feel and is never perfectly level, so if an absolutely flat surface is required, you may want to consider another material.
- Concrete will always have small cracks, as some cracking is normal for all cement surfaces.

An artfully realized desert labyrinth constructed of stone and decomposed granite (Design: Debra Huffman).

Walking a labyrinth, in contrast, is a left-brain activity. There are no decisions for the labyrinth walker, just a looping path that leads to the center and back. Walking through a labyrinth is meant to be a contemplative process. As Tucson landscape architect Debra Huffman notes, "Walking a labyrinth is a walk that you take with yourself; you walk to the center and walk back out by yourself."

Huffman, who has designed and built labyrinths in two of her own gardens, loves the feeling they create in her yard. "In our first house, we built a labyrinth that was part of our patio. So we sat on it and lived on it. I feel like the labyrinth in our current home has settled our house." Huffman's labyrinth is a seven-circuit design that she constructed using small rectangular pieces of stone surrounded by decomposed granite.

In a garden, the labyrinth can bring a feeling of order and calm to the riot of cactus and desert shrubs and trees that populate desert landscapes. They are one of the rare design elements that fit into both formal and informal gardens.

In Huffman's garden, a large blue palo verde tree overhangs her labyrinth, casting a dappled shade on the stone pattern. During spring, the palo verde blossoms fall and cover the labyrinth in yellow. In the morning and evening light, the stones stand out like ancient symbols; the labyrinth feels like the heart of the garden. "When we walk it, we walk it intentionally," says Huffman, "but I'm also content just to look at it."

Seating

Good seating is one of the most neglected aspects of a garden. Without it, people will simply pass through a space rather than linger. The relatively mild winters in the hot-garden region lure us outside for more of the year than in more northerly climes. For backyard parties, you see the importance of comfortable seating as your fire burns lower, the empty bottles accumulate, and the stories get longer.

MASONRY Durable and solid, masonry seating has its charms. It can be made from all manner of materials from stuccoed cement block to stone to recycled bricks and bottles. On the downside, it can be cold or hot, it is not portable, and without pillows or backs, it may not provide comfort for extended periods. Masonry can also look smart with bright colored tiles. Southwestern gardens often include low masonry seat walls called *bancos*. Bancos can be great seating, but they must be situated in the right spot, as they cannot be moved into the sun or shade.

WOOD When it comes to building materials for outdoor furniture in desert climates, wood is the redheaded stepchild. Concerns about dry rot, termites, and sun damage tend to steer people toward plastic, steel, and aluminum—materials that look good but lend themselves to mass production rather than personalization.

A bold tile bench at the Rio Grande Botanic Garden, Albuquerque.

Which brings us back to good old wood. Yes, wood requires more upkeep in the desert than some other materials, but it also has big advantages for the do-it-yourselfer.

Consider the following: wood is easy to work with, wood is cheap, wood does not get scorching hot in the summer sun, and wood can be painted bright colors to match almost any garden decor or house trim. In addition, there is a long tradition of wooden garden furniture design that makes many stylish plans available to the slightly ambitious homeowner.

One of the best chair plans comes from *Sunset* magazine, which designed a Western version of the Adirondack chair. Another smart design comes from New York City's beloved Wave Hill garden. Wave Hill offers a plan based on a 1918 design by the acclaimed Dutch architect Gerrit Rietveld; the original Rietveld

> ### Tips for Making Wooden Furniture
>
>
>
> - Use screws instead of nails.
> - Pre-drill screw holes to avoid splitting the wood.
> - If you are painting, use a good-quality primer before applying your finish coats.
> - Painted wood will need touching up or repainting every three to five years.
> - If you are leaving a natural finish on your wood, use redwood or cedar.
> - Natural finishes may require periodic oiling.

A pair of Sunset chairs at home on the author's porch.

This salvaged bench highlights the character of multiple layers of paint at the Rademacher garden.

ABOVE: A pared-down steel table in Marfa, Texas.
BELOW: A pair of freshly repainted 50s "Motel Chairs" fit well in Tucson Botanical Garden's Barrio Garden.

Wave Hill chair is part of the permanent collection of the Museum of Modern Art.

- Plans for the Sunset Chair (free on the Internet, or $3.50 by mail):www.sunset.com/sunset/web/marketplace/store/Plans_Projects/Chair/Chair.html
- Plans for the Wave Hill (Rietveld) chair ($10, plus shipping): www.wavehill.org/shop/WaveHillChairPlans.html

STEEL AND ALUMINUM Metal furniture can be a bargain and usually doesn't need regular refinishing. Steel furniture, a mainstay of Southwestern outdoor living, is available in Mexico or from resellers north of the border. Like wood furniture, it is portable and paintable. Steel may rust if the finish wears off, whereas aluminum typically needs no maintenance and is lightweight and easy to move. Many steel café chairs incorporate plastic and synthetic fabric panels into their design. These can be comfortable, colorful, and economical options for gardeners on a budget (and who isn't?).

Nightscaping and Lighting

The combination of hot days, mild evenings, and bold plant shapes begs for the addition of outdoor lighting in many Southwestern yards. Outdoor lighting can reclaim outdoor living spaces by extending their usability well into the night. Because many families spend their daytime hours at work, it only makes good sense to spend some money on lights that make the garden usable during the hours you are at home.

"Nightscaping" is the term used by designers to describe the illumination of the garden after dark through the installation of lighting. It has three essential objectives:

- First, garden lighting aims to create a mood or an effect in the garden. An example of "effect lighting" would be hanging a pendant light in a mesquite tree to create a pool of light beneath the canopy. Effect lighting is done mainly for aesthetics and is what makes the garden interesting at night.
- Second, lighting helps direct foot traffic along pathways in the yard. Pathway lights should be placed wherever there is an elevation change (such as steps), at the entry to walkways, and near pools and fountains.
- Last, landscape lighting seeks to make the garden safer by illuminating dark areas, thereby eliminating places for burglars to hide.

Although all three objectives may be taken into account when designing a lighting plan, the most dramatic results come from effect lighting.

In desert landscaping, some of the most theatrical lighting effects come from imitating nature. In nature there are two main

At the Inn at Loreto in Loreto Bay, Baja, strategically placed lighting makes this outdoor room feel warm and inviting after dark.

> ### Dark Skies Ordinances
>
>
>
> Because of our exceptionally dark skies, infrequent cloud cover, and low humidity, many Southwestern settlements have observatories nearby. Light pollution from cities—and even gardens—can compromise astronomy research. For this reason, cities such as Tucson have passed dark skies ordinances that prohibit certain kinds of outdoor lighting. In general, these ordinances usually prohibit lighting that is unshielded (without a shade), and lighting that shines up (above the horizon). For these reasons, always check your local codes before spending money on lights. In my design practice, I rarely have trouble with the code because the lights I recommend to clients are fully shielded and shine down.

sources: downlighting and backlighting. Downlighting is best described as how a full moon makes your plants look at night; it is a source of light from above. Backlighting is the silhouetting of cacti, succulents, or trees against a bright background. With bold and spiky plants like ocotillo, backlighting can create dramatic shadows.

Another popular form of outdoor lighting throughout the Southwest and Mexico is string lights. These can be as simple as Christmas lights or as architectural as lights suspended with steel cables. String lights usually sag in the center and can evoke everything from a Paris café to a neighborhood taco stand or Day of the Dead festival. String lights are fun and informal and fit in with the spirit of barrio gardens. It sounds trite but it's true: illuminating your garden at night allows you to truly see your yard in a new light.

Firestyle

Several years ago, I took my family to Alamos, Mexico, in the southern part of Sonora, for the holidays. Invited to a family party by friends, we celebrated the New Year outdoors in the courtyard of an old Colonial villa near the town square. We ate tacos among the mango and avocado trees, listened to roaming musicians, and warmed ourselves by the multiple fire pits arranged around the patio. We all look back fondly on that night, but what stayed with us most were the fires. Even in southern Sonora, the nighttime winter temperatures can get chilly. A warm hearth welcomes visitors. We smelled the smoke in our hair and clothes for the remainder of the trip, and each whiff of smoke brought smiles to our faces. Ever since that party, the glory of outdoor fireplaces, fire pits, and ovens has been seared into my garden-design sensibilities.

I began watching how people flocked to an outdoor fire—even in the desert. When a new high-end supermarket with a café with outdoor seating and a fire feature was completed, I was amazed to see how many people gathered around the outdoor fireplace as if they had never seen flames before. It struck me that this fire seemed to attract more people than many of the million-dollar storefronts in the same complex. People are consistently mesmerized by fire. Somewhere in our genes, way down deep, we must be programmed to follow warmth. Just because our longing for fire is primitive, though, doesn't mean that our fire pits and outdoor fireplaces need to look old-fashioned.

In Marfa, Texas, at the Thunderbird Motel, they have a minimalist square steel box as a fire pit. Designed by Christie Ten

Building a wood-fired oven outdoors creates another excuse to spend time in the garden.

An outdoor patio at the Thunderbird Motel, Marfa, Texas (Design: Christine Ten Eyck).

Eyck, the Thunderbird Motel's fire-pit area is a model of simplicity. The blackened box pares down fire to its simplest elements: wood, fire, and box. Even a minimalist fire pit can cause us to recall grilled food and camping trips. Also in Marfa, at a residence near the courthouse, a clean-lined L-shaped seating area with a fireplace as the focal point is an excellent choice. Our feelings about flickering flames make the prospect of constructing a backyard fire pit or outdoor oven as delicious as a well-browned marshmallow. Good fires, good friends, and good food—all primitive and contemporary needs of the human animal.

Ramadas

In other parts of the country they might call them pergolas, garden pavilions, outbuildings, lean-tos, or sheds, but in the Southwest we usually call shade structures in our gardens *ramadas*. The importance of shade in desert gardens should not be underestimated. If you plan on spending time outside in the summer during daylight hours, you'd better find some shade (or at least a wide-brimmed hat), or you just might bake your brainpan. While this shade doesn't have to be provided by a ramada—a tree canopy, umbrella, or even your house might do—a ramada offers some significant advantages. Chief among those is that a ramada provides a garden destination—a way to lure people deeper into your garden toward

A rock ramada at the DeArmond Garden in Tucson evokes the spirit of historic 1930s-era National Park structures (Design: Jeffrey Trent).

a shady spot with seating. Ramadas provide a place for cooking, dining, tea-sipping, lounging, sunrise or sunset viewing, reading, potting, and storage.

Ramadas come in a wide range of styles—from vine-covered rustic structures of twisted mesquite to solid masonry units with steel roofs. When planning for a ramada, consider the following:

- The relationship between the ramada and the house is important. Try to match materials (roofing, rock facing, stucco, etc.) whenever possible to integrate the two. When siting the ramada, ask yourself if you want it to be hidden from the house or a visible central feature. Make sure the scale of the ramada doesn't overwhelm the house.
- Double up on function. A carport bay that is open to the backyard can be a great ramada and is easily dressed up with patio furniture. If your ramada has a wall or two, consider hiding storage there. The barbecue grill often fits nicely in the ramada as well.
- If you have strong prevailing winds, consider making one or two solid walls as a windbreak.
- Account for how people will get to the ramada. Where will your pathway(s) be?
- When selecting vines for a ramada on the south side of your home, consider planting winter-deciduous vines that will allow the winter sun to warm your home while blocking out the summer sun.

At White Sands National Monument in New Mexico, space-age ramadas attached to concrete pads seem as at home as flying saucers and aliens.

Peeled lodgepoles provide rusticity and shade in a garden full of natives at Denver Botanic Gardens.

Fountains and Water Features

I should confess that, as much of a desert rat as I am, I love water. I'm a swimmer, and nine months out of every year I tromp on over to our community pool to swim laps each morning. Moving as fast as I can through clear water is my meditation. Some of my favorite Sonoran Desert places—San Carlos, Sonora, and Loreto Bay, Baja—are spots where sea and desert bump up against each other, and you can swim in water next to incomparable desert geology and flora. There is almost nothing as exhilarating. But the reality of living in the desert is that most of us will not be able to claim the Gulf of California, or even a swimming pool, as part of our desert gardens. Instead, if a water feature is to be part of our gardens, we should imitate nature. In nature, water oozes out of seeps in rock cracks, snakes its way through slot canyons, or rushes briefly and violently down normally dry arroyos. Visible water is usually ephemeral rather than perennial, and scarce rather than abundant. All of this might seem obvious until you drive up to a house in the desert and find something that resembles a junior version of the Trevi fountain. I've got nothing bad to say about the actual Trevi fountain—it looks great in Rome, but big Italianate fountains are generally out of place in desert gardens. What *does* look good? Small and subtle fountains. Here are a few tips and design ideas:

- *Suggest* water by making artful rainwater-harvesting basins that are empty most of the time but create excitement when they fill with rain.
- Remember that deeper ponds with less surface area conserve water better than wide, shallow ponds.

ABOVE: A small but deep limestone water feature at Lady Bird Johnson Wildflower Center in Austin. BELOW: A stock tank fountain surrounded by deer grass and fitted with a copper and slate fountain attachment (Design: Scott Calhoun).

A painted stock tank fountain at the Rademacher garden in Phoenix.

- Keep the size of the water feature in scale with the size of your home. As a rule of thumb, fountains should be less than $\frac{1}{3}$ the height of the home.
- In informal gardens, fountains are often best tucked into corners or placed beside walkways rather than used as centerpieces.
- Use native water plants in and around your feature.
- Ornamental grasses often look at home next to water features.
- Repurpose round galvanized stock tanks as fountains; they are a nod to the West's ranching heritage and reflect a circle of blue—like a giant telescope mirror held up to the sky. They can be painted to dress them up and integrate them with the colors of your home.

This south-facing wall and planter at Tucson Botanical Gardens, filled with cool-season growers, proves that veggie gardening doesn't have to be plain or unduly messy.

NATIVES FOR WATER If you're looking for plants to grow in and/or around a water feature, consider these natives:

Plant Name	Mature Height x Width	Cold Hardiness (degrees F)	Water Use (*see pages 165–166)	Scott's Notes
Clover Fern (*Marsilea macropoda*)	8" x 2'	0	3	Good ground cover for boggy spots.
Desert Lobelia (*Lobelia laxiflora*)	1' x 2'	0	3*	Will take water edges or drier shade.
Golden Columbine (*Aquilegia chrysantha*)	2–3' x 2–3'	–20	3+*	Native to hanging gardens in canyons. Takes shade.
Rocky Mountain Iris (*Iris missourensis*)	2–3' x 1'	–20	3+*	Native iris, good for boggy spots.
Scarlet Monkey Flower (*Mimulus cardinalis*)	1–2' x 1–2'	–20	3+*	Will grow in wet rockwork.
Seepwillow (*Baccharis glutinosa*)	8–10' x 6–8'	7	3+*	Will grow in water.
Yerba Mansa (*Anemopsis californica*)	18" x 18"	–20	3*	Will grow in water.

Living with Veggies

In the "Designing with Desert Plants" chapter of this book, I made a point of highlighting a number of edible ornamental landscape plants, but what if you want a traditional vegetable or herb garden in your hot garden? Here are a few considerations:

LOCATION From personal experience, I find it best to locate your veggie garden as close to your kitchen as possible—preferably in a place where you will walk by the garden as you come and go. The farther from the kitchen the garden is, the less likely it is to be planted, watered, weeded, and harvested. That said, the garden

Stock tanks can also be repurposed into handsome raised veggie gardens (Design: Greg Corman).

also needs full sun (a little late-afternoon shade is okay, but don't put your garden beneath large trees or shrubs) and access to regular water.

SOIL FOR VEGGIES When it comes to growing traditional vegetables, good rich soil that is high in organic matter (the sort that is very uncommon in this region) is key to getting good results. There is nothing you can do to the plants after a veggie garden is planted that will affect the production of the garden as much as what you do to soil *before* you plant. In the hot-garden region, that means adding lots of composted organic material to the soil. Because you will need to replenish soils and nutrients each season in your beds, a compost pile is an excellent way to create rich soil on-site.

IN-GROUND PLANTING VS. RAISED BEDS If you are planting in the ground, you need to break up the existing soil (dig a test hole, fill it with water, and make sure that the water is gone within 24 hours—or ideally, two hours) and thoroughly incorporate compost throughout the soil. In compacted soils this is hard work. Provided your drainage is good, in-ground growing gives you the opportunity to plant in depressions that will capture rainwater. Some Native American tribes create gardens with square basins called "waffle beds." The downside to in-ground veggie gardens is that in heavy or poorly drained soils, the plants will fail to thrive. For those instances, raised beds might be a better choice.

Raised beds and containers give you total control of your soil conditions and ensure good drainage. Raised beds can be constructed of lumber, masonry, or—my favorite method—steel stock tanks. Stock tanks, which come in both oval and round sizes, come almost ready-made and often look smart in the context of larger desert gardens. To prepare a stock tank for planting, poke numerous holes in the bottom of the tank (the pointed end of a digging bar works well here), lay down hardware cloth over the new holes (this is to prevent rodents from getting into the beds), set the tank on a few bricks (to provide a small airspace so that tree roots will not invade the bed), and fill with pure well-rotted compost or an organic potting soil/compost mix.

PLANTING SEASONS Newcomers often remark that veggie gardening here is just like anyplace else, only with different planting times. We really can grow food year-round here. My favorite gardening time is the winter, when chartreuse salad greens brighten up beds and working outside is a pleasure. The planting and harvest times listed here are for Tucson, but they can be pushed forward or backward based on elevation and first and last frost dates (in the colder regions, some fall planting dates are pushed into spring). In most of the hot-garden region we have two main growing seasons: a cool season and a warm season. (These times will not apply to the higher, colder parts of the region, where we follow a planting timeline similar to that of the American Midwest.) Here are planting lists for each season:

- **Cool-weather veggies and herbs** (*plant in fall, harvest in winter or spring*): beets, cabbage, carrots, cilantro, fava beans, garbanzo beans, garlic, greens, kale, leeks, lentils, lettuce, onions, parsley, peas, radishes, spinach, Swiss chard, turnips, wheat.
- **Warm-weather veggies and herbs** (*plant in spring, harvest in summer or fall*): amaranth, basil, beans, black-eyed peas, chile and bell peppers, corn, cucumbers, eggplant, herbs, okra, gourds, melons, peppers, pumpkins, sunflowers, squash, tomatoes.

A Little Art

I'm no art critic, and sometimes I'm unsure if *any* art belongs in gardens. With that confession, this section on art will be brief. Along with the requisite bougainvillea and citrus tree, I think every newcomer to the hot Southwest must be receiving a complimentary steel Kokopelli or coyote (with the de rigueur bandana, of course) to plop in their yard from the chamber of commerce. I'm certainly not making light of the horny humpbacked flute player or trickster, but I'm wondering if maybe interesting plants might be better than having a graven image of an ancestral Puebloan flute player in the yard? I'm just saying… I do like rusted objects in a garden. What's wrong with a giant rusty sunflower or gate? In a climate as dry as ours, a little rust is not distressing in the least.

When it comes to art, there is nothing better than a useful object artfully rendered. That is, art that is functional. Designer/plantsman Dan Johnson's handmade wooden gate—an homage to the Santa Rita prickly pear—is precisely such a piece. The stylized wooden gate gets its magic from a combination of zigzag pickets, vivid paint color, and not least of all, a wooden prickly pear whose topmost pads take a half-turn to fit between the pickets.

GROW SOME BALLS Of course, some art's only function is to delight, which is exactly what Gene Joseph's big recycled propane tank balls do. Round objects seem to fit in well in hot gardens. A few years back, before steel prices spiked, Gene, the owner of Plants for the Southwest, purchased a large quantity of perfectly round propane tanks on the cheap. Since then, he has been turning them into garden art. They can be pierced and used as sputnik-style lights, cut in half for a fire feature, or simply rolled out into the garden. If nothing else, rolling a big ball into your front yard is bound to raise your neighbor's eyebrows. Who said art isn't fun?

Gene Joseph showing off one of his recycled propane tank balls ready for installation in a garden.

Designer Greg Corman highlights a pair of cantera stone balls by creating a curved bed with a mass-planting of gorilla's armpit.

Another ball option is cantera stone. Landscape designer Greg Corman used a sweep of gorilla's armpit (see Weird Plants, pages 79–80 and 110) to curve around two cantera spheres to excellent effect. As is often the case, plants and art are best together.

Yet another option is the oblong ball (or egg). Designer Carrie Nimmer has craftily nestled a weathered ceramic egg under her screwbean mesquite tree in a nest of purple heart (*Setcreasea pallida*).

Shrines

When we think about what conveys a sense of regionalism in hot gardens, we may think about succulent plants with bold shapes, seasonal wildflowers, or dry rocky arroyos, but in many Southwestern yards, a personal spiritual element graces the garden: the shrine. Garden shrines range from the miniature to the

Vintage VW hubcaps imported from Texas, an upturned bathtub, and steel flowers bring some serious shrine fun into the Rademacher garden.

In the tiny Sonoran village of La Aduana near Alamos, an informal shrine to the Virgin of Guadalupe is festooned with Christmas lights and planted with a variety of cactus species.

grand, the solemn to the irreverent, and the private (backyard) to the public (front). Tucson's most noted (or is it notorious?) shrine, El Tiradito, is dedicated to a sinner. A shrine in the Barrio Garden at Tucson Botanical Gardens is draped with flowers, Christmas lights, and photographs, but as the Day of the Dead approaches, bride and groom skeletons, in gown and tuxedo, flank the shrine.

In contrast to the light-hearted Day of the Dead shrines, many shrines are places for reflection. I've been hiking deep in the thorn-scrub near Alamos, Sonora, and come across a beautiful

At Tucson Botanical Gardens, this shrine is constructed of traditional adobe block.

tiled blue-and-white shrine to *La Virgen*—candles still burning. The scene gave me pause, and though I'm not Catholic, I considered crossing myself for good luck. It almost goes without saying, but the Virgin of Guadalupe has to be the number-one theme of shrines in the hot-garden region, with St. Francis and Elvis polling second and third.

As I reported in my first book, I have a shrine in my own garden dedicated to dirt, which I found just as worthy of celebration as Elvis. The point is, we all have something that we celebrate, remember, or treasure, and there is nothing wrong with dedicating a little space for a creative shrine. After all, isn't gardening supposed to be spiritual?

The Junk Garden

Whether you're searching for an old car grille to decorate a wall or some rusted bedsprings to use as a trellis, you should be happy you live in the arid Southwest. With its proximity to a variety of architectural, industrial, and military salvage yards, the hot-garden region just might be the epicenter for junk gardening.

Garden junk can be divided into two categories: decorative and useful, although many pieces straddle the line between these two. At Val Little's Tucson garden, she incorporated rusted bedsprings into a fence and allowed vines to wind their way through the unusual screen. Little also uses bedsprings as the "roof" for an inventive ramada supported by agricultural augers and paved with old water-meter lids. The combination works well. "I see," you say

Val Little's tidy junk garden is complete with water-meter-lid paving and a bedspring ramada.

to yourself, "recycling *is* the aesthetic!" In her Phoenix garden, Janet Rademacher took an old plow disc, stuck it upright into the ground, and filled the discs with bird seed, making an interesting feeder. On the decorative side of the spectrum, Rademacher's garden is also home to a car door and rusted propane tanks riddled with bullet holes.

Landscape designer Greg Corman loves scouring the salvage yards for hidden treasures for the gardens he designs. "The trick is to get creative," says Corman. "You have to be able to look at something and see it for something other than what it is. For instance, I found a big steel parts bin that I'm planning on potting with a large specimen plant. Carefully selected junk gives a garden more personality and is a smart way to recycle materials."

Gunslinging banditos and salvaged propane tanks riddled with bullet holes are part of the *mise-en-scène* under the canopy of a mesquite in Janet Rademacher's Phoenix garden.

Some Junk Ideas

- Used brick makes for an Old World look as a paving surface on patios.
- Iron fence panels can easily be converted into trellises.
- Clay roof tiles stood on end make neat garden borders.
- 55-gallon drums in bright weathered colors can be insulated with foil-backed bubble wrap insulation (to protect plant roots from extreme heat) and used as pots.
- Old bedsprings make good fence panels that double as trellises.
- Old furniture and wood can be repainted or refurbished to add a vintage touch.

GLASS IN THE GARDEN Developed over 2,000 years ago with the advent of glassblowing, the bottle has become a ubiquitous part of American culture. An object both common and mysterious, the bottle is now making its way into our gardens as folk art. The bottle as garden art got its movie debut in the film *Ray*: the camera pans in front of a young Ray Charles in a rural Alabama yard standing beneath a dead tree festooned with colorful bottles. The "bottle tree" in *Ray* is rooted in the African-American tradition of placing upside-down bottles in trees, where they are believed to catch evil spirits. I know I'm a sucker for this kind of garden lore, but it makes perfect sense to me, considering that liquor bottles originally contained spirits. Empty a bottle of spirits, put it in a tree, and what will you capture? *More* spirits—and even better, *evil* ones! As far as I'm concerned, this is exactly the kind of tradition that can make a garden more interesting.

Although the bottle-tree tradition started in the South and Caribbean, modern bottle sculptures are making their way into desert gardens: glass is the new garden jewelry. As fine as it is, the bottle tree is not the only way to bring bottles into your garden. If you take the concept of the outdoor room, bottles can be used in the ceiling, walls, and floor.

Using block walls as her canvas, nurserywoman Janet Rademacher artfully placed cobalt-blue bottles in the coils of a rusted set of bedsprings and hung the whole assemblage on her masonry wall as both trellis and bottle art. The idea of stringing

In winter, the stark branches of a deciduous tree can be jazzed up with cobalt blue bottles (Design: Libby Davison).

Another Libby Davison invention is this rhythmic series of cobalt blue bottles upended on steel curlicue rods against a wall.

In a paved surface, the bottoms of round and square bottles make fascinating additions to brick patios and seat walls. In Susan Mathew's Bisbee garden, antique square-bottomed bottles are arrayed with brick for a unique and old-fashioned look. In the Tucson Botanical Garden's Barrio Garden, a line of upended bottles forms a novel border for a planting bed.

This nearly goes without saying, but one of the joys of working with bottles in a garden is that you get to consume whatever is in them before putting them into service. If you are using a large number of bottles that contain wine or beer, you might even have to invite friends over for a most enjoyable garden "work" party. As Janet Rademacher remarks, "We needed lots of Tequiza bottle caps, and we must have drunk it for a month."

Selecting your bottles is a matter of personal taste, but you may want to stick with a theme. Cobalt-blue bottles, or the familiar feminine hourglass figure of Coca-Cola bottles, look good in groups. In any case, use bottles you like, and remember to keep the most interesting ones out of your recycling bin for future garden projects.

Emerald slag glass serves as a jewel-like border in the blue garden at Lotusland.

colorful bottles along a bleak barbed-wire fence is also becoming chic and is featured in Terance Conran's *Essential Garden Book* as a way of bringing ornament to the boundaries of a property.

In Libby Davison's Tucson backyard, she creates a jewel-like rhythm by hanging cobalt-blue bottles in her backyard mesquite tree as well as artfully arranging the bottles upside-down on rusty rebar stakes.

In my own garden, I've taken my daughter's collection of Mexican soda bottles and suspended them with baling wire from our steel ramada, lacing the whole assembly with white Christmas lights. Overhead, especially when lit by sparkling lights, bottles make fine bedazzlements. When you have bottles, you have an excuse to keep decorating with ornaments and electric lights long past the holiday season.

Attracting Desirable Wildlife

We often think of plants and animals as two separate and unconnected groups, but in fact the two are intimately connected. As recent research by Dr. Doug Tallamy suggests, bringing wildlife into your garden begins by planting native plants that are uniquely equipped to attract specific pollinators, especially butterfly larvae. Tallamy's research masterfully shows the connections between native plants and their attendant insects, which become food for birds and other wildlife. Tallamy's contention is that 90 percent of all insects are specialists that have evolved to eat specific native plants, and that absent those native plants, we have fewer insects in our gardens (particularly butterflies) and fewer birds to feast on those insects. Tallamy says that native plants produce 35 times more larval bird food than exotics. If that is not an argument for bird lovers to plant natives, I'm not sure what is! Here is an admittedly incomplete catalog of animals that will add to the richness of your desert garden:

BEE COOL WITH NATIVE BEES Native bees are the unsung pollinating champions of desert gardens. One native bee, the mighty blue orchard mason bee, does the work of 120 European bees. The services bees provide ensure that plants set fruit and make seed to produce the next generation of plants. With European honeybee populations in decline, now is a great time to reconsider native pollinators in home gardens. The Southwest is blessed with spectacular bee diversity. Bee researcher Steve Buchman writes (in *A Natural History of the Sonoran Desert*), "The region around Tucson is thought to host more types of bees than anywhere else in the world, with the possible exception of some deserts in Israel."

We have 45 genera of Southwest native bees with names like cactus bee, leafcutter bee, and mason bee. Most of these bees are solitary and live in burrows either in the ground or in wood or masonry nests.

The tunneling activity of bees that live underground aerates the soil and allows water from shallow rains to infiltrate it. In addition, the bees' nitrogen-rich poop fertilizes adjacent plant roots.

Other bee species, such as mason bees and leafcutter bees, prefer to make nests in round holes. When I was working at Civano

A simple bee condominium at the Arizona-Sonora Desert Museum.

Nursery in Tucson, I noticed that the feeding tubes of our empty hummingbird feeders kept getting stuffed with leaves—the work of leafcutter bees making nests.

Bee Food

If you are already committed to growing some of the native plants mentioned thus far in the book, your garden will be pre-equipped for feeding bees. Basically, native bees need plants that produce lots of nectar and pollen. Trees like catclaw acacia are famous for the honey made from their flowers, and to get near one in bloom is to hear the loud buzz of pollination. Whitethorn acacia, blue palo verde, tenaza, mesquite and ironwood are other good nectar trees for bees. Other excellent plants for native bees include salvias and

Apart from their eye-popping colors, barrel cactus flowers provide native bees with nectar.

penstemons, indigo bush, lupine, creosote bush, Arizona poppy, scorpion weed (*Phacelia crenulata*), and flattop buckwheat. An excellent exotic for nectar is 'Dark Knight' bluebeard, also sometimes called blue mist (*Caryopteris* x *clandonensis* 'Dark Knight').

Housing

Some solitary bees don't go to the trouble of digging out their own nest holes, but instead look for the abandoned exit holes of beetles and boring insects in tree branches. You can simulate these exit holes in your own garden by building or purchasing bee-block-

Ungulates like this pronghorn antelope are common visitors to the higher grassland fringes of the hot-garden region.

style homes. To make your own bee house, simply drill a grid of $5/16$-inch holes, 2–3 inches deep and $3/4$ inch apart, in a block of wood at least 4 inches deep and 8 inches long, and hang it off the ground in a protected location. Or you can purchase mason-bee homes in ready-made wooden styles or in terra-cotta pipes.

Aloes make good cool-season hummingbird plants, blooming in spring before most natives.

Pollinator Panels

Another particularly desert-appropriate option is to make a "pollinator panel" from the dried bloom stalks of desert spoon (*Dasylirion* sp.) and century plants (*Agave* sp.). After collecting the dried stalks, drill a series of 5/16-inch holes up and down them. Lash the stalks together with twine or baling wire and suspend them a few inches off the ground against a fence. The resulting panel provides a handsome, rustic screen and high-rise bee accommodations. Having native bees in your yard will increase fruit and seed production in your garden.

BACKYARD BUTTERFLIES Flowers are nice, but what if they could fly? "Flying flowers" is how some butterfly gardeners describe the winged wonders that visit their gardens. Tucson resident Karen Hillson, who happens to be the editor of *Butterfly Gardener* magazine, has attracted 50 different species of butterflies to her yard just by using a wide variety of desert-adapted plants.

"There are two types of plants you can use to draw butterflies: nectar plants and larval food plants," Hillson explains. Nectar plants are the flowers that adult butterflies visit for nourishment, while larval food plants are what caterpillars eat before they metamorphose into winged adults. "I suggest that gardeners plant both

A western tiger swallowtail feeding on Rocky Mountain penstemon.

A congregation of cloudless sulphur butterflies, which arrive by the thousands from Mexico, feed on native senna species and mud.

Powerful Butterfly Plants

- **Milkweeds** Our desert milkweed (*Asclepias subulata*) and pine-leaf milkweed (*Asclepias linaria*) are sure bets for attracting both queen and monarch butterflies.
- **Native "stinky" passion vine** (*Passiflora foetida*) According to the Arizona Native Plant Society's publication, *Desert Butterfly Gardening*, "Every butterfly garden should include this vine." The gray-green foliage of this rambling plant is punctuated by lavender flowers. The gulf fritillary butterfly ignores the flowers, but the young caterpillars love munching on the leaves.
- **Butterfly mist** (*Ageratum corymbosum*) and **'Boothill'** (*Conoclinium greggii*) are two more commercially available butterfly magnets that do well in much of the region.

Queen butterflies flock to white ball acacia flowers.

types of plants. Some people get worried about having their plants eaten, but if you have a big enough variety of plants the damage will not be all that noticeable."

Hillson began educating herself about butterfly plants using the Arizona Native Plant Society's booklet *Desert Butterfly Gardening*, which provides excellent lists and photos of desert-adapted plants and the species of butterflies they attract. "You find that you get addicted to the plants," says Hillson, whose backyard is a rollicking collection of carefully selected butterfly plants transected by stepping stones that allow up-close viewing.

Many butterflies are very particular about the type of flowers they frequent. Hillson points out a saltbush (*Atriplex canescens*) in her yard that is one of the few food plants for the smallest butterfly on Earth, the western pygmy blue, which is only about as big as your pinkie fingernail. Another showy Arizona butterfly, the pipevine swallowtail, relies on just one plant for larval food, the southwestern pipevine (*Aristolochia watsonii*). "The native pipevine used to be very hard, if not impossible, to find in local nurseries; now it is being grown by Tohono Chul and is more widely available," says Hillson.

There are also a few plants to avoid in a butterfly garden; "Australian sennas have toxins that kill young caterpillars." Hillson suggests planting native desert sennas instead, such as *Senna covesii* and *S. leptocarpa*.

If you plant your butterfly garden in spring, have a little patience. Hillson says that summer through fall is the big butterfly season in most areas of the hot-garden zone: "Around the monsoon is when we begin to see large numbers of cloudless sulphurs and sleepy orange butterflies."

BIRDS The Southwest is full of bird lovers and bird experts, and lots of people own expensive binoculars with which to view birds to add to their "life lists." Bird lovers congregate here because we have a fair number of birds that come into the region from Mexico, and this is the only place in the states you can see many of

Raptors like this American kestrel are great for keeping garden rodents in check.

Lynn Hassler's Top 20 Bird-Habitat Plants

Since different desert birds have a variety of feeding preferences, author, birder, and horticulturist Lynn Hassler recommends the following plants for different birds.

Trees and Large Shrubs

Blue palo verde (*Parkinsonia florida*): shelter, cover, and nesting sites; nectar, insects
Desert hackberry (*Celtis pallida*): shelter, cover, and nesting sites; berries
Velvet mesquite (*Prosopis juliflora*): shelter, cover, and nesting sites; nectar, insects, seeds
Wolfberry (*Lycium freemontii*): shelter, cover, and nesting sites; nectar, berries, insects

Medium shrubs

Baja fairy duster (*Calliandra californica*): nectar, insects, seeds
Pink fairy duster (*Calliandra eriophylla*): nectar, insects, seeds

Small shrubs

Autumn sage (*Salvia greggii*): nectar, insects
Chuperosa (*Justicia californica*): nectar, insects
Mexican flame (*Anisacanthus wrightii*): nectar, insects

Sculptural plants

'Blue Elf' aloe (*Aloe* x 'Blue Elf'): nectar
Deer grass (*Muhlenbergia rigens*): seeds; shelter and nesting material
Engelmann's prickly pear (*Opuntia engelmannii*): fruit, insects, seeds
Ocotillo (*Fouquieria splendens*): nectar, insects; song perch
Saguaro cactus (*Carnegiea gigantea*): nectar, insects, fruit, seeds; nesting sites and shelter

Perennial wildflowers

Brittlebush (*Encelia farinosa*): insects, seeds
Desert zinnia (*Zinnia acerosa*): insects, seeds
Dogweed (*Thymophylla pentachaeta*): insects, seeds
Firewheel (*Gaillardia pulchella*): insects, seeds
Parry's penstemon (*Penstemon parryi*): insects, nectar, seeds
Tropical sage (*Salvia coccinea*): insects, nectar, seeds

Desert Birds by Food Preference

Seed-eaters: doves, quail, finches, sparrows, cardinals, pyrrhuloxias
Fruit-eaters: mockingbirds, thrashers, phainopeplas, house finches
Nectar-eaters: hummingbirds, orioles, verdins
Insect-eaters: cactus wrens, verdins, Gila woodpeckers (most birds eat insects at some time or another)

---

them. I don't pretend to be any sort of bird expert, preferring a more laid-back sort of birding that revolves around observing which sorts of birds I enjoy in my garden. My list is more of a backyard bird list than a life list.

After about eight years, my observations are thus: I very much enjoy the company of cactus wrens, curve-billed thrashers, hummingbirds, finches, cardinals, phainopeplas (looks like a black cardinal), quail (although they are voracious wildflower-seed eaters), Cooper's hawks, roadrunners, and both white-winged and mourning doves (although, like the Gila woodpecker I am about to mention, they do wake you up early). I have seen vermillion flycatchers in one client's garden but never in my own, although I would like to.

The cactus wren is noisy and inquisitive and fun to have as a weeding companion in a garden. He makes noise as if he is bossing all the other birds around. In my garden he likes to hop around and eat bugs and dig in the gravel. He makes nests in cholla cactus out of anything available, including plastic plant-stick tags. The roadrunner also is a good garden companion, and like the cactus wren, he is curious. When I was managing Civano Nursery, I once witnessed a roadrunner voraciously consume a 32-ounce cupful of grubs that we had extracted from a garden bed, which to my mind was the best and highest use for said grubs. My other garden encounter with a roadrunner was less pleasant, although I still took it as an auspicious sign. I was walking atop a 5-foot-high block wall, measuring a garden area for a client, when the client's dog flushed out a large roadrunner poking around in the backyard. Without warning, this supposedly ground-dwelling bird flew up and hit me square in the back, nearly causing me to fall off the wall. With ruffled feathers, he flew off to an adjacent mesquite tree. It struck me that this particular roadrunner was not nearly as cagey as his cartoon depiction would lead one to believe. I had

Cardinal illuminating a *Bursera* species.

A Cooper's hawk enjoys a dove picnic on my patio table.

been struck by a doofus of a bird who could barely escape the jaws of the family dog and could not avoid flying into a tall workman in his flight. Roadrunners do kill and consume rattlesnakes, although I sincerely doubted this one had the agility for the task. The coyote would surely get *this* bird, but I kind of liked this roadrunner anyway and thought that getting broadsided by him (and not falling off the wall) could only portend good luck.

Less-desirable visitors have included the Old World house sparrows, which make a mess and are prolific to the point of boredom, and pigeons, about which I don't really have to say much. One native bird I respect and like to watch—at someone else's garden—is the Gila woodpecker, a red-caped flicker that for some reason loves making a banging rat-a-tat-tat on my steel roof with his beak early in the morning. Being a woodpecker, he also knocks painted splinters off my roof fascia looking for bugs. Still, he is better than sparrows and pigeons.

In a garden, I much prefer planting plants to attract birds, rather than using feeders. In addition to attracting pigeons and exotic house sparrows in large flocks, the birdseed that falls on the ground attracts pack rats, which in turn attract rattlesnakes. If you feel compelled to feed birds, avoid the large quail blocks that tend to spill seed everywhere in favor of a more selective bird feeder that will get you more finches, cardinals, and wrens.

LIZARD LOUNGES The lizard just may be the most pleasant reptile to have hanging around the backyard. Some mornings I awake to tree lizards climbing my window screens, and I love to watch their curved-tail silhouettes in the morning light. I've even spotted a rather large common collared lizard trying unsuccessfully to catch a breakfast of queen butterfly in my backyard recently. Other than the tree lizard, good species include the chuckwalla, common collared lizard, spiny lizard, and horned lizard (better known as the "horny toad" and an insatiable consumer of ants).

The best way to attract lizards, and keep them happy in your garden, is to make rockworks and walls on which they can alternate between sun and shade. When I saw a large dome-shaped Andy Goldsworthy rock sculpture in the National Gallery in Washington D.C., it occurred to me that this was the perfect lizard hotel (although a very costly one), with its many voids and crags. In your garden, cairn-like structures are effective and provide lots of plants and the associated bugs for them to eat (you usually don't have to worry about this part). Provide quality lizard accommodations and the lizards will arrive.

A portly chuckwalla takes in the sun on a warm rock.

This spiny lizard hangs in a parenthesis from a creosote branch.

It is fair to note that two species of lizards, the Gila monster and Mexican beaded lizard, are venomous—although being bitten by one is quite a feat, since they move rather slowly and have to actually gnaw on you to inject venom.

SONORAN DESERT AND SPADEFOOT TOADS We are mostly not perverts here in the Southwest, although we do talk an awful lot about toad sex just because it is so much fun. I have yet to hear a Southwestern biologist say anything about what toads eat (other than "insects"), although I'm sure they know, because they are so eager to tell us about toad coupling, which I have to admit is a pretty fascinating subject. Toads are great in your garden because 99 percent of the time they are underground hibernating, and the 1 percent of the time they spend above ground they are eating bugs and mating. In the Sonoran and Chihuahuan deserts nearly all toad activity is relegated to the summer monsoon season. Some say that toads respond to the moisture in the soil as their cue to wake up and find a mate, while other researchers say that it is actually the rhythm that hard rain makes on the ground that stirs them. In either case, the male toad wakes up with a hard-on, so to speak.

In my neighborhood and garden, I've observed two species of toads: the Sonoran Desert toad (*Bufo alvarius*, formerly called Colorado River toad) and Couch's spadefoot (*Scaphiopus couchi*), and I find them both enormously enjoyable garden residents. I see the Sonoran Desert toad, one of the biggest toads in North America, more frequently. Frankly, he is hard to miss, especially when he perches himself on the ledge of our backyard fountain to admire his warty countenance in a mirrored door that is part of our landscape. I'm hoping that he is not mistaking his own reflection for one of an attractive female. He likes to occasionally hop down into our fountain to cool off. Most important, he doesn't bother my plants and most likely helps the general ecology of my garden by gulping down insects and pooping out toadilizer, if you will.

The Couch's spadefoot is more elusive until big rains come to produce decent puddles that stick around for a few days. Which brings us back to toad sex. These desert puddles, particularly large ones, attract droves of spadefoots, and at night their lovesick calls, which to my ear sound like nothing if not bleating sheep, fill the moist air. With a flashlight, a curious human can follow the "beeeh, beeeh" call to a pool filled with toadus flagrante (which biologists call *amplexus*), always in the male-on-top position. But variations apply, as described here by Ellen Meloy: "doggie style describes the act adequately, with forelegs steadying the load. Using his nuptial pads—love thumbs with good grip—the male clasps his mate by her waist (inguinal amplexus) or more forward (auxiliary) or by the throat (cephalic) or chest (pectoral)."

In gardens, sculpting basins to collect rainwater (see p. 165–167) is a great way to water your garden and create some very good toad habitat. If you build it, they will come. One important thing to remember is that Sonoran Desert toads produce a powerful toxin (bufotoxin) that can be harmful to dogs that try to bite or catch them (and to people, if you handle or, heaven forbid, kiss or lick them). Other than that, toads are great for gardens.

Repelling Less-desirable Wildlife

In my first book, *Yard Full of Sun*, I addressed the subject of wildlife in gardens by describing one of my midnight showdowns with javelinas (hairy snouted creatures that locals sometimes refer to as pigs, but which actually belong to the peccary family). In a somewhat nonchalant manner, I once labored under the delusion that the pigs and I could share the garden; that was before the more frequent visits of a band of pigs cost me many good nights' sleep. The point of my javelina story is mainly to illustrate that not all wildlife is compatible with desert gardens and gardeners. After all, how much love do any of us have for a bark scorpion in our bedrooms or brown recluses behind our couches? I suspect that even the most compassionate and well-meaning PETA members would not hesitate to flatten scorpions and poison spiders on the heel of a shoe if they found them inside their homes. So in this section, I cover two species that I have found relatively incompatible with humans in desert gardens. Since rabbits have already been discussed in the Wildflowers section, I'll leave that topic well enough alone here.

JAVELINAS Yes, they are charming in a rather piggish way, but if you value your agaves (or pansies and petunias, which they consider as fine as French mesclun greens) you will not purposefully attract javelinas into your garden—especially by feeding them. Several restaurants around the perimeter of Tucson used to feed

Javelinas can be unwelcome garden visitors.

table scraps to roving bands of javelinas each evening to entertain their dinner guests, who could gaze out the picture windows at gorging hairy pigs (I'm not sure why this practice was considered appetizing). One of these restaurants was near my home, and I suspect that this irresponsible feeding trained entire generations of javelinas to forage for trash rather than settle for their regular diet of prickly pear cactus, bean pods, and native plant roots. The pigs became expert at getting into my garage, toppling my giant green City of Tucson trash can, and enjoying messy and raucous refuse dinners on the concrete floor. For dessert, they enjoyed sampling the roots of several hundred dollars' worth of rare agaves I had recently transplanted. I have since managed to fence out the javelinas, which is good because my attention has been needed on the pack rat front. The best defense against javelinas is a good fence; where complete enclosure is not possible, consider a cylinder of chicken wire or hardware cloth, anchored firmly to the ground with stakes or rebar, around new plantings.

THE TALE OF THE PACK RAT OR "RUN BROTHER RUN"

It should first be stated that this is a cautionary, yet true, tale of the life and death of pack rats in a garden. It is not for the faint of heart or tight of pocketbook, and calling it a children's story might be a stretch. What I *can* say is that while the white-throated wood rat (*Neotoma albigula*), better known as the pack rat, is an undeniably cute creature with big black eyes, this gives you no clue as to the ambition of his den building, or pack-rattery, if you will.

My first up-close and personal experience with *Neotoma albigula* involved laundry. As I was removing a load from our dryer, which is located in our carport area, I noticed a mesquite-bean pod sticking out of a small louvered vent on the side of the dryer. Hmmm, that's strange, I thought to myself. I pulled the bean pod through the slot, but as I slid it out it was followed by another. After retrieving a screwdriver, I removed the vent and as I did, a Las Vegas–quantity jackpot of mesquite-bean pods and cholla-cactus stems poured out. My dryer, a cube with an inner cylinder, was packed full of pack rat booty. I spent the rest of the afternoon disassembling my dryer on the carport floor and banging on its sides, cursing and sweating, trying to get the last of the pods and cholla out. I was like a frustrated kid slamming the side of a vending machine that wouldn't vend. I turned the box upside down and walloped it with all my might until I could extract no more. I ended up with an enormous mountain of pods and cholla stems—over half the volume of a large City of Tucson trash can. How could a less-than-a-pound animal stuff all this in my dryer, I wondered? Just as I was ready to reassemble the machine, I noticed a pair of big black eyes staring at me from the back corner of my dryer. Using the end of a broomstick, I did my best to terminate the rat with a swift poke, only to miss and have him sprint across the garage and make a spectacular leap onto a 4-foot-high storage shelf.

I began trapping the white-throated wood rat with a conventional rat trap baited with peanut butter. I had my successes and considered the situation under control—until, that is, the morning I started up my diesel Jetta and backed down my driveway, only to notice a stream of diesel fuel trailing from beneath the car. I stopped and opened the hood. As I did, I observed a strange heft and sag to the insulation lining the underside of the hood. I noticed two round holes from which, you guessed it, bean pods were hanging. Then I spied a hopeful sign, the long tail of *Neotoma albigula* hanging out one of the holes. Grabbing a shovel, or more specifically the flat side of the blade, I attempted to send this wood rat with a taste for fuel lines into the next world. My swing was strong and well placed, but the structural steel beams in the hood prevented me from landing a solid blow. Instead, he jumped—leaped, really—from the engine compartment and ran around the side of the house while I pursued him hotly with my shovel, until I lost his trail. Four hundred dollars' worth of fuel-line work later, I began my trapping rituals again, vigilantly baiting both heartful (live) and heartless (dead) traps with peanut butter each night, which is where I stand now.

The moral of this story is that, sadly, the pack rat is an animal that should not be attracted to gardens or homes. This is why it is wise to keep prickly pear and cholla cactus nicely cleaned up (that is, remove any current or potential nesting material from the base of the plant) and to leave your car hood open at night, as people do all over the rural areas of southern Arizona.

Precious Water

4
Precious Water: Conserving H₂O by Design

And the dry beauty—let Plato teach us to love that also, duly.

—Walter Pater

WATER AND HUMAN HABITATION have long been married in the arid Southwest. Where you find water, people settle. In Arizona, Native Americans and, later, Anglos found the Salt River valley irresistible. Before it was dammed, the wide Salt River meandered through what are now Mesa, Tempe, and Phoenix as a sometimes dangerous river with ferries to breach it. It was diverted into canals, many of which were simply rehabbed channels left by the ancient Hohokam people. In my father's youth in the 1950s, the canals still had dirt banks, and large cottonwood trees cast shade on the water. These were the days before the widespread construction of backyard swimming pools, and the vein-like canals of Maricopa County doubled as refreshing swimming holes for children and fishing spots for adults. These canals, and the agriculture that accompanied them, profoundly changed the desert landscape. As Sylvester Baxter, the secretary of the Hemenway Expedition in 1888, wrote:

The traveler enters the valley of the Rio Salado [Salt River] surrounded by wide reaches of sagebrush and greasewood interspersed with thickets of mesquite. A dreary, unpromising spectacle! He thinks, and here, the tawny ground beneath the bushes has all the unfertile aspect of the traditional desert, to eastern eyes. A moment more, and behold a transformation as sudden and as magical to the astonished vision as was ever worked by change of scene on theatre stage! The desert has vanished, and smooth fields expand with the floor like evenness of a Kansas prairie as far as the eye can see toward the distant bases of surrounding mountains. Under the calm blue of the Arizona midwinter sky the young grain spreads away in broad acres of tender green; sleek kine are browsing contentedly in the rich alfalfa pastures and long straight lines

A small-scale fountain with rain lilies and 'Silver Falls' dichondra (Design: Scott Calhoun).

of Alamos and Lombardy poplars intersect the fields in pleasant perspectives. It is a picture of peace and plenty.

The magic has been wrought by the touch of life-bringing water, which sparkles on all sides in the tree-bordered canals that spread their contents over the land in rapid streams… Daily the rich fields widen and the desert shrinks… the river's capacity for irrigation is still beyond estimate.

Today, Phoenix supplements Salt River water with water from the Colorado River via the Central Arizona Project, or as it is commonly known, the CAP. The CAP is a massive $3.6 billion cement-lined canal that brings Colorado River water from Lake Havasu east to Phoenix and then south to Tucson. The naturalist Peter Warshall says, "We have created the largest hydrologic infrastructure in history. The longest Roman aqueducts were only 30 to 50 miles long." Compare that with the 336-mile-long, 16.5-foot-deep CAP. Even with Herculean projects like the CAP, though, our demand for water is outstripping supply. It occurs to me that most of the alfalfa and cotton fields are going or gone, replaced by houses, and as surely as Baxter describes the transformation of "dreary" thickets of mesquite into farmland, the mesquite is making a big-time comeback—this time as a residential landscape tree!

In fact, a certain thornless mesquite hybrid is the most popular nursery-grown tree in the state, and our native mesquite (*Prosopis juliflora*) can command prices of several thousand dollars when sold as mature salvaged specimens. I guess what I'm saying is that there is no use getting too nostalgic about the good old days of cottonwood trees and cotton fields, because we have made the choice, for better or worse, to grow houses now, and in the yards of those new residences, we are most likely going to be planting desert plants where water-intensive crops once grew. Think of it as the revenge

The water situation in the hot-garden zone is sure to bring more succulents, xeric shrubs, and rockery into the region's new gardens.

of the desert! And the reason for the desert's revenge (which if you haven't guessed, I feel is an event to be celebrated) is that in stark contrast to Baxter's observation that the Salt River's capacity for irrigation is "beyond estimate," the water resources for the entire Southwest are now over-allocated and stretched to the limit. The Southwestern states employ armies of water policy makers, lawyers, and hydrologists to fight for what they believe is their fair share of Colorado River water, and in most of these states, conservation programs that include residential elements are the norm.

As I write, Las Vegans are frantically re-plumbing Lake Mead for fear the lake's rapidly dropping level will fall below the level of the current intake pipe. In addition, the Southern Nevada Water Authority is paying people, by the square foot, to remove turf grass and replace it with drought-tolerant landscaping. As Nevada historian Dennis McBride remarks, "Hoover Dam is the dealer, Vegas is the crack whore." In spite of these challenges, Pat Mulroy, the head of the Southern Nevada Water Authority, remains hopeful about the future growth of Las Vegas—an attitude largely based on the ability of residents to adapt. She comments that residents have removed enough high-water-use grass to stretch halfway around the world. To this, my questions are: What are they replacing the grass with? Is it more drought-tolerant? Do the new plantings create a Mojave Desert sense of place?

Perhaps Arizona governor Janet Napolitano said it best when she called for the creation of a culture of water conservation. I liked this phrasing because the word "culture" connotes much about how our habits might need to change. A culture that values conservation would most likely value our native plants and the patterns of the natural landscape.

The other common source for water in our deserts is groundwater, which we are also outstripping nature's ability to replenish. In Sonora, Mexico, farmers who used to hit water in the Hermosillo aquifer at 35 feet, today have to pump it from 400 feet deep! It seems to me that this ancient and pristine water should be saved for drinking.

Given the water situation on and below the ground, how do we go forward in our Southwestern gardens? The answer, which is obvious but not often practiced, is that we grow appropriate things and we do it more efficiently.

In the hot-garden zone, we are beginning to design some of the most water-thrifty gardens on earth. This new paradigm has two main tenets: look good and use a lot less water than traditional landscapes. Since we take such extraordinary measures to deliver water to our cities, isn't it fair to ask how we are using it? Considerable water goes to agricultural and commercial users, but seeing that the average homeowner has little direct influence over those uses, I'll focus on what we have absolute control of: residential use. In the Southwest, the amount of water we use varies from city to city. In Tucson, we use 114 gallons per person per day (gpcd); in Las Vegas, 174; in Albuquerque, 110 (according to a study called Water in the Urban Southwest, by Western Resource Advocates). Because of proactive municipal conservation programs, these residential-use numbers have fallen in recent years, but before we congratulate ourselves too much we should consider that residents of another civilized arid place, western Australia, use only 82 gpcd.

Because 50 to 60 percent of the potable water delivered to Southwestern households is used outdoors in our landscapes, that means that we use between 57 gallons gpcd (Tucson) and 105 gpcd (Las Vegas) of imported water outdoors each day. If you imagine someone physically delivering this amount of water, stacking it in your backyard in 55-gallon drums every day, you begin to grasp the volume of water we use outdoors in our gardens, and it is no small quantity.

Watering the Hot Garden

Everyone wants to know how long and how often to water his or her plants, which is a much trickier question than you might think. Even with plants with similar water requirements, variables like soil type, exposure, and seasonal temperatures all play a part. So nobody can honestly tell you to "water once a week for an hour" without knowing quite a bit about your garden situation. With that caveat, I offer the following guidelines:

WATERING FREQUENCY In this book, in which nearly all of the plants listed are low-water-use, I'm using the Arizona Department of Water Resources/Tucson Active Management Area's

"Low Water Use Drought Tolerant Plant List" guidelines, which assign drought-tolerant plants the numbers 1, 2, and 3 to indicate their water requirements. Tucson averages around 12 inches of rain a year, so if you live in a drier or wetter part of the hot-garden zone, you will need to increase or decrease the frequency of your watering accordingly. The watering frequency is as follows:

1. Very low: irrigate every three to four weeks during the growing season after establishment
2. Low: irrigate every two to three weeks during the growing season after establishment
3. Moderate: irrigate weekly during the growing season after establishment

Any of these numbers with an asterisk beside it designates a number I have estimated myself, not from the ADWR guidelines.

DEPTH AND DURATION There is an easy rule of thumb—the "1–2–3 Rule"—for how long you should water your ground covers, shrubs, and trees. Ground covers should be watered to a depth of one foot, shrubs to a depth of two feet, and trees to a depth of three feet. To determine that you have watered to that depth, use a soil probe, which is a rod (a long screwdriver or sharpened piece of rebar works) that you poke into the soil. The probe will move easily through wet soil and stop at dry. Once you have determined how long to water to get it to the desired depth, you never have to change how long you water that plant, only how often.

ACCOUNTING FOR RAIN People say there is no accounting for rain in this region, but I beg to differ! One of the best things you can do to help yourself water consciously is to buy a rain gauge and keep track of precipitation. If you are watering on a schedule

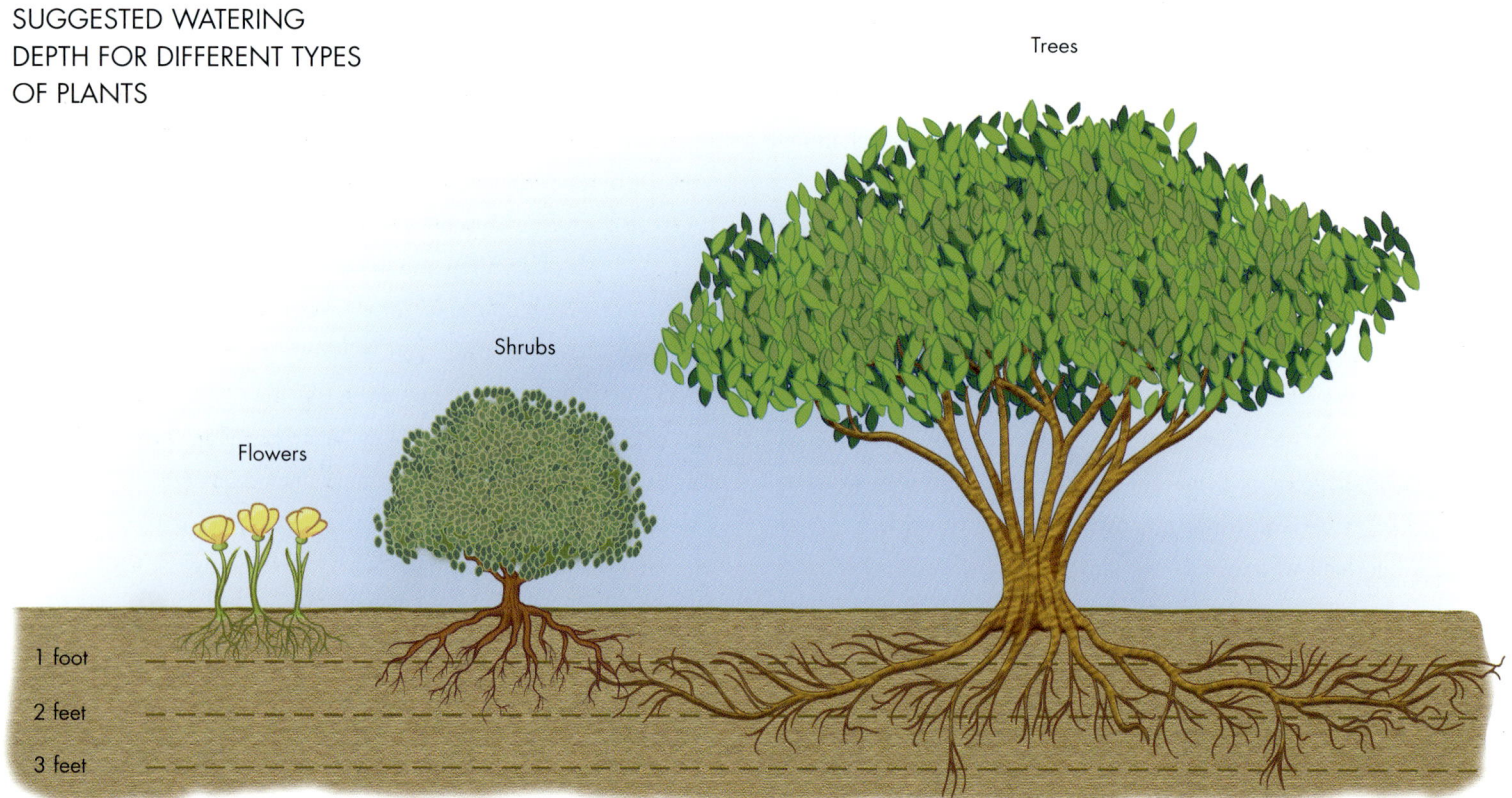

SUGGESTED WATERING DEPTH FOR DIFFERENT TYPES OF PLANTS

GENERAL PLACEMENT OF IRRIGATION SYSTEM COMPONENTS
(Not to Scale)

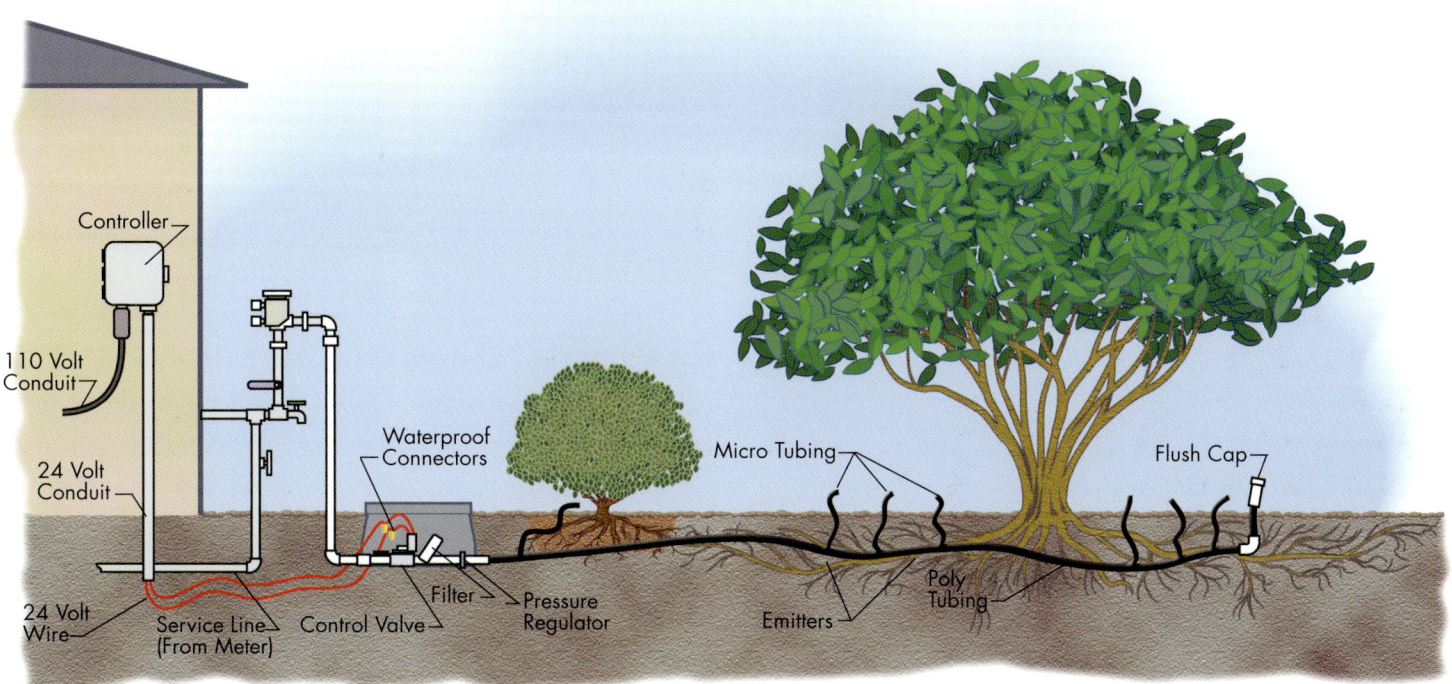

or with an automatic timer, make sure you turn off the system when you get significant rainfall, which I define as more than half an inch. If it rains half an inch, skip at least the next irrigation.

WATERING METHODS Assuming that you have already bought into my advice to plant your garden with appropriate low-water-use plants, the next step is to match those plants with an appropriate watering system. Here are three ways to water more consciously:

1. Well-managed drip irrigation
2. Hybrid rainwater/drip irrigation
3. Raingarden (no-irrigation garden)

Well-managed Drip Irrigation

Even in deserts, relatively inefficient methods of irrigation are still common. The least efficient method is flood-and-furrow irrigation. If farmers switched even to low-pressure sprinklers, they would reduce water use by 30 percent; if they shifted to drip irrigation, what Lester Brown, author of *Plan B 3.0* calls, "the gold standard of irrigation efficiency," they could cut water use in half. In desert landscapes, a water-wise garden watered with drip irrigation can reduce water use by at least 75 percent when compared with turfgrass. Drip technology pinpoints the delivery of water exactly to a plant's root zone and makes it possible to grow plants without flooding or sprinkling a large area. In many ways, it is an ideal watering method for desert gardeners who space their plants a little farther apart and don't need to blanket an entire area with water. For desert landscaping, the general layout of a system is as illustrated here.

TIPS FOR DRIP SYSTEMS Make sure your system has a minimum of two valves: this will give you one valve and line for trees and large shrubs, which prefer deep and less-frequent watering, and one valve and line for ground covers, which need shallower and more frequent watering. Always use a backflow preventer (a device to keep water in the irrigation lines from being siphoned back into your drinking water).

- Do not exceed 200 feet of poly tubing from the valve to the flush cap.
- Do not exceed a total flow rate of 200 gallons per hour per valve.
- Micro tubing should be limited to lengths of six feet or less.
- Rather than a controller, consider manual ball valves with shut-off timers that require you to be more conscious of your watering habits and are less prone to clogging, or sticking on.
- If you do purchase a controller (an automatic irrigation timer), get a model that is easy to program and allows you to space out watering to one-month intervals. Controllers should be reprogrammed four times annually to account for seasonal water needs.
- Make the system easily expandable so as trees mature you can add extra drip emitters.
- Succulents like agaves and hesperaloes usually like the same irrigation frequency as trees and can be watered on the tree line.
- Here is a guideline for the number of emitters needed for mature plants:

Plant Type	Canopy Diameter	Number of Emitters	Emitter Flow Rate (gallons/hour)
Small Shrubs/ Ground Cover	1–3'	1	1
Large Shrubs	4–6'	2–3	2
Small Trees	7–10'	3–5	2–4
Large Trees	11–14'	4–6	2–4
	15–20'	6–12	2–4
	21'+	12+	4

One of the downsides to drip systems on automatic timers is that they can waste a lot of water if they are not managed properly. Ask any landscape contractor in the region, and he or she will have a story about someone drowning their native plants because the irrigation controller was never changed from a schedule designed to establish new plants several years earlier. Sometimes saving water is not about how the ship is built but about how we sail the ship. This is one of the reasons that I advocate the use of manual valves that require you to look at your plants and observe when they *need* water rather than because a timer says it's Thursday at 6:00 a.m.

Hybrid Rainwater/Drip Irrigation

A hybrid rainwater/drip garden recognizes that during the establishment period, and occasionally during severe droughts, even the most xeric plants will need supplemental watering. A hybrid rainwater/drip system stores rainwater in tanks, and when the tanks have rainwater in them, that water is pumped though your drip system to your plants. When the rainwater level in the tank falls to nearly empty, a float valve in the tank turns on and partially fills the tank with potable water so that you can continue to water (without creating redundant systems) during times of drought. Another advantage of the hybrid rainwater/drip system is that you can use a standard irrigation timer that will automatically turn your irrigation valves on and off (of course, this still requires you, the homeowner, to thoughtfully program your timer). The configuration of the drip system can be conventional—like the system shown in the diagram—and it makes managing your rainwater less of a hands-on activity. Unfortunately, a hybrid rainwater/drip system has some of the same drawbacks as a regular drip system: it requires the homeowner to program a clock and monitor the conditon of drip irrigation lines and emitters. If the clock is not programmed effectively, this sort of system could waste a good amount of potable water. Managed correctly, it would be a

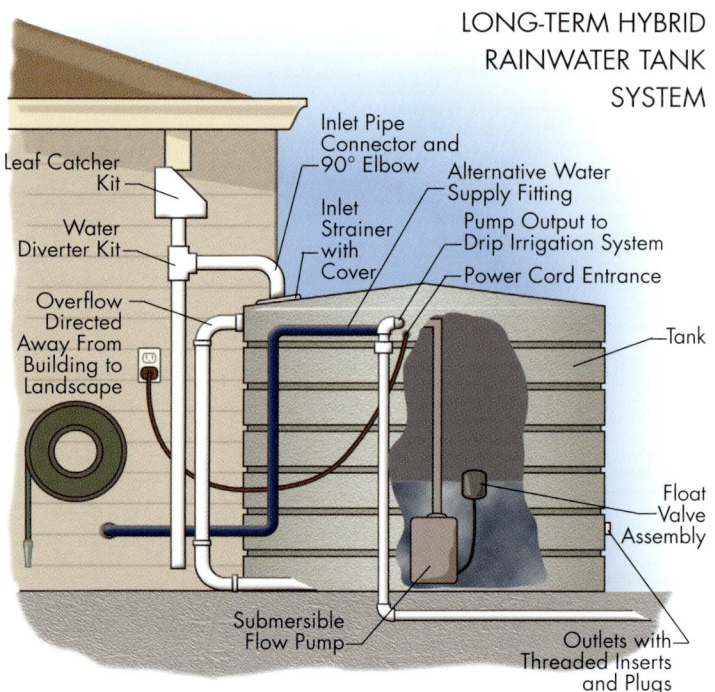

LONG-TERM HYBRID RAINWATER TANK SYSTEM

giant step forward for residents of the Southwest. Expect to see this sort of system mandated on new residential construction in a hot-garden-zone municipality near you soon.

Desert Raingarden

Gardens designed to survive without regular irrigation are known across much of the country as "raingardens." Although the phrase "desert raingarden" might seem like an oxymoron, with careful planning such a garden can be built. By design, the raingarden is the most water-efficient type of garden you can install. Long-term (because of salt buildup and water scarcity), raingardens are probably the only truly "sustainable" gardens our region will support. A raingarden will be composed of the very toughest and most drought-tolerant native plants and will use a high percentage of the superstars of drought tolerance: cacti and other succulents. The reason many cacti and succulents are uniquely suited to hyper-arid conditions is that they have a metabolism (called "CAM") that allows them to make sugars only at night, which greatly reduces water loss. Just as in the desert, plants in a no-drip garden should be spaced farther apart and planted in areas that will take advantage of rainwater runoff from adjacent land, rocks, and structures. Because these plants won't have an IV of supplemental watering, a desert raingarden will have more pronounced periods of vibrancy and dormancy (growth and drought), depending on the season and available moisture.

Even with its virtues, a desert raingarden will not be for everyone. Creating a no-drip garden in places like Palm Springs or Las Vegas, where they average around five inches of rain annually, is more difficult by several magnitudes than installing a raingarden in somewhere like Marfa, Texas, where they get over 15 inches a year. On a 7,000-square-foot lot, the following table illustrates the yearly rainfall in gallons that you can expect to receive in various hot-garden cities. This number is good to keep in the back of your mind as a baseline goal for the water needs of your landscape.

To determine this number for your own lot, roof, or garden, do the following calculation (see page 181 for sample rainfall figures):

CATCHMENT AREA (in square feet) x AVERAGE YEARLY RAINFALL (in feet*) x 7.48 = TOTAL ANNUAL RAINWATER (in gallons)

*To convert yearly rainfall in inches to feet, simply divide by 12. For example, Albuquerque receives 8.88 inches of rain per year, divided by 12 = .74. If we take that .74 and do the calculations for a 7,000-square-foot catchment area, the math looks like this:

7,000 square feet x .74 inches/year x 7.48 = 38,746 gallons/year.

KNOW YOUR WATERSHED When you become conscious of the rainwater resources right on your property, you become the owner of your own little water company and the manager of your own watershed. To manage your watershed effectively, you first need to know how water flows across your property. This is best done in the middle of, or just after, a major storm (avoiding lightning storms!). Note where water runs off and where water pools.

Think of the roof of your home as a small mountain—the highest point on your property. Where does that water go? That is a good spot to begin to slow the water down. Always begin slowing the water down at the highest point you can. Then have a plan for that water to flow to another lower basin.

Rainwater from the roof of this Albuquerque live/work space is directed to tree-lined permeable parking areas (Design: Chris Calott).

CONSIDER AESTHETICS Although digging many small deep basins may be effective, you don't want your front yard to look like a newly swept mine field with a tree planted next to each former mine hole. Instead consider bordering and retaining basins with an elegant radius curve, raised pathways and more gentle organic depressions. Think about what shapes and depths look natural. Just as exaggerated hills and contours built in a landscape simply for aesthetic effect can look silly, so can basins that are built solely with the goal of saving water rather than contributing to the overall beauty of the garden.

SLOW DOWN THE WATER Whenever possible, you want to spread out the water to percolate into the soil. It should not be channeled where it can run fast with powerful erosive force. Passive earthworks combined with smart mulching provide the simplest and most economical way to slow down and spread out the rainwater that falls on your property. Passive earthworks are simply berms and basins made of dirt that steer water around your lot. To reduce the velocity of fast-moving rainwater, you want to avoid sending rainwater through straight, narrow drainage ways; instead use a shovel to dig a series of connecting basins that cause rainwater meander to planted areas before leaving your property. It is usually better to move water from high points to low points in a zigzag pattern rather than a straight line. This is akin to a trail on steep mountain terrain with lots of switchbacks—the switchbacks provide a gentle and less erosive descent. Mulches, both organic and inorganic, also slow down water when they are spread over the surface of your garden. Organic mulch (typically chipped and shredded wood that is often a free byproduct available from tree services) laid down four inches thick serves as a sponge that will both slow water down and reduce evaporation. The role that inorganic materials (rocks) can play in rainwater harvesting will be discussed later in this chapter.

PLAN FOR OVERFLOW In a really big rain event, say one inch in 30 or 40 minutes, almost any rainwater basin will be inundated and will overflow. When these once-in-every-five- or ten-year thunderstorms strike, you may encounter the sort of ferocious water velocity that causes some streets in desert cities to run like rivers. When designing and constructing your rainwater system, you should plan for this. As you create basins that overflow from one to the next, make sure that the overflow from the final basin runs to the street rather than back toward your foundation.

Raingarden Design Tips

- Direct runoff from all nonirrigated garden spaces (gravel areas, patios, pathways, ramadas) toward shallow basins with plants in and around them.
- Locate basins at least 10 feet from foundations, 20 feet if you have a basement.
- Plant trees on the perimeters of basins, or in domes within basins, rather than in basin bottoms.
- Create a conceptual plan of your yard showing existing structures, plants, and circulation patterns around the property. Depict high and low points, noting where water collects and runs off your property. Capture rainwater that runs off of hard surfaces (roofs, patios, pathways) in basins and with berms. Consider installing a holding tank, either above or below ground, with an overflow directed into a basin or series of basins.
- Make sure to plan for overflow during extreme storm events.
- Make a plant list, restricting yourself to the most xeric native plants that grow in your region for the high spots in the landscape.
- If you are using tanks, locate them so the water can easily be directed to planted areas.

This graceful sunken rock spiral absorbs rainwater collected from the roofs of adjacent buildings at the Desert Botanical Garden in Phoenix. It is planted with deer grass, desert willows, and other native plants (Design: Christine Ten Eyck).

MAINTENANCE After a big rain event like the one I just mentioned, you will need to reassess your berms and basins, and possibly do a little repair work if there has been erosion damage. After a few big storms, you should be able to modify and fortify your berms and basins to handle the flow.

RAINWATER HARVESTING ROCKWORK Have you ever been hiking and noticed how many plants like to grow in and around rocks? I often find penstemons, agaves, hedgehogs, and resurrection fern growing in rock fissures and around the base of

Tips for Using Rocks to Harvest Water

- Dry streambeds should suggest a real streambed.
- Slope rocks toward plants.
- The faster the water flow, the larger the rocks you should use.
- When you select gravel, remember that smaller gravel has more surface area, but larger gravel has more air pockets.

rocks. The fact is, rocks harvest water and can be tilted to direct water into little planting pockets. As a bonus, many xeric plants love the quick drainage and shadowy nooks that rocks supply. As I have become more active in the North American Rock Gardening Society, I've noticed that the ways we typically arrange rocks in Southwest landscapes often are not thoughtful and actually misdirect water *away* from plants rather than toward them! So, on the following page is a diagram of how to set retaining boulders in a fashion that makes them harvest water.

Yerba mansa is planted in pockets along the rainwater harvesting spiral (Design: Christine Ten Eyck).

SLOPED ROCKWORK WITH PLANTING POCKETS

Raingarden Plant Selection and Considerations

The heart of water conservation in Southwest gardens is plant selection. Simply put, but sometimes not understood, it is impossible to build a desert-appropriate, low-water-use garden with high-water-use plants. Duh. This doesn't mean that you can't include a few plants with higher water requirements, but rather that those plants should be very limited and grouped together. Keep in mind that your oasis areas will never fend for themselves.

- Start with small plants that will take less water to establish. If you can find plants in grow tubes (or grow them from seed in grow tubes) this gives you a good root-to-shoot ratio. In the cooler (but not wetter) climate of Denver, some native plant gardeners have started entire gardens with plants grown in grow tubes, planted them in late spring when the ground was still wet from snow, watered them once and then let them fend for themselves. In the hot-garden regions, this techique is best done in the fall (with both plants and seeds). One additional advantage of planting from grow tubes is that you can dig your holes by attaching an auger to a cordless drill, which will make quick work of digging.

After a big storm your earthworks may need repair. In the author's garden, shown below, raised pathways were breached during a gully washer. The level of the pathways was later raised to withstand larger rainfall events.

- Plant in the fall or winter months for easier establishment.
- Don't assume that all of the plants for sale in local nurseries are suitable for our climate, especially for raingardens. If you are unsure, find expert help (and refer to the lists provided in this chapter).
- Although the majority of the plants you will use will be xeric, if you are using planting basins, the trees and shrubs located at the bottoms of these basins must be able to withstand both periodic flooding and drought. (See the Bottom-of-the-Basin Plants list.) For tree species not on this list, plant them *beside* the basins.
- Remember that native trees will grow more slowly and mature at smaller sizes in rainfall-only gardens.
- Be prepared for some plants to go through seasonal drought dormancy.

Basin bottoms can also be mulched with organic materials as demonstrated above (Design: Watershed Management Group).

ANATOMY OF A BASIN The basic planting areas within a rainwater-harvesting basin are as follows:

- **Berms:** Sloped areas around the edge of a basin designed to hold back water until it percolates down into the soil. In big storm events, the soil that makes up berms takes up water through capillary action but is not saturated for more than a couple of hours. Many succulents, particularly agaves, generally like conditions on berms.
- **Bottoms:** The lowest part of the basin, where the water is held for the longest period (note: it should not stand for more than 24 hours) and the soil is the most water-logged after storm events. The plants grown in the bottoms of basins need to be adaptable to periods of both drought and deluge. Most succulents, such as cacti and agave, dislike conditions in the bottoms. Trees such as mesquites and desert willows, which are prone to periodic flooding in their natural habitats, are well adapted to bottom growth.
- **Domes:** A mounded area within the bottom that reduces the amount of water-logging that plants get. It is wetter than a berm but is a better area to plant most trees than a bottom, as the crown of the tree stays above the water level.

Rainwater-harvesting basins don't have to be large or complex to be effective. You are not building a mini Hoover Dam; you are just watering some trees, shrubs, and sculptural plants.

BOTTOM-OF-THE-BASIN PLANTS AND BESIDE-THE-BASIN PLANTS Some plants (listed on pages 178–179 and 179–180) have proven successful in growing in the bottom of rainwater-catchment basins where they are periodically flooded. The plants were tested in basin bottoms surrounded by berms, where water is held to percolate into the soil. During rainy periods, water may submerge some or all of the plant up to 24 hours. Other plants fare best *beside* the basin, in the berms, where their roots can reach the water but the above-ground parts of the plants are not standing in it. These lists come from Russ Buhrow, curator of plants at Tohono Chul Park, whose Sin Agua garden provided much of the following data, and from my own design projects, where I've noted what has thrived and what has failed.

GETTING RAINGARDEN PLANTS ESTABLISHED The first two years in your raingarden will most likely require a little watering work on your part. You may feel like an indentured water mule after the first summer, but if you've selected your plants carefully you won't have too much watering to do the second and third years. Buckets, hose timers, and ollas are three tools that can help you on the road to establishment, as outlined on the following two pages.

If trees are to be located within basins, make sure that they are a species that is able to withstand periodic flooding.

The Poor Man's Drip System

The poor man's drip system is a 5-gallon bucket with a small hole drilled through the side of the container, right at the bottom. This system is good for a few plants but will wear you out if you have to water a large number of plantings. Just as with a drip emitter, the water will come out slowly and percolate deeply around the root zone. It also turns off by itself.

Hose-Timers

Maximize the utility of your hose with timers (like egg timers for your hose that turn it off after a set time period) and well-placed soaker hoses and hose-end sprinklers that can ease new gardens through establishment and help germinate wildflower seeds. Use sprinklers only before sunup or after sundown in calm weather to minimize evaporation loss.

Ollas

Ollas (pronounced OY-ya) are porous clay vessels, which can be buried underground and filled with water that wicks through the clay to water surrounding plant roots. Ollas water from the inside out. This ancient method, which is believed to have begun in western China, was adopted by ancient Romans to water grapes and olives. In fact, buried clay pots have been found in situ at the base of olive trees. Today, starting in New Mexico, ollas are making a comeback in gardens. In a warehouse in a working neighborhood on Albuquerque's east side, a micro-enterprise called Agua de Vida (under the guidance of East Central Ministries) is giving people good work, handcrafting beautiful ollas modeled after pumpkins and gourds. In fact, the best way to visualize how ollas function is to picture a pumpkin buried nearly up to its stem, with plants around its perimeter. Now imagine that the pumpkin is made from clay and the stem is a small hole used to fill the clay pumpkin with water. Here are some useful facts about ollas:

Roots form dense mats around porous clay ollas, allowing for very efficient watering.

- They are excellent for growing chiles, squash, eggplant, greens, herbs, and many other herbaceous plants.
- Ollas can be used to help establish woody plants and trees, but as these plants grow they may break the olla.
- Ollas can save up to 85 percent when compared with traditional sprinkler-type watering systems.
- When using ollas in containers, use pots that are twice the diameter of the olla.
- To minimize evaporation and mosquitos, cap your olla with a stone or stopper.
- Buy ollas made from food-grade clay.
- The water from an olla spreads out to a distance equal to the radius of the olla (from the edge of the olla)—so for example, if your olla is a foot in diameter, your damp ground should be about two feet across, with the mouth of the buried olla in the center.
- Ollas are available from ½ quart to 1½ gallon capacity.
- Ollas should be buried as high as possible to encourage lateral spread of water. The portion of the olla above the soil level can be sealed with a silicone-based sealant to minimize evaporation.
- Ollas can be grouped in squares, in circles, or in lines. Four ollas will water about seven pepper plants.

Rainwater-harvesting Cisterns

So, you've designed and planted a garden chockful of local plants and installed some rainwater basins to help water them, and then the month of May comes along. May is a month when many hot-garden cities average around zero inches of rain. It is also a month in which plants' watering needs begin to substantially increase with the arrival of hot weather. So what's a desert rat to do? The answer, in part, may be a rainwater-harvesting tank that fills up from the rainwater runoff from your roof. Tanks can be made of many different materials from concrete to plastic to steel, but the main purpose of installing one is to extend the length of time that you have rainwater available to water your garden. If your tank is big enough, you might even make it through the month of May.

ABOVE: In the Huxman garden, the wet-downspout culvert-style cistern became the centerpiece of the garden rather than something to be hidden (Design: Scott Calhoun). BELOW: A mix of wildflowers including brittlebush and a 'Desert Museum' palo verde tree are well positioned to take advantage of the rainwater from the adjacent cistern.

SITING CULVERT-STYLE TANKS In my design practice, I often use metal culverts, upended into cement, as tanks. When using this sort of tank, there are two options: a dry-downspout or wet-downspout installation. In a dry-downspout installation, the culvert-style tank needs to be located near the downspout that will be feeding it. In a wet-downspout system, the culvert-style tank can be located within a couple of hundred feet of the downspout, provided that your desired location is not above the downspout.

COUPLING A TANK WITH BASINS The ideal way to design your raingarden is to have the water from your cistern (both overflow and spigot) flow into a basin or series of linked basins. This is the easiest method with the least duplication.

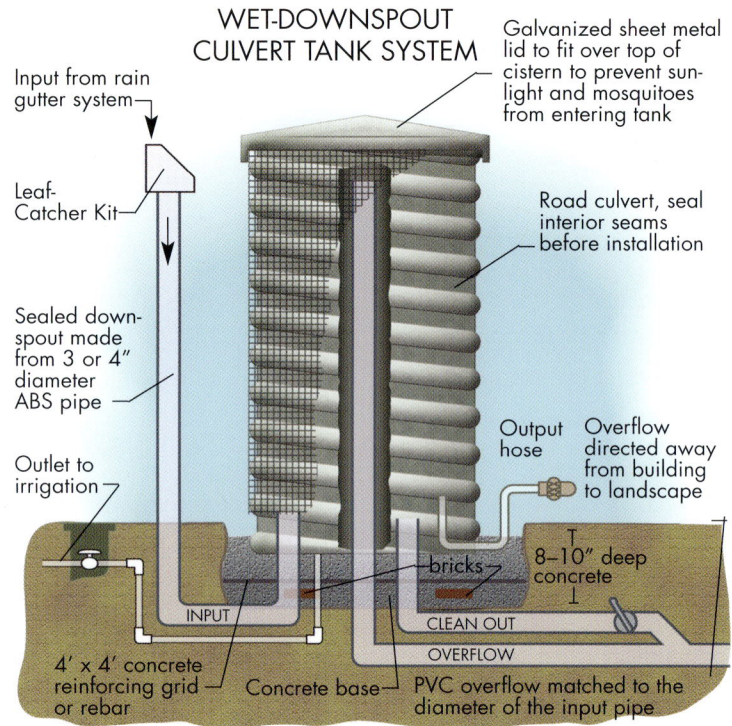

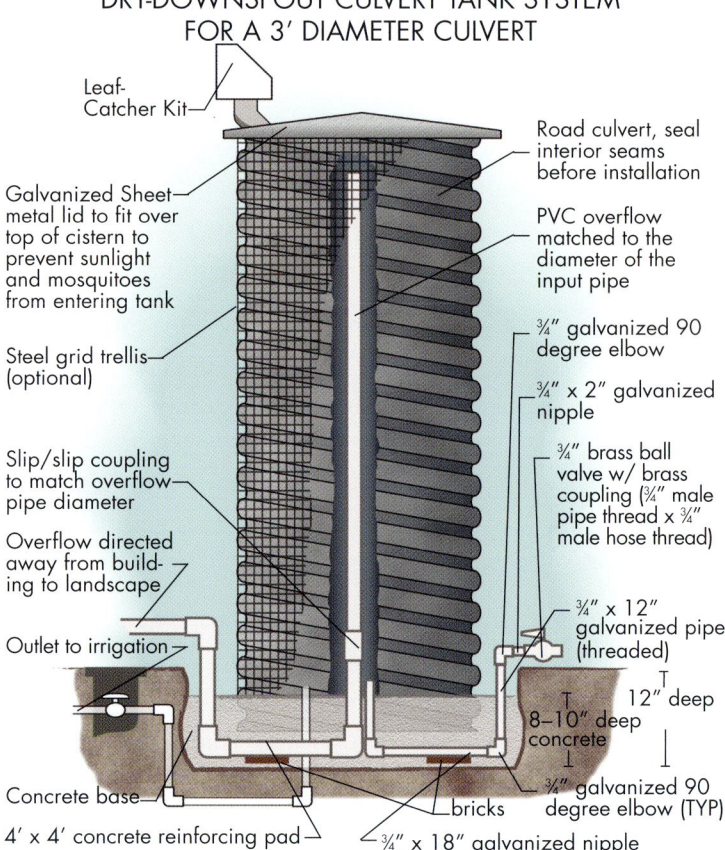

Comparison of Four Efficient Landscape Irrigation Strategies

	Efficient Drip Irrigation	Rainwater Earthworks
Ease of Implementation/Cost	Conventional and well-documented installation practices. Easily contracted or DIY. The least expensive option.	Simple to construct and maintain with a shovel and wheelbarrow. Materials are inexpensive (or free) but the labor can be onerous depending on soil conditions.
Location of Use	Very flexible. Can be automated and water any part of a garden regardless of gravity. Plants with higher water needs can be planted in higher densities.	Must be 10 feet away from home foundations, and plants should be in the vicinity of the catchment area. May be impractical in small yards with slow drainage.
Maintenance	Needs a yearly flush and inspection for animal damage to poly lines and for clogged emitters. Timers should be reset four times per year, seasonally.	No moving parts. Repair erosion damage after major storm events.
Impact on Groundwater Supplies	Uses groundwater (unless hooked up to a rainwater tank).	Does not affect groundwater, but may recharge shallow aquifers.
Water Quality	Salt will eventually build up in soils, depending on the hardness of the municipal water.	Excellent, very low in salts, preferred for growing plants.
Duration of Water Availability	Constant, so long as you are paying your water bill and there are no regional shortages or restrictions!	Limited, depending on soil type, top dressing (mulch), weather, and plant uptake.

	Rainwater Tanks	Graywater
Ease of Implementation/Cost	More complex installation. More expensive to install than earthworks, on par with a DIY drip system.	Can be difficult and costly to retrofit existing homes, depending on layout of rooms and plumbing configuration.
Location of Use	Good for small yards. With gravity-fed tanks, plants should be located either at grade or below tanks and within hose reach. Effective when used in combination with earthworks.	Should not be used on veggie root crops (e.g. carrots, radishes); may be used on many native plants and fruit trees. Graywater should not stand.
Maintenance	Every-other-year cleaning. Valves should be protected from hard freezes.	System may require occasional cleaning of lint (from systems originating in washers).
Impact on Groundwater Supplies	Does not affect groundwater.	Reuses groundwater.
Water Quality	Excellent, very low in salts, preferred for growing plants.	Depends on the type of household soaps and detergents used. Usually higher salt content than tap water.
Duration of Water Availability	Extended, depending on the size of tank and frequency of rainfall.	Varies with occupants' habits.

Plant Charts

Raingarden Plant Selection: Bottom-of-the-Basin Plants

Common and Botanical Names	Plant Type	Russ and Scott's Notes
Apache Plume (*Fallugia paradoxa*)	Shrub	White flowers and pink seed plumes.
Arizona Wild Cotton (*Gossypium thurberi*)	Shrub	Attracts cardinals and has red color in late summer, early fall.
Big Root (*Jatropha macrorhiza*)	Perennial	With pink flowers and waxy leaves.
'Boothill' (*Conoclinium greggii*)	Perennial	Attracts clouds of butterflies, summer only.
Clover Fern (*Marsilea macropoda*)	Ground cover	Clover-like foliage, will go drought-dormant, takes shade.
Coahuilan Rosewood (*Vaquelinia corymbosa heterodon*)	Small tree	Striking serrated evergreen foliage.
Deer Grass (*Muhlenbergia rigens*)	Grass	Stalwart ornamental grass with graceful seed spikes.
Desert Sunrise (*Amoreuxia palmatifida*)	Perennial	Winter-dormant tuberous perennial with orange and red flowers.
Desert Willow (*Chilopsis linearis*)	Tree	Flowers visited by hummingbirds and native bees.
Devil's River (*Zexmenia hispida*)	Perennial	An easy, tough ball-shaped plant with golden flowers.
Flattop Buckwheat (*Eriogonum fasciculatum poliofolium*)	Perennial	Dense blue-green bush with pink flowers; deer food.
Foxglove Penstemon (*Penstemon cobaea*)	Perennial	Hummingbird plant.
Giant Morning Glory (*Ipomoea longifolia*)	Perennial	Summer root perennial with 4-inch trumpet flowers.
Goodding's Verbena (*Glandularia gooddingii*)	Perennial	Great winter–spring bloomer with lilac flowers.
Guardiola (*Guardiola platyphylla*)	Perennial	Reseeds, attracts butterflies to nectar.
Hummingbird Trumpet (*Zauschneria californica*)	Perennial	Magnificent hummingbird plant that looks good draping over walls. Can be used as a ground cover.
Kidneywood (*Eysenhardtia orthocarpa*)	Small tree	Great butterfly-attracting patio tree.
Limber bush (*Jatropha cardiophylla*)	Shrub	Tropical-looking during the monsoon season.

Common and Botanical Names	Plant Type	Russ and Scott's Notes
Mariola (*Parthenium incanum*)	Shrub	Small silver shrub, very rabbit-resistant.
Oreganillo (*Aloysia wrightii*)	Shrub	Attracts small butterflies and goldfinches.
Parish's Wolfberry (*Lycium parishii*)	Shrub	A good wildlife plant with silver succulent leaves.
Podwing Vine (*Nissolia schottii*)	Vine	Twining vine with yellow flowers; rabbit food.
Sacred Datura (*Datura wrightii*)	Perennial	Huge white flowers that inspired Georgia O'Keeffe.
Scarlet Penstemon (*Penstemon barbatus*)	Perennial	Hummingbird plant.
Shrubby Senna (*Senna wislizenii*)	Shrub	Larval food for sulfur butterflies.
Southwestern Pipevine (*Aristolochia watsonii*)	Vine	Food for the pipevine swallowtail butterfly.
Tarbush (*Flourensia cernua*)	Shrub	Chihuahuan Desert indicator species.
Texas Kidneywood (*Eysenhardtia texana*)	Small tree	Great butterfly bush. Can make a small patio tree.
Velvet Mesquite (*Prosopis juliflora*)	Tree	Tough native tree, beautiful wood that can be used for furniture and firewood, and bean pods that can be eaten.
Western Spiderwort (*Tradescantia occidentalis*)	Perennial	Blue-purple flowers every morning when moist.
Wright's Goldenrod (*Solidago wrightii*)	Perennial	Reseeds, attracts butterflies to nectar.
Yellow Bells (*Tecoma stans*)	Shrub	Freezes to ground in cold winters; resprouts.
Yerba Mansa (*Anemopsis californica*)	Perennial	Native to alkaline seeps, zinc-oxide-white flowers, takes shade.

Raingarden Plant Selection: Beside-the-Basin Plants (Plants for Berms)

Common and Botanical Names	Plant Type	Russ and Scott's Notes
Baja Fairy Duster (*Calliandra californica*)	Shrub	Red-bottlebrush-flowered hummingbird and butterfly plant.
Bee Bush (*Aloysia gratissima*)	Shrub	Attracts small butterflies and goldfinches.
Chiltepin (*Capsicum annuum*)	Shrub	Native hot pepper, good for birds and for salsas.
Desert Agave (*Agave deserti*)	Succulent	Good residential-scale agave, 1–3 feet at maturity.

Common and Botanical Names	Plant Type	Russ and Scott's Notes
(Beside-the-Basin Plants, continued)		
Desert Hackberry (*Celtis pallida*)	Tree	A great bush for quail and for screening.
Desert Honeysuckle (*Anisacanthus thurberi*)	Shrub	Hummingbird plant.
Desert Lavender (*Hyptis emoryi*)	Shrub	Hummingbird shrub; gets frost damage in cold years.
Desert Milkweed (*Asclepias subulata*)	Perennial	Great butterfly plant, but aphids like it too.
Desert Rose Mallow (*Hibiscus coulteri*)	Summer annual	Pale yellow flowers that fade to red as they close. Monsoon bloomer.
Dogweed (*Thymophylla pentachaeta*)	Ground cover	Blooms a lot; weedy, easily controlled.
Globemallow (*Sphaeralcea ambigua*)	Perennial wildflower	Available in many flower colors from white to orange to red.
Ironwood (*Olneya tesota*)	Tree	The premier native shade tree for the Sonoran Desert.
Mountain Cassava (*Manihot davisiae*)	Perennial	Summer root perennial with dramatic foliage.
Ocotillo (*Fouquieria splendens*)	Stem succulent	Classic zigzag-branching hummingbird plant.
Pink Fairy Duster (*Calliandra eriophylla*)	Shrub	Hummingbird and butterfly plant.
Prairie Zinnia (*Zinnia grandiflora*)	Ground cover	Wonderful ever-blooming golden ground cover.
Soap Tree Yucca (*Yucca elata*)	Succulent	Native trunk-forming yucca with cream-colored flower bayonets.
Southwest Coral Bean (*Erythrina flabelliformis*)	Shrub	Heart-shaped bright green leaves and lipstick-red flowers make it superb for summer gardens.
Sundrops (*Calylophus hartwegii*)	Perennial	Lots of color throughout the warm season.
Superstition Mallow (*Abutilon palmeri*)	Perennial	Velvetine silver leaves and orange flowers. Survives extreme drought once established.
Toumey Agave (*Agave toumeyana*)	Succulent	Clumper, forming colonies to 6–10 feet in time.
Trixis (*Trixis californica*)	Perennial	Covered with yellow flower heads in spring.
Western Soapberry (*Sapindus saponaria drummondii*)	Tree	Medium-sized deciduous shade tree. Excellent but hard to find.

Desert Raingardens: Annual Rainfall for Southwest Cities

City	Annual Normal Precipitation (in inches)	Yearly Gallons of Rainwater from a 7,000-sq.-ft. Lot
Albuquerque, NM	8.88	38,746
Barstow, CA	4.40	19,199
Bishop, CA	5.26	22,951
Blythe, CA	3.60	15,708
Carlsbad, NM	12.92	56,374
Cottonwood, AZ	11.84	51,662
Death Valley, CA	2.26	9,861
Douglas, AZ	12.8	55,851
El Paso, TX	9.43	41,146
Fresno, CA	10.90	47,560
Hawthorne, CA	4.39	19,155
Inner Grand Canyon (Phantom Ranch), AZ	8.38	36,565
Kanab, UT	13.49	58,861
Kingman, AZ	10.47	45,684
Lancaster, CA	7.75	33,816
Las Cruces, NM	8.35	36,434
Las Vegas, NV	4.13	18,021
Moab, UT	9.80	42,761
Needles, CA	4.54	19,810
Page, AZ	6.46	28,187
Palm Springs, CA	5.47	23,867
Pecos, TX	10.59	46,208
Phoenix, AZ	7.66	33,423
Roswell, NM	13.05	56,942
Safford, AZ	8.91	38,877
St. George, UT	8.23	35,910
Tuba City, AZ	6.47	28,230
Tucson, AZ	12.00	52,360
Yuma, AZ	3.17	13,832

ABOVE: Ollas ready to be fired in a kiln. BELOW: Firecracker penstemon positioned to harvest rainwater from an adjacent boulder.

EXTREME TOOLS FOR THE HOT GARDEN

WHAT KIND OF SOIL DO I HAVE? Before you go out and buy a pickup-load of new tools, assess your soil conditions.

Begin by digging several small test holes with a shovel in different parts of the yard. If just making a one- or two-inch-deep divot requires slamming the point of the shovel into the ground at full force several times, you most likely have some kind of hardpan (compacted clay, sometimes with rocks). In addition to your shovel, hardpan requires either a digging bar or a jackhammer, or perhaps both. Clay is easy to identify because it will form a ball (or roll into a ribbon) in your hand when it is wet.

If you can dig easily with a regular shovel and your soil will not make a ball in your hand when wet, your soil has a high sand content. This is good news, because sandy soils, while they require more frequent watering, are much easier to dig in than clay soils. Sandy usually will not require the use of special tools.

The worst sort of soil to discover in your desert garden is caliche. Caliche is a gray-white cement-like substance that feels just as if you have hit a large rock when you strike it with a pick. The good news (though "good news" and "caliche" are two terms seldom used together) about caliche is that it is usually very localized and probably doesn't cover your entire yard. Also, caliche may be only a few inches thick, in which case you should be able to break through it without too much fuss; otherwise, bust out the digging bar or jackhammer.

As I mentioned earlier, old-timers know, and newcomers soon learn, that planting plants in the Southwest is often more akin to mining than gardening. Visions of soft brown soil that is easily tilled and cultivated are quickly replaced with the hard realities of compacted clay, rock, and caliche. This is the kind of soil that eats regular gardening tools for breakfast. Forget the little stamped-steel hand cultivator you brought from Illinois and the "Garden Weasel" you purchased from an infomercial; put on your prospector's hat and get some serious tools for digging in the desert. Like the miner, you need to have a full arsenal of weapons at your disposal to attack your excavation project. The following three tools are the favorite big guns of the landscape trade:

JACKHAMMER/DEMOLITION HAMMER *Weight: 12–42 lbs.*
The formidable electric jackhammer fitted with a spade bit is the *T. rex* of gardening tools. As landscape contractor Marc White comments, "If you can't use dynamite, a jackhammer is the next best thing. It is less wear and tear on your body [than using a pick]. Even though a jackhammer is heavy, it is easy to use." Jackhammers make quick work of stubborn hardpan soils and will even go through caliche. They can be used to dig trenches as well as holes for plants. "In a three-hour $60 [jackhammer] rental period, a homeowner could dig most of their irrigation trenches and the holes for their large trees," says Andy Bessey, owner of Desert Horticulture Landscaping.

The downside to jackhammers has always been their weight. Just carrying a jackhammer from the car to the backyard starts your back feeling the heft. Many landscapers rely on the trusty Mikita 1500 jackhammer, which weighs in at a chunky 42 pounds. Thankfully, recent innovations have brought to the market smaller and lighter jackhammers that are more in line with homeowners' needs. DeWalt and Hilti tools both make small demolition hammers that are nearly 30 pounds lighter than traditional landscape jackhammers; for most homeowner gardening projects, these little jackhammers are perfect. Even though the little jackhammers are smaller, they are still costly, so you may want to consider renting if you don't have an ongoing use for an expensive demolition tool.

Safety tips for using electric jackhammers include wearing safety goggles, steel-toed boots, and the all-important earplugs. Since jackhammers are loud, don't start hammering away at the crack of dawn if you want to stay on good terms with the neighbors.

The use of jackhammers for landscaping is pretty well confined to the Southwest, where our soils are too tough for simple shovels. In other parts of the country, jackhammers are used to demolish old concrete patios, foundations, and walls; in the hot-garden zone, they are the workhorses of the landscape industry.

PICK AND MATTOCK PICK *Weight: 2.5–6 lbs.*
The pick is not the easiest tool to handle, but when wielded properly it inflicts the same force as a jackhammer: it is essentially a human-powered jackhammer. A variation of the pick—the

mattock pick—is a popular firemen's tool that has a pointed pick on one end and a 4-inch blade for trenching on the other. Andy Bessey advises that you select a good, heavy pick with a long enough handle to get the job done. "Don't get a little tool that looks like it was made for children. An undersized tool, even if it is lighter, will take longer to do the job." Of all the tough tools mentioned here, the pick is the most economical for the homeowner. Picks are available with either wood or plastic handles.

DIGGING BAR *Weight: 14 or 17 lbs.*

Although it looks like a medieval implement of war or something Darth Maul (this is the second geeky *Star Wars* reference, for those of you who are counting) used against the Jedi, the digging bar really is a gardening tool. It is a simple steel bar with one pointed end and one blade-shaped end. Like the jackhammer, it works in an up-and-down motion, with your arms, rather than electricity, providing the power. Raising and dropping one of its ends into the dirt breaks up tough soil.

Digging bars come in two weights: 14 and 17 pounds. The 14-pound model is slightly easier to handle but doesn't inflict the same sort of blow as the 17-pound model. If you can comfortably handle the larger tool, you will get more digging done faster. Digging bars are also used to dig postholes, and one can be used as a lever to position large landscape boulders in your yard.

Although a 14- or 17-pound tool may not sound that portly, the first time you hold one, the first thing you notice is the heaviness of the steel. It is a tool that my father, who once spent a full day on the end of one, calls "the death stick." The tool feels like it was built for a shot-putter, but as you use it, you notice how effective that dead weight is at dislodging rocks and breaking through caliche. Using a digging bar for an hour is at least as good as the equivalent time spent on the biceps machine at the gym.

These big, powerful tools can turn an otherwise daunting job into a quick morning's work. So next time you feel like your dirt has got you licked, get a bigger jackhammer, pick, or digging bar, and show your hardpan who's boss. After all, extreme gardening conditions call for extreme tools.

SURGICAL CACTUS AND SUCCULENT TOOLS

Early in my desert gardening career, I found myself sporting a set of linear scars on my hands and forearms, consistent with intravenous heroin use, after I weeded around my cactus and agave plants. This happened each growing season until I saw a local cactus-grower employing a pair of extra-long surgical tweezers to remove some nasty spurge from the base of a golden barrel cactus. I went out right away and bought a set of 12-inch tweezers, which I later replaced with an even larger 18-inch set. With tweezers this long, reaching weeds in the deepest nook of a hedgehog cactus became painless. Weeding with tweezers is a little like playing the board game "Operation," except that when I make a mistake in the cactus I let loose a string of profanity rather that having the patient's lightbulb nose turn red.

For agaves, whose dead—yet still "armed"—leaves accumulate around the bottom of the plant, a long-handled saw is called for. I found a great model on the Internet (see the Cactus Pruning Tools in the Resources section for listing). It is designed for working around large cactus and agave plants and has a long handle with a heavy-duty angled serrated blade. With it I'm able to reach down to the base of an agave plant and saw away without leaving a fresh set of "tracks" on my forearms. In addition to the long-handled saw, a good pair of heavy-duty welding gloves are great for handling cactus. These welding gloves are standard issue for "cactus rangers"—members of the Tucson Cactus and Succulent Society, who know a little about handling cacti. This band of volunteers has saved over 40,000 (and counting!) cacti from the developer's blade since 1999.

ACKNOWLEDGMENTS

The multi-year process of completing this book has been an exhilarating, mind-expanding, and occasionally tedious ride. I couldn't have done it without the help of my publishers: I thank Ross Humphreys and Susan Lowell for their continued inspiration, support, and encouragement. I'd also like to thank Lisa Anderson, whose tireless pursuit of clarity has once again helped bring a crazy and disparate project to fruition, and Caroline Cook, whose organizational input was key.

The following desert rats and government agencies were so generous with their knowledge, time, and gardens that I'm not exactly sure how to thank them other than to list them prominently here: Wynn Anderson, Rita Jo Anthony, the Arizona Department of Water Resources (both the Phoenix and Tucson active management areas), Christina Bickelmann, Simmons Buntin, Russ Buhrow, Greg Corman, David Cristiani, Libby Davison, Mark Dimmitt, Jane Evans, John Fairey, Ron Gass, Peter Gierlach, John Greenlee, Russ Harrison, Lynn Hassler, Karen Hillson, Sean Hogan, Debra Huffman, Gene Joseph, Panayoti Kelaidis, Brad Lancaster, Val Little, Charles Mann, Jim Martinez, George Montgomery, Carrie Nimmer, Jill Nokes, Bob Perrill, Janet Rademacher, David Salman, Mark and Margaret Sitter, Greg Starr, Robin Stinnett, Dennis Swartzell, and Jon Weeks.

Portions of this book originally appeared in *The Arizona Daily Star*, *Horticulture* magazine, and *Tucson Home* magazine.

RESOURCES

Purveyors of Plants for the Hot Garden

ARIZONA

Arid Lands Greenhouses
3560 West Bilby Road
Tucson, AZ 85746
520-883-9404

B & B Cactus Farm
11550 East Speedway Boulevard
Tucson, AZ 85748
520-721-4687, www.bandbcactus.com

Bach's Cactus Nursery
8602 North Thornydale Road
Tucson, AZ 86742
520-744-3333, www.bachs-cacti.com

Civano Nursery
5301 South Houghton Road
Tucson, AZ 85747
520-546-9200, www.civanonursery.net

Desert Survivors Native Plant Nursery
1020 West Starr Pass Boulevard
Tucson, AZ 85713
520-361-3071

Harlow Gardens
5620 East Pima Street
Tucson, AZ 85712
520-298-3303, www.harlowgardens.com

Landscape Cacti
7711 West Bopp Road
Tucson, AZ 85735
520-883-0020

Mesquite Valley Growers
8005 East Speedway Boulevard
Tucson, AZ 85710
520-721-8600

Miles To Go Cactus and Succulent Webalog
520-682-7272, www.miles2go.com

Mountain States Wholesale Nursery (wholesale only, but a good source of information)
Litchfield Park, AZ
www.mswn.com

Plants for the Southwest
50 East Blacklidge Drive
Tucson, AZ 85705
520-628-8773

Shady Way Gardens
566 West Superstition Boulevard
Apache Junction, AZ 85220
480-288-9655

Southwest Gardener
2809 North 15th Avenue
Phoenix, AZ 85007
602-279-9510, www.southwestgardener.com

Spadefoot Nursery
8897 East Walnut Trail
Pearce, AZ 85625
520-824-3247

Starr Nursery
3340 West Ruthann Road
Tucson, AZ 85745
520-743-7052, www.starr-nursery.com

Sticky Situation
Tucson, AZ
520-743-9761, www.stickysituation.com

Tanque Verde Greenhouses
10810 East Tanque Verde Road
Tucson, AZ 85749
520-749-4414, www.cactus-mall.com/tanque-verde/

CALIFORNIA

Greenlee Nursery
15993 El Prado Road
Chino, CA 91708
www.greenleenursery.com

San Marcos Growers
125 South San Marcos Road
Santa Barbara, CA 93160
www.smgrowers.com

NEW MEXICO

Bernardo Beach Native Plant Farm
3729 Arno Street NE
Albuquerque, NM
505-345-6248, www.bernardobeachnatives.com

Plants of the Southwest
3095 Agua Fria Road
Santa Fe, NM 87507
505-438-8888, www.plantsofthesouthwest.com

Santa Fe Greenhouses, DBA High Country Gardens
2902 Rufina Street
Santa Fe, NM 87507
800-925-9387, www.highcountrygardens.com

TEXAS

Yucca Do Nursery
FM 359 and FM 3346
Hempstead, TX 77445
979-826-4580, www.yuccado.com

OUTSIDE THE SOUTHWEST

Cistus Nursery (rare yuccas and agaves)
22711 Northwest Gillihan Road
Sauvie Island, OR 97231
www.cistus.com

Peaceful Valley Farm & Garden Supply (fruiting olives)
125 Clydesdale Court
Grass Valley, CA 95945
www.groworganic.com

Plant Delights Nursery (for agaves)
9241 Sauls Road
Raleigh, NC 27603
919-772-4794, www.plantdelights.com

Cactus-pruning Tools and Other Hard Goods

Blue Orchard Mason Bee Nest
www.highcountrygardens.com

Cactus Pruning Tools
www.cactuspruner.com

Rainbow Gardens Bookshop (plus cactus-pruning tools and barrel cactus slings, by appointment only)
3620 West Sahuaro Divide
Tucson, AZ 85742
520-577-7406, www.rainbowgardensbookshop.com

Seeds

ARIZONA

Native Seeds/SEARCH
525 North 4th Avenue (retail outlet)
Tucson, Arizona 85705
520-622-5561, www.nativeseeds.org (catalog orders)

Southwestern Native Seeds
P.O. Box 50503
Tucson, Arizona 85703
www.southwesternnativeseeds.com

Wildseed
6615 South 28th Street (mail order only)
Phoenix, Arizona 85042
602-276-3536

CALIFORNIA

S&S Seeds Inc.
P.O. Box 1275
Carpinteria, CA 93014
805-684-0436, www.ssseeds.com

Seedhunt
P.O. Box 96
Freedom, CA 95019
www.seedhunt.com

Theodore Payne Foundation
www.theodorepayne.org

NEW MEXICO
Plants of the Southwest
3095 Agua Fria Road
Santa Fe, NM 87507
800-788-7333, www.plantsofthesouthwest.com

TEXAS
Native American Seed
Junction, TX
800-728-4043, www.seedsource.com

Must-See Hot Gardens

ARIZONA
Arizona-Sonora Desert Museum
2021 North Kinney Road
Tucson, AZ 85743
520-883-1380, www.desertmuseum.org

Boyce Thompson Arboretum
37615 U.S. Highway 60
Superior, AZ
520-689-2723, www.btarboretum.org

Desert Botanical Garden
1201 North Galvin Parkway
Phoenix, Arizona 85008
480-941-1225, www.dbg.org

Tohono Chul Park
7366 North Paseo del Norte
Tucson, AZ 85704
520-742-6455, www.tohonochulpark.org

Tucson Botanical Gardens
2150 North Alvernon Way
Tucson, Arizona 85712
520-326-9686, www.tucsonbotanical.org

CALIFORNIA
The Huntington Library, Art Collections, and Botanical Gardens
1151 Oxford Road
San Marino, CA 91108
626-405-2100, www.huntington.org

The Living Desert Zoo and Gardens
47-900 Portola Avenue
Palm Desert, CA 92260
760-346-5694, www.livingdesert.org

NEVADA
Arboretum at UNLV
University of Nevada, Las Vegas
4505 South Maryland Parkway
Las Vegas, NV 89154
702-895-3392
www.unlv.edu/facilities/landscape/arboretum.html

Ethel M Chocolate Factory and Botanical Cactus Gardens
2 Cactus Garden Drive
Henderson, NV 89015
702-435-2655, www.ethelm.com

Springs Preserve
333 South Valley View Boulevard
Las Vegas, NV 89107
702-822-7700, www.springspreserve.org

NEW MEXICO
Rio Grande Botanic Garden
903 10th Street SW
Albuquerque, NM 87102
505-764-6200, www.cabq.gov/biopark/garden/

TEXAS
Chihuahuan Desert Gardens
Centennial Museum (the corner of University and Wiggins)
University of Texas, El Paso
El Paso, TX 79968
915-747-5565
http://museum.utep.edu/chih/gardens/gardens.htm

Lady Bird Johnson Wildflower Center
4801 La Crosse Avenue
Austin, TX 78739
512-292-4100 , www.wildflower.org

Peckerwood Garden
20571 F.M. 359
Hempstead, TX 77445
979-826-3232, www.peckerwoodgarden.com

SUGGESTED READING

Calhoun, Scott. *Chasing Wildflowers: A Mad Search for Wild Gardens*. Tucson, AZ: Rio Nuevo Publishers, 2007.

———. *Yard Full of Sun: The Story of a Gardener's Obsession That Got a Little Out of Hand*. Tucson, AZ: Rio Nuevo Publishers, 2005.

Felger, Richard; Johnson, Matthew B.; Wilson, Michael F. *The Trees of Sonora, Mexico.* New York: Oxford University Press, 2001.

Irish, Gary, and Mary F. Irish. *Agaves, Yuccas, and Related Plants: A Gardener's Guide*. Portland, OR: Timber Press, 2000.

Irish, Mary. *Arizona Gardener's Guide*. Nashville, TN: Cool Springs Press, 2002.

———. *Gardening in the Desert: A Guide to Plant Selection and Care*. Tucson, AZ: The University of Arizona Press, 2000.

Lancaster, Brad. *Rainwater Harvesting for Drylands*, Volumes 1 and 2. Tucson, AZ: Rainsource Press, 2006, 2008.

MacKay, Pam. *Mojave Desert Wildflowers*. Helena, MT: Falcon, 2003.

Mielke, Judy. *Native Plants for Southwest Landscapes*. Austin, TX: University of Texas Press, 1993.

Morrow, Baker H., and V. B. Price. *Anasazi Architecture and American Design*. Albuquerque, NM: University of New Mexico Press, 1997.

Nabhan, Gary P. *Gathering the Desert*. Tucson, AZ: The University of Arizona Press, 1985.

Nelson, Kim. *A Desert Gardener's Companion*. Tucson, AZ: Rio Nuevo Publishers, 2001.

Niethammer, Carolyn. *American Indian Cooking*. Lincoln, NB: University of Nebraska Press, 1999.

———. *The Prickly Pear Cookbook*. Tucson, AZ: Rio Nuevo Publishers, 2004.

Phillips, Judith. *Natural by Design: Beauty and Balance in Southwest Gardens*. Santa Fe, NM: Museum of New Mexico Press, 1995.

———. *Plants for Natural Gardens: Southwestern Native and Adaptive Trees, Shrubs, Wildflowers and Grasses.* Santa Fe, NM: Museum of New Mexico Press, 1995.

Phillips, Steven J., and Patricia W. Comus. *A Natural History of the Sonoran Desert*. Tucson, AZ: Arizona-Sonora Desert Museum Press; Berkeley, CA: University of California Press, 2000.

Quinn, Meg. C*acti of the Desert Southwest*. Tucson, AZ: Rio Nuevo Publishers, 2002.

———. *Wildflowers of the Desert Southwest*. Tucson, AZ: Rio Nuevo Publishers, 2000.

———. *Wildflowers of the Mountain Southwest*. Tucson, AZ: Rio Nuevo Publishers, 2003.

Springer, Lauren. *The Undaunted Garden: Planting for Weather-Resilient Beauty*. Golden, CO: Fulcrum Publishing, 1994.

Starr, Greg. *Cool Plants for Hot Gardens: 200 Water-Smart Choices for the Southwest*. Tucson, AZ: Rio Nuevo Publishers, 2009.

Tallamy, Douglas W. *Bringing Nature Home: How Native Plants Sustain Wildlife in Our Gardens.* Portland, OR: Timber Press, 2007.

Tatroe, Marcia. *Cutting Edge Gardening in the Intermountain West.* Boulder, CO: Johnson Books, 2007.

Turner, Raymond M., Janice E. Bowers, and Tony L. Burgess. *Sonoran Desert Plants, An Ecological Atlas.* Tucson, AZ: The University of Arizona Press, 1995.

Wasowski, Andy, and Sally Wasowski. *The Landscaping Revolution: Garden with Mother Nature, Not Against Her.* Chicago, IL: Contemporary Books, 2000.

Wasowski, Sally. *Native Landscaping from El Paso to L.A..* Chicago, IL: Contemporary Books, 2000.

West, Steve. *Northern Chihuahuan Desert Wildflowers: A Field Guide to Wildflowers and Other Plants of the Desert and Its Parklands.* Helena, MT: Falcon, 2000.

GENERAL INDEX
(NOTE: also see Table of Contents for additional broad subject categories.)

agave propagation, radical, 65
agave weevil, 65
Albuquerque planting theme, 89
annual rainfall, hot-garden cities, 181
architecture and landscape, 32
basins for watering plants, 170, 173
basins, preferred plants for bottoms, 173, 178
bees, 151-153
berms, 170, 173
berms, preferred plants for, 179
birds, attracting, 154-156
bulbs for desert gardens, 61-62
butterflies, attracting, 153
cactus salvage, 71
cactus tools, 182, 183, 185
charismatic megaflora, 24
cholla buds, as food, 76-77
chuperosa leaves as food, 47
citrus, care and planting, 84-86
color wheel, 118
comparison of landscape irrigation strategies, 177
dates, California fan palm, as food, 82
decomposed granite, 131, 133
dg, *see* decomposed granite
dormancy, as design element, 56-57
El Paso planting theme, 87
fall color, 46-47
fruit trees, 83-87
gravel, 133
hedgehog fruit, 72
homeowners' associations, issues with, 55, 56
hot-garden region, defined, 10-14
jackhammers, 182
javelinas, 158-159
labyrinths, 31, 33, 134-135
Las Vegas planting theme, 90
lizards, 157
Mediterranean plants, 83
mesquite beans as food, 44
mesquite beans, milling, 45
moon cactus fruit, as food, 52
mulch, 132-134
ocotillo fencing, 79
ollas, 174-175
Outback shrubs, 83
pack rats, 159
Palm Springs planting theme, 89
palm trimming, 81-82
palo verde peas as food, 42
passion flower as food, 51
patio design tips, 134
pests, *see* javelinas; pack rats; rabbits; agave weevil
pincushion cactus fruit, as food, 78
plant numerology, 34-35
poor man's drip system, 174
prickly pear cactus, harvesting fruit, 74
pruning tips, 48
   (*also see* palm trimming; yucca trimming)
quiz for "Discovering Your 'Big Here,'" 31-32
rabbits, 55
rainwater, gallons per year calculation, 169
recipes (*also see* cholla buds; chuperosa leaves; dates, California fan palm; hedgehog fruit; mesquite beans; moon cactus fruit; palo verde peas; passion flower; pincushion fruit; prickly pear fruit)
   Scott's Prickly Pear Lemonade, 76
   Spicy Ice-Box Pickled Cholla Buds, 77
   Spinach and Soap Blossom Salad, 70
riprap, 134
rockwork, for slowing rain water, 171
ruderals, 62
Santa Fe planting theme, 90
soil amendment, 92
soil preparation, 91, 182
soil type, assessing, 182
solar arc, 40
temperature highs and lows, hot-garden cities, 17-18
Tipton method, 92
toads, Colorado River, 157
toads, spadefoot, 157
trees as air conditioning, 40
Tucson planting theme, 88
USDA hardiness zones, 17-18
vining and creeping cacti, 51
water features, native plants for, 143
watering basin, anatomy of, 173
wildflower seeds, care and sowing, 53-55
woody lilies, 63
yucca flowers as food, 70
yucca trimming, 70

INDEX OF PLANT NAMES
(NOTE: **boldface** *numbers denote pictures.)*

Abutilon palmeri, 99, 180
Acacia
   angustissima, 99 (*also see* white ball acacia)
   berlandieri, 94
   constricta, 95 (*also see* whitethorn acacia)
   farnesiana, 95, 124
   greggii, 94 (*also see* catclaw acacia)
   occidentalis, 96
   rigidula, 94
   willardiana, 42, 95, 124, 129 (*also see* palo blanco)
Acalypha monostachya 'Raspberry Fuzzies', 87, 100
Achnatherum hymenoides, 110
Adam's tree, 109
Agastache x 'Desert Sunrise', 91
agave, 49, 62, 63-66, 103-104, 153, 159, 168, 171, 173, 183
Agave, **63-66**
   americana, 65
   americana marginata, 65, 104
   americana mediopicta, 65, 104, 124 (*also see* white stripe agave)
   bovicornuta, 104 (*also see* cow's horn agave)
   bracteosa, 104
   chrysantha, 89, 103
   colorata, 103
   deserti, 103, 179
   geminiflora, 104 (*also see* twin-flowered agave)
   gentryi 'Jaws', 103
   guiengola, 103
   havardiana, 90, 104
   macroacantha, 103
   murpheyi, 103
   neomexicana, 88, 103
   ocahui, 103
   ovatifolia, 104, 123
   palmeri, 103
   parryi, 104, 122
   parryi huachucensis, 103
   parryi truncata, 103
   parviflora, 104
   pelona, 103
   potatorum, 103
   salmiana ferox 'Green Goblet', 104
   schidigera 'Durango Delight', 103
   'Sharkskin', 104
   toumeyana, 180
   utahensis, 90, 104
   victoriae-reginae, 104 (*also see* Queen Victoria agave)
   vilmoriniana, 103 (*also see* octopus agave)
   weberi, 104, 129 (*also see* Weber's agave)
Ageratum corymbosum, 153
Ajo lily, 61, **62**
algerita, 91, 96
alichoche, 102
Allonia incarnata, 61
aloe, 64, **83,** 112-113, **152**
Aloe
   barbadensis, 112
   dichotoma, 112
   ferox, 112
   striata, 112, 124
   variegata, 112
   x 'Blue Elf', 112, 155
Aloysia gratissima, 179
Aloysia wrightii, 77, 98, 179
Ambrosia dumosa, 99
Amoreuxia palmatifida, 178
Anemopsis californica, 143, 179

INDEX

Anisacanthus thurberi, 180
Anisacanthus wrightii, 98, 155
Antigonon leptopus, 101
Apache plume, 90, 178
'Apricot Glow' torch cactus hybrid, 72
Aquilegia chrysantha, 126, 143
Arctomecon californica, 90
Argemone platyceras, 102
Argentine giant, 73, 107
Aristida purpurea, 111
Aristolochia watsonii, 101, 154, 179
Arizona grape ivy, **51,** 89, 101
Arizona poppy, 59, 152
Arizona queen of the night, 51, 102
Arizona rainbow hedgehog cactus, 106
Arizona rosewood, 96
Arizona wild cotton, 178
arroyo lupine, 52, 53, 58
artichoke agave, **8,** 103
'Art's Seedless' desert willow, 90, 95
Asclepias linaria, 88, 153
Asclepias subulata, 153, 180
Aster bigelovii, 60
Atriplex canescens, 97, 154
Atriplex confertifolia, 98
Atriplex family, **45**
Atriplex hymenelytra, 90, 97
Atriplex nummularia, 111
Aussie ranger, 111
autumn glow, 110
autumn sage, 46, 96, 155
    'Furman's Red', 46
    'Purple Haze', 46
    'Sierra Linda', 46
    white autumn sage, 126
Baccharis glutinosa, 143
Baccharis x 'Starn', 100
bahia, 102
Bahia absinthifolia, 102
Baileya multiradiata, 57, 89, 123
Baja fairy duster, 96, 155, 179
Baja fire barrel, 106
Baja "Punk Rock Hairdo" barrel cactus, 106, 123
bamboo muhly, 110
banana yucca, 69, 89, 105
'Barbara Karst' bougainvillea, 101
barestem larkspur, 57
barrel cactus, 70-71, 106, **152**
Bauhinia lunarioides, 94
Bauhinia mexicana, 94
beaked yucca, 27, **67,** 68, 105, 121, 122, 124
bear grass, **49,** 63, 66, 89, 104
beavertail prickly pear, 75, 90, 108
bee bush, 179
bell-flowered hesperaloe, 104
Berberis fremontii, 91 (also see *Berberis trifoliata*)
Berberis trifoliata, 96 (also see *Berberis fremontii*)
Berlandier acacia, *see* guajillo
Berlandiera lyrata, 59
Big Bend agave, *see* Havard agave
Bigelow nolina, 104
Bignonia capreolata 'Tangerine Beauty', 102 (also see 'Tangerine Beauty' crossvine)
big root, 178
big sacaton, 110, 126
blackbrush acacia, 94

black dalea, **46,** 96
blackfoot daisy, **30,** 59, 90
blazing star, 102
blue barrel, 106
bluebush, 111
blue catmint, 91
blue dicks, 52, 61, 132
'Blue Elf' aloe, 112, 155
blue grama grass, 58, **80,** 91, 110
blue nolina, 66, 105
blue palo verde, 41, 88, 95, 135, 151, 155
blue ranger, 48
blue sotol, *see* desert spoon
boojum tree, 78, 81, 109
'Boothill', 153, 178
Bothriochloa barbinodis, 110
bougainvillea, *see* 'Barbara Karst' bougainvillea
Bougainvillea 'Barbara Karst', 101
Bouteloua chondrosioides, 111
Bouteloua curtipendula, 111 (also see sideoats grama)
Bouteloua gracilis, 91, 110 (also see blue grama grass)
Brahea armata, 111, 124
Brahea edulis, 111
Brazilwood, 94
'Bright Lights' cosmos, 59, 60
brittlebush, 57, 89, 132, 155, **175**
broom dalea, 59
'Bubba' desert willow, 87, 94
buckthorn cholla, 108
Buddleia marrubifolia, 99
buffalo gourd, 100
bulbine, 112
Bulbine frutescens, 112
Bursera microphylla, 89, 94
bush muhly, 90, 110
butterfly agave, **65,** 103
butterfly mist, 153
Caesalpinia
    cacalaco, 94
    mexicana, 94
    paraguariensis, 95
    pulcherrima, 98 (also see red bird of paradise)
    pulcherrima 'Phoenix', 98
    x 'Sierra Sun', 95
Calibanus hookeri, 110 (also see gorilla's armpit)
California fan palm, 81, 82, 89, 111
Callaeum lilacaena, 101
Callaeum macropterum, 102
Calliandra californica, 96, 155, 179
Calliandra eriophylla, 98, 155, 180
Calochortus kennedyi, 62 (also see mariposa lily)
Calylophus hartwegii, 87, 100, 180 (also see sundrops)
candelilla, 109
cane beardgrass, 110
cane cholla, 108
canyon morning glory, 101
canyon penstemon, 57, 123
cape aloe, 112
Capsicum annuum, 97, 179
cardinal penstemon, 57, 87
Carnegiea gigantea, 107, 155 (also see saguaro cactus)
Caryopteris x *clandonensis* 'Dark Knight', 91, 152
cascalote, 94
catclaw acacia, 94, 151
cat's claw vine, 50, 101
Celtis laevigata reticulata, 89, 94, 96

Celtis pallida, 155, 180 (also see desert hackberry)
century plants, **63,** 65, 104, 153 (also see agave)
Cephalocereus senilis, 107, 124 (also see old man of Mexico)
Cercis canadensis mexicana, 94
Cercocarpus ledifolius, 94
Cereus hildmannianus, 107
Cereus hildmannianus f. *tortuosus*, 110
Cereus peruvianus f. 'Monstrose', 109, 121 (also see curiosity cactus)
Cerro Guiengola agave, 103
chamisa, *see* rabbitbrush
chia, 57
Chihuahuan orchid shrub, 94
Chihuahuan primrose, 100
Chihuahuan sage, 99
Chilopsis linearis, 178 (also see desert willow)
Chilopsis linearis 'Art's Seedless', 90, 95
Chilopsis linearis 'Bubba', 87, 94
Chilopsis linearis 'Lucretia Hamilton', 94
Chilopsis linearis 'Warren Jones', 96
chiltepin, 97, 179
Chinquapin oak, 95
chocolate flower, 59
Choisya dumosa, 98
cholla cactus, 70, 76-77, 108-109, 156, 159
Chrysactinia mexicana, 59, 90, 121, 124
chuperosa, 47, 89, 97, 155
cimarron sage, 99
cinch weed, 59
Cissus trifoliata, 89, 101 (also see Arizona grape ivy)
citrus, 83, 84-86
citrus, dwarf, 84
claret cup cactus, **72,** 90, 106, 124
Cleistocactus strausii, 107, 124 (also see snow pole)
Clematis drummondii, 101
Cleveland sage, 97
cliff rose, 70
climbing janusia, 101
clover fern, 100, 143, 178
Coahuilan rosewood, 178
Colorado four o'clock, 59, 124
columnar cactus, 70, 73-74, 107-108
Comanche prickly pear, 90, 108
compact ranger, 99
compass barrel, 52, **71,** 90, 106
Condalia warnockii, 99
coneflower, *see* Mexican hat
Conoclinium greggii, 153, 178
Cooperia drummondii, 61
coral aloe, 112, 124
coral bean trees, 120
coral bells, 126
Cordia boissieri, 95
Cordia parvifolia, 97 (also see little-leaf cordia)
corky seed pincushion, 109
Coryphantha recurvata, 109
Coryphantha vivipara, 109
Cosmos sulphureus 'Bright Lights', 59
cotton-top cactus, 90, 106
Coulter's lupine, *see* arroyo lupine
Coville barrel, 70-71, 106
cow's horn agave, 64, 104
cow tongue prickly pear, 108, 124
cream cactus, 109
creeping devil, 102

creosote bush, 12, 88, 89, 97, 152, **157**
Crossosoma bigelovii, 98
Cucurbita foetidissima, 100
curiosity cactus, **80,** 109, 118, 121
curl-leaf mountain mahogany, 94
Cylindropuntia
   acanthocarpa, 108
   arbuscula, 108
   articulata inermis, 108
   echinocarpa, 108
   imbricata, 109
   leptocaulis, 108
   papyracantha, 108
   spinosior, 108
   versicolor, 108 (*also see* staghorn cholla)
Dakota verbena, 59, 90
Dalea
   bicolor bicolor, 46, 98
   capitata 'Sierra Gold', 100
   frutescens, 46, 96
   greggii, 87, 100
   pulchra, 97
   scoparia, 59
   versicolor sessilis, 98
'Dallas Red' lantana, 124
damianita daisy, 59, 90, 121, 124
'Dark Knight' bluebeard, 91, 152
Dasylirion quadrangulatum, 105 (*also see* toothless spoon)
Dasylirion sp., 66, 104-105, 153
Dasylirion texanum, 90, 105
Dasylirion wheeleri, 88, 105
Datura wrightii, 60, 91, 102, 179 (*also see* sacred datura)
deer grass, 47, **58,** 110, **142,** 155, **171,** 178
Delphinium scaposum, 57
desert agave, 103, 179
desert bluebells, **57,** 71
desert Christmas cholla, 108
desert four o'clock, *see* Colorado four o'clock
desert hackberry, 45, 155, 180 (*also see* netleaf hackberry)
desert holly, 90, 97
desert honeysuckle, 180
desert larkspur, *see* barestem larkpur
desert lavender, 89, 180
desert lobelia, 143
desert marigold, 57, 89, 123
desert milkweed, 153, 180
Desert Museum hybrid palo verde, **41,** 95, **175**
desert rose mallow, 180
desert sage, 90, 97
desert senna, 59, **60,** 154
desert spoon, **49, 66,** 88, 105, 153
desert sunflower, 102
desert sunrise, 178
'Desert Sunrise' hummingbird mint, 91
desert willow, **43, 171,** 173, 178 (*also see Chilopsis linearis* sp.)
desert zinnia, 57, 155
devil's claw, **54,** 59 (*also see* yellow devil's claw)
devil's river, 178
devil's tongue barrel cactus, 106
Dichelostemma pulchellum, 61 (*also see* blue dicks)
Dichondra argentea 'Silver Falls', 100, 124 (*also see* 'Silver Falls' dichondra)

dinner plate prickly pear, 108
Dioon edule, 111, 123
Dioon spinulosum, 111 (*also see* spiny dioon)
Diospyros texana, 95
Dodonaea viscosa, 97
dogweed, 60, 89, 155, 180
'Durango Delight' agave, 103
'Dusky Blue' yucca, 105
dwarf rabbitbrush, 60
dwarf rosemary, 83, 112
Ebenopsis ebano, 96
Echinocactus grusonii, 106
Echinocereus
   engelmannii, 107 (*also see* strawberry hedgehog)
   fendleri, 106
   ledingii, 107
   nicholii, 106
   pantalophus, 102
   polycephalus, 90, 106
   rigidissimus, 106
   stramineus, 107 (*also see* strawberry hedgehog)
   triglochidiatus, 90, 106, 124 (*also see* claret cup cactus)
   triglochidiatus 'White Sands', 107
Echinopsis pachanoi, 107
elephant's food, 112
elephant tree, 42, **88,** 89, 94
'El Toro' bull grass, 110
Emory oak, 95
Encelia farinosa, 57, 89, 155 (*also see* brittlebush)
Enceliopsis argophylla, 90
Engelmann's prickly pear, **52,** 74, 90, 108, 118, **119,** 124, 128, 129, 155
Ephedra nevadensis, 90, 98
Ephedra viridis, 89, 124
'Epic' torch cactus hybrid, 72
Eremophila hyrgrophana, 111
Eremophila maculata 'Valentine', 111 (*also see* 'Valentine' emu bush)
Eremophila x 'Summertime Blue', 111
Ericameria laricifolia, 60, 99
Ericameria nauseosa speciosus, 70
Ericameria nauseosus, 91
Ericameria nauseosus nauseosus, 60
Erigeron divergens, 102
Eriodictyon angustifolium, 90, 99
Eriogonum corymbosum nilesii, 90, 97
Eriogonum fasciculatum poliofolium, 88, 97, 178 (*also see* flattop buckwheat)
Erysimum asperum, 59
Erythrina flabelliformis, 110, 180
Erythrina sp., 120
escarpment live oak, 96
Eschscholtzia mexicana, 58
Euphorbia antisyphilitica, 109
Euphorbia heterophylla, 103
Euphorbia rigida, 112
evening rain lily, 61
evergreen sumac, 87, 97
Eysenhardtia orthocarpa, 94, 178
Eysenhardtia texana, 179
fairy duster, **45,** 52 (*see also* Baja fairy duster)
Fallugia paradoxa, 90, 178
Faxon's yucca, 91, 105
Fendler's hedgehog, **72,** 106
Ferocactus

   cylindraceus, 90, 106 (*also see* compass barrel)
   emoryi, 106
   glaucescens, 106
   gracilis coloratus, 106
   latispinus, 106
   pringlei, 106
   rectispinus, 106, 123
   stainsii, 106
   wislizeni, 89, 106, 121
Ficus petiolaris, 110
fig, 83, **85,** 86, 87 (*also see* Indian fig)
fire barrel, 32, 70, 106
firecracker penstemon, 58, 69
firewheel, **52,** 58, 155
fishhook barrel, **70-71,** 89, 106, **121**
fishhook pincushion, 109
flattop buckwheat, 72, 88, 97, 152, 178,
Flourensia cernua, 179
foothills palo verde, **42,** 43, 59, 64, 73, **93,** 94
Fouquieria, 77
   columnaris, 109 (*also see* boojum tree)
   diguetii, 109
   macdougalii, 109
   splendens, 89, 109, 122, 128, 155, 180 (*also see* ocotillo)
four wing saltbush, 97
foxglove penstemon, 178
fragrant ranger, 48, 99
fragrant sage, *see* fragrant ranger
frogfruit, 100
'Furman's Red' autumn sage, 46
Gaillardia pulchella, 58, 155
Garrya flavescens, 90, 98
Geraea canescens, 102
giant flowered purple sage, 97
giant hesperaloe, 105
giant morning glory, 178
giant penstemon, 58
Glandularia gooddingii, 58, 178
Glandularia pulchella, 100
globemallow, 55, 58, **79,** 180
'Glorious' torch cactus hybrid, 72
'Gold Star' yellow bells, 97, 124
golden barrel, **34,** 70, 71, 106
golden beehive cactus, 109
golden columbine, 126, 143
golden hedgehog, 106
golden leadball tree, 87, 94
goldeneye, 97
golden-flowered agave, 89, 103
Goodding's verbena, **52,** 58, 178
gopher plant, **83,** 112
gorilla's armpit, 80, 110, **145,** 146
Gossypium thurberi, 178
grapefruits, **84**
gray creeping germander, 112
gray oak, 89, 96
'Green Cloud' Texas ranger, **47,** 48, 99, 130
green desert spoon, 90, 105
green-flowered pincushion, 109
'Green Goblet' hardy century plant, 104
grizzly bear prickly pear, 108
Guadalupe palm, 111
Guaiacum coulteri, 97
guajillo, 94
guardiola, 178

Guardiola platyphylla, 178
guayacan, 97
'Hacienda Creeper', 101, **126**
Haematoxylum brasiletto, 94
Hamelia patens, 99
Harriman's yucca, 105
Harrisia bonplandii, 102
Harrisia martini, 102, 123
Harvardia pallens, 95 (*also see* tenaza)
Havard agave, 90, 104
hedgehog cactus, 72, 106-107, 171
Helianthus maximiliana, 91, 124
Hesperaloe, 66, 67, 104-105, 168
    campanulata, 104
    funifera, 105
    nocturna, 105
    parviflora, 105
    parviflora 'Yellow', 105 (*also see* yellow hesperaloe)
Hesperocallis undulata, 61
Heuchera sanguinea, 126
Hibiscus coulteri, 180
Hill Country penstemon, **116**, 129
'Hills of Santa Cruz' olive, 112
'Honeydew Melon' Indian fig, 75
honey mesquite, *see* Texas honey mesquite
hop bush, 97
'Houdini' sage, 99
Huachuca agave, 103
hummingbird trumpet, 89, 178
Hyptis emoryi, 89, 180
Indian fig, 75, 108, 127, **128**
Indian rice grass, 110
indigo bush, 97, 152 (*also see* trailing indigo bush)
Ipomoea barbatisepala, 101
Ipomoea coccinea hederifolia, 101
Ipomoea longifolia, 178
Iris missourensis, 143
ironwood, 43, 51, **81**, 82, **83**, 89, 96, 123, 151, 180
Janusia gracilis, 101
Jatropha cardiophylla, 88, 97, 110, 178
Jatropha macrorhiza, 178
'Jaws' agave, 103
jet-tipped agave, 103
jimson weed, *see* sacred datura
jojoba, 97
Joshua tree, **68**, 69, 90, 105
Joshua tree, Las Vegas area, 90
'June Noon' torch cactus hybrid, 72
Justicia californica, 89, 97, 155 (*also see* chuperosa)
Justicia candicans, 98
Justicia sonorae, 98
Kallstroemia grandiflora, 59
kidneywood, 94, 178
kokerbom, 112
kumquats, 84
Lantana camera 'Dallas Red', 124
Lantana camera 'Radiation', 121
Larrea tridentata, 88, 89, 97 (*also see* creosote bush)
Las Vegas bear paw poppy, 90
Las Vegas buckwheat, **26**, 90, 97
lavender spice Mexican oregano, 97
Leding hedgehog, 107
lemons, 84
Leucaena retusa, 87, 94
Leucophyllum, 47, 59 (*also see* Texas ranger)
    candidum, 100
    frutescens, 47, 48
    frutescens 'Compacta', 99
    frutescens 'Green Cloud', 48, 99
    frutescens 'White Cloud', 100
    laevigatum, 99
    langmaniae, 100, 129
    langmaniae 'Lynn's Legacy', 100
    pruinosum, 99
    revolutum 'Houdini', 99
    zygophyllum, 99
limber bush, 88, 97, 110, 178
limequats, 84
limes, 85
little-leaf cordia, 45, 97
little-leaf sumac, 98
Lobelia laxiflora, 143
Lophocereus schottii, 107, 121 (*also see* senita)
'Louis Hamilton' globemallow, 58
'Lucretia Hamilton' desert willow, 94
lupine, 58, 132, 152
Lupinus sparsiflorus, 58
Lupinus succulentus, 58
Lycium freemontii, 99, 155
Lycium parishii, 179
'Lynn's Legacy' ranger, 48, 100
Macfadyena unguis-cati, 101 (*also see* cat's claw vine)
'Macho Mocha' mangave, 110
Maireana sedifolia, 111
Mamillopsis senilis, 109
Mammillaria, 77, 125
    candida, 109
    grahamii, 109
    heyderi, 109
    macdougalii, 109
    parkinsonii, 109
    tetrancistra, 109
    viridiflora, 109
Manfreda maculosa, 110
Manfreda x 'Macho Mocha, 110
Manfreda x 'Silver Leopard', 110
Manihot davisiae, 180
'Manzanillo' olive, 112
mariola, 89, 179
mariposa lily, **61**, 62
Marsilea macropoda, 100, 143, 178
Martin's harrisia, 51, 102, 123
Maurandya antirrhiniflora, 49, 101 (*also see* twining snapdragon vine)
Maximilian's sunflower, 91, 124
medicinal aloe, 112
Melampodium leucanthum, 59, 90
Merremia aurea, 102 (*also see* yellow morning glory)
mescal ceniza, 103
mescal pelon, 103
mesquite, 29, 30, 44, 45, 50, 64, 151, 164
Metzelia involucrata, 102
Mexican bird of paradise, 94
Mexican blue palm, **81**, 111, 124
Mexican blue penstemon, **9**
Mexican blue sage, 98
Mexican blue yucca, **69**, 105
Mexican buckeye, 87, 98
Mexican elderberry, 94
Mexican evening primrose, 100
Mexican feather grass, 27, **64**, **91**, 110, **122**
Mexican fencepost, **35**, **74**, 107
Mexican flame, 98, 155
Mexican flame vine, **3**, 101
Mexican gold poppy, 52, **53**, 58
Mexican hairy barrel, 106
Mexican hat, **59**, 60, 61
Mexican orange, 98
Mexican orchid tree, 94
Mexican poppies, *see* Mexican gold poppy
Mexican redbud, 94
Mexican sunflower, **60**
Mexican tree ocotillo, **77**, 109
milk-chocolate spine prickly pear, 75, 108
milkweed vine, 101
Mimulus cardinalis, 143
Mirabilis multiflora, 59, 124
'Mission' grape, 102, **126**
'Mission' olive, 112
Mojave aster, 90
Mojave lupine, *see* arroyo lupine
Mojave yucca, 90
Monterey blue dalea, 46, 98
moon cactus, **52**, 102
Mormon tea, 89, 90, 98, 124
moss verbena, **49**, 100
mottled yucca, 105
mountain cassava, 180
mountain delight dalea, 98
mountain yucca, 105
Muhlenbergia
    capillaris 'Regal Mist', 111 (*also see* 'Regal Mist' muhlenbergia)
    dumosa, 110
    emersleyi 'El Toro', 110
    lindheimeri, 110
    porteri, 90, 110
    rigens, 110, 155, 178 (*also see* deer grass)
    rigida, 111
Murphy's agave, 103
Nama hispidum, 58
Nashville muhly, 111
Nassella tenuissima, 110, 122 (*also see* Mexican feather grass)
native fleabane, *see* spreading fleabane
native passion flower, 51, 101, 153
Nepeta x *faassenii* 'Select Blue', 91
netleaf hackberry, 89, 94, 96
New Mexico agave, 88, 103
night-blooming cereus, 107
night-blooming hesperaloe, 105
Nissolia schottii, 179
nolina, **66**, 104-105 (*also see* bear grass)
Nolina bigelovii, 104
Nolina matapensis, 105
Nolina microcarpa, 89, 104 (*also see* bear grass)
Nolina nelsoni, 105 (*also see* blue nolina)
Nolina texana, 90, 105
ocahui, 103
ocotillo, **10**, **51**, 77, **78-79**, 89, 109, 122, **128**, 129, 139, 155, 180
octopus agave, **65**, 103
Oenothera caespitosa, 59, 89
Oenothera speciosa, 100
Oenothera stubbei, 100
Old Man of Mexico, 74, 107, 124
Old Man of the Andes, 74, 107

Old Man of the Mountain, 107
old man pincushion, 109
old man saltbush, 111
Olea europaea, 112 (*also see* olive)
Olea europaea 'Hills of Santa Cruz', 112
Olea europaea 'Manzanillo', 112
Olea europaea 'Mission', 112
Olea europaea 'Swan Hill', 112
olive, 112
Olneya tesota, 89, 96, 123, 180 (*also see* ironwood)
Opuntia
   basilaris, 90, 108 (*also see* beavertail prickly pear)
   bigelovii, 76
   comanchica, 90, 108
   engelmannii, 90, 108, 124, 128, 129, 155 (*also see* Engelmann's prickly pear)
   engelmannii lindheimeri, 108
   engelmannii linguiformis, 108, 124
   erinacea, 108
   ficus-indica, 108, 128 (*also see* Indian fig)
   robusta, 108
   violacea gosseliniana, 108
   violacea macrocentra, 108
   violacea santa-rita, 89, 108 (*also see* Santa Rita prickly pear)
oranges, 85
'Orange Slush' Indian fig, 75
oreganillo, 77, 98, 179
Oreocereus celsianus, 107 (*also see* Old Man of the Andes)
Oreocereus trollii, 107
organ pipe cactus, **73,** 74, 107
Orthocarpus purpurascens, 58
Our Lord's candle, 105
Outback cassia, 111
owl's clover, 58
owl's eyes, 109
Pachycereus marginatus, 107 (*also see* Mexican fencepost)
Pachycereus schottii monstrosus, 107, 123 (*also see* totempole cactus)
pale-leaf yucca, **67,** 69, 105
palma de la virgen, 111 (*also see* Dioon edule)
Palmer's agave, 103
palo blanco, **40,** 42, 95, **124,** 129
palo brea, **9, 43,** 96
pancake cactus, 109
'Papago Pink' globemallow, 58
'Papaya' Indian fig, 75
paper flower, 60
paper-spined cholla, 108
Parish's wolfberry, 179
Parkinsonia florida, 41, 88, 95, 155 (*also see* blue palo verde)
Parkinsonia microphyllum, 94 (*also see* foothills palo verde)
Parkinsonia praecox, 96 (*also see* palo brea)
Parkinsonia x 'Desert Museum', 95 (*also see* Desert Museum hybrid palo verde)
Parry's agave, 104, **122**
Parry's penstemon, **7,** 58, **73,** 89, 129, 155
Parthenium incanum, 89, 179
Parthenocissus 'Hacienda Creeper', 101, 126
partridge breast aloe, 112
Passiflora foetida, 101, 153 (*also see* native passion flower)

passion flower, *see* native passion flower
passion vine, *see* native passion flower
Pectis papposa, 59
Pedilanthus macrocarpus, 110 (*also see* slipper plant)
pencil cholla, 108
Peniocereus greggii, 102 (*also see* Arizona queen of the night)
Penstemon
   amphorellae, **9, 61**
   baccharifolius, 60, 124
   barbatus, 179
   cardinalis, 57, 87 (*also see* cardinal penstemon)
   cobaea, 178
   eatonii, 58, 69
   palmeri, 58
   parryi, 58, 89, 155 (*also see* Parry's penstemon)
   pseudospectabilis, 57, 123 (*also see* canyon penstemon)
   strictus, 91 (*also see* Rocky Mountain penstemon)
   superbus, 58, 129
   triflorus, **116,** 129
Perovskia atriplicifolia, 91
Phacelia campanularia, 57 (*also see* desert bluebells)
Phacelia crenulata, 152
'Phoenix' bird of paradise, 98
'Phoenix' hybrid mesquite, 96
Phylla nodiflora, 100
pincushion cactus, 77-**78, 125**
pine-leaf milkweed, 88, 153
pink fairy duster, 98, 155, 180
pink rain lily, 62
piñon pine, 91, 95
Pinus edulis, 91, 95
podwing vine, 179
Poliomintha maderensis, 97
pomegranate, see 'Wonderful' pomegranate
Populus deltoides wislizenii, 91, 96
Portulacaria afra, 112
'Prairie Sunset' rain lily, 62
prairie zinnia, 60, 69, 100, 180
prickly pear cactus, 70, 74, **75,** 76, **83,** 108, 124
prickly poppy, 102
Proboscidea altheaefolia, 61
Proboscidea parviflora, 59 (*also see* devil's claw)
Prosopis glandulosa, 89, 96, 124
Prosopis juliflora, 88, 96, 155, 164, 179 (*also see* velvet mesquite)
Prosopis pubescens, 89, 95 (*also see* screwbean mesquite)
Prosopis velutina, see Prosopis juliflora
Prosopis x 'Phoenix', 96
prostrate germander, 112
prostrate three leaf sumac, 91, 98
Psilostrophe cooperi, 60
Psorothamnus spinosus, 89, 95
Punica granatum 'Wonderful', *see* 'Wonderful' pomegranate
purple aster, 60
'Purple Haze' autumn sage, 46
purple heart, 146
purple mat, 58
purple orchid vine, 101
purple three awn, 111
Purshia mexicana, 70
Queen Victoria agave, 63, 104
queen's wreath, 101
Quercus

   emoryi, 95
   fusiformis, 96
   grisea, 89, 96
   muehlenbergii, 95
   turbinella, 90, 95
rabbitbrush, 91 (*also see* dwarf rabbitbrush; whitestem rabbitbrush)
'Radiation' lantana, 121
ragged rockflower, 98
Raspberry Fuzzies copperleaf, 87, 100
Ratibida columnaris, 60 (*also see* Mexican hat)
red bird of paradise, **47, 73,** 98
red-flowered prickly pear, 108
red hesperaloe, 66, 67, 105, 123
red justicia, 98
'Red Slush' Indian fig, 75
red yucca, *see* red hesperaloe
'Regal Mist' muhlenbergia, **80,** 111, 121
Rhus microphylla, 98
Rhus ovata, 98
Rhus trilobata 'Autumn Amber', 91, 98
Rhus virens, 87, 97
Rio Bravo sage, 100, 129
Rio Grande cottonwood, 91, 96
rock fig, 110
rock penstemon, 60, 124
Rocky Mountain iris, 143
Rocky Mountain penstemon, 91, **153**
'Roger's Red' California grape, 102, **130**
rose, climbing, 126
Rosmarinus officinalis 'Irene', 112 (*also see* dwarf rosemary)
Rosmarinus officinalis 'Tuscan Blue', 112
Russian sage, 91
Sabal uresana, 111
sacahuista, 90, 105
sacred datura, **8,** 60, 91, 102, 179
saguaro cactus, 30, 73, 107, 155
saltbush, **45,** 97, 154
Salvia
   chamaedryoides, 98
   clevelandii, 97
   coccinea, 61, 155
   columbariae, 57
   dorrii dorrii, 90, 97
   farinacea 'Texas Violet', 87
   greggii, 46, 96, 155
   greggii 'White', 126
   pachyphylla, 97
   x 'Trident', 99
Sambucus nigra cerulea, 94
San Pedro, 107
Santa Cruz striped agave, 104
Santa Rita prickly pear, **75,** 89, 108, 129, 145
Sapindus saponaria drummondii, 87, 96, 180
'Sapphire Skies' yucca, 105
Sarcostemma cynanchoides, 101
scarlet creeper, 101
scarlet monkey flower, 143
scarlet penstemon, 179
scorpion weed, 152
screwbean mesquite, 42, 89, 95, 146
scrub oak, 90, 95
seepwillow, 143
Senecio confusus, 101 (*also see* Mexican flame vine)
senita, 73, 107, 121

Senna covesii, 59, 154 (*also see* desert senna)
Senna leptocarpa, 154
Senna oliogophylla, 111
Senna wislizenii, 89, 98, 179
Setcreasea pallida, 146
shadscale saltbush, 98
sharkskin agave, **64, 91**, 104
shrubby germander, 112
shrubby senna, 89, 98, 179
'Sicilian Port Wine' Indian fig, 75
sideoats grama, **10,** 111
'Sierra Gold' dalea, 100
'Sierra Linda' autumn sage, 46
'Sierra Sun' hybrid bird of paradise, 95
silk tassel tree, 90, 98
silver cholla, 108
'Silver Falls' dichondra, **49,** 100, 124, **163**
'Silver Leopard' tuberose, 110
'Silver Peso' Texas mountain laurel, 95
Simmondsia chinensis, 97
skeletonleaf goldeneye, 87
slipper plant, **79,** 80, 110
smoke tree, 89, 95
snowball cactus, 109
snow pole, **73,** 74, 107, 124
soap tree yucca, 67-68, 70, 90, 106, 180
soapweed, 69-70
Solanum tridynamum, 102
Solidago wrightii, 179
Sonoran justicia, 98
Sonoran nightshade, 102
Sonoran palmetto, 111
Sophora secundiflora, 87, 95 (*also see* Texas mountain laurel)
Sophora secundiflora 'Silver Peso', 95
sotol, *see* desert spoon
southwest coral bean, 110, 180
southwestern pipevine, 101, 154, 179
Sphaeralcea ambigua, 58, 180 (*also see* globemallow)
spider agave, 104
spiny dioon, **81,** 111
spiny star, 109
Sporobolus wrightii, 110, 126
spreading fleabane, 102
spruce cone cholla, 108
sprucetop grama, 111
staghorn cholla, **76,** 108
stem succulents, 62, 77-78
Stenocereus eruca, 102
Stenocereus thurberi, 108 (*also see* organ pipe cactus)
"stinky" passion flower, *see* native passion flower
strawberry hedgehog, 72, 107
succulent lupine, 58
sugar bush, 98
'Summertime Blue' emu bush, 111
sundrops, 87, **91,** 100, 180
sunray, 90
'Sunrise' bells, 99
superb penstemon, **58,** 129, **130**
Superstition mallow, 99, 180
'Swan Hill' olive, 112
sweet acacia, 95, 124
tangelos, 84, 85
'Tangerine Beauty' crossvine, **50,** 102
tangerines, 84, 85

tarbush, 179
Tecoma stans, 87, 179 (*also see* yellow bells)
Tecoma stans 'Gold Star', 97, 124
Tecoma x 'Sunrise', 99
teddy bear cholla, 76
Telesiphonia brachysiphon, 61
tenaza, 95, 151
Teucrium aroanium, 112
Teucrium chamaedrys 'Prostratum', 112
Teucrium fruticans 'Azurea', 112
Texas ebony, 43, 96
Texas firecracker bush, 99
Texas honey mesquite, 89, 96, 124
Texas kidneywood, 179
Texas mountain laurel, 42, **43,** 87, 95
Texas olive, 95
Texas persimmon, 95
Texas ranger, **47**-48, **60,** 99-100
Texas tuberose, 110
Texas violet sage, 87
Thompson hybrid desert broom, 100
Thompson yucca, 106, **122**
'Thunder Cloud' Texas ranger, **48,** 100
Thymophylla pentachaeta, 60, 89, 155, 180
Tithonia rotundifolia, 60
toothless spoon, 66, 105
torch cactus hybrids, 72, 107
totempole cactus, 73, 107, **123, 124**
Toumey agave, 180
Tradescantia occidentalis, 179
trailing four o'clock, 61
trailing indigo bush, 87, 100
tranquility tree, 95
tree bear grass, 105
tree catclaw, 96
tree cholla, 109
Trichocereus hybrids, 107 (*also see* torch cactus hybrids)
Trichocereus terscheckii, 107 (*also see* Argentine giant)
'Trident' sage, 99
trixis, 89, 180
Trixis californica, 89, 180
tropical sage, 61, 155
trumpet bush, *see* yellow bells
tufted evening primrose, 59, 89
turpentine bush, 60, 99
'Tuscan Blue' rosemary, 112
tuxedo spine prickly pear, 108
twin-flowered agave, 64, 104
twining snapdragon vine, 49, 79, 101
twisted cereus, 110
twisted yucca, 106
Ungnadia speciosa, 87, 98
Utah agave, 90, 104
'Valentine' emu bush, 83, 111
valesia, 99
Valesia glabra, 99
Vaquelinia californica, 96
Vaquelinia corymbosa heterodon, 178
variegated century plant, 104 (*also see* Agave americana marginata)
velvet mesquite, **50,** 88, 96, 155, 179
Verbena bipinnatifida, 59, 90
Viguiera parishii, 97
Viguiera stenoloba, 87
virgin's bower, 101

Vitis californica 'Roger's Red', 102, 130
Vitis vinifera 'Mission', 126
'Volcano Sunset' torch cactus hybrid, 72
Warnock condalia, 99
'Warren Jones' desert willow, 96
Washingtonia filifera, 81, 89, 111 (*also see* California fan palm)
Weber's agave, 63, 65, 104, **129**
Western blue flag, *see* Rocky Mountain iris
western soapberry, 87, 96, 180
western spiderwort, 179
western wall flower, 59
whale's tongue agave, 104, **123**
white autumn sage, 126
white ball acacia, 99, **154**
white bursage, 99
'White Cloud' Texas ranger, 100
white rain lily, 126
'White Sands' claret cup, 107
whitestem chamisa, *see* whitestem rabbitbrush
whitestem rabbitbrush, 70
white stripe agave, 65, 104, 124
whitethorn acacia, 95, 151
white trumpet, 61
wild poinsettia, 103
wolfberry, 99, 155
wooly butterfly bush, 99
'Wonderful' pomegranate, **86,** 87
Wright's goldenrod, 179
Xylorhiza tortifolia, 90
yellow bells, **65,** 87, 179
yellow devil's claw, 61
yellow hesperaloe, 105, 123
yellow morning glory, **50,** 102
yellow orchid vine, 102
yerba mansa, 143, **171,** 179
yerba santa, 90, 99
Yucca,
   baccata, 69, 89, 105
   brevifolia, 69, 105 (*also see* Joshua tree)
   brevifolia jageriana, 90
   elata, 70, 90, 106, 180 (*also see* soap tree yucca)
   endlichiana, 105
   faxoniana, 91, 105
   glauca, 69-70
   harrimaniae, 105
   linearifolia 'Dusky Blue', 105
   pallida, 69, 106
   rigida, 105 (*also see* Mexican blue yucca)
   rostrata, 68, 105, 124 (*also see* beaked yucca)
   rostrata 'Sapphire Skies', 105
   rupicola, 106
   schidigera, 90
   schottii, 105
   thompsoniana, 106 (*also see* Thompson yucca)
   whipplei, 105
Zauschneria californica, 89, 178
Zephranthes candida, 126
Zephranthes grandiflora, 62
Zephranthes x 'Prairie Sunset', 62
Zexmenia hispida, 178
Zinnia acerosa, 57, 155
Zinnia grandiflora, 60, 69, 100, 180